Already Enough

Love Yourself Messy

by Miriam MacMillan

For Hattie,
Thanks for always
Being So lovely ♡

Enjoy, Miriam x

Dedication

For Ethan, Niamh, Noah, Eli, Jesse, Indie, and my little sparkle.

How do I describe in words how much you all mean to me? You all have taught me what true unconditional love is and means. You have also taught me more about myself more than you will ever know.

Thank you for all being beautiful sparks of joy in my life and loving me through all my messy moments.

Thank you for filling my heart with laughter, fun and everyday magic in all your unique, individual ways.

I wanted to prove to you that no matter how much the world is going to shit around you and no matter how messy your life is, if you face your fears, take inspired action, trust in perfect timings, and love yourself...you can achieve anything.

Always BE yourselves, love yourselves and have fun... even when you're feeling messy.

I hope this book serves as a reminder to you of just how fucking amazeballs, gorgeous, worthy and deserving of love you all are.

Also, sorry not sorry about the swears.

Table of Contents

Legal Disclaimers

Foreword

By Mel

Where do I start? From the beginning?

I've known Mirrie for 23 years, since our teens. Fast forward to 2013, two years after reconnecting again as adults, we slowly but surely began walking barefoot down a path of true friendship to the point in 2020 where we uncovered our soul connection. To say that, today, she's one of the biggest loves of my life is an understatement.

When Mirrie first conceived the idea of this book, many (many) moons ago, we were worlds and realities away from where we are now; both in our personal lives and friendship. Although she laments/jokes about it having taken five years to write, edit, add to, edit, reframe, edit, etc., it's been a tale of epic proportions and countless repetitive questions of "are you sure?" from the Universe (Big U) that have transformed this book from brilliant into the gem you're holding (even if metaphorically) in your hands today.

I'm blessed with the unique vantage point of not just witnessing this journey but being the recipient of enough of her "nukes" to blow me into the depths of true self-love and how that impacts on each and every connection we share in life.

Adulting is, as the meme goes, "one star, not recommended," but it's the hand we've been dealt. Life gets in the way of so many important things but none more so than our relationship with ourselves. Yet it's this relationship and coexistence which is the one and only that is truly lifelong. One we cannot escape. So how do you live with, let alone love, your imperfect self?

Loving yourself messy is, in my humble opinion, one of the hardest things to do in this world we live in. The thing is, though, when you have someone championing you and reminding you at every turn how incredible you are and how your ugly actually makes you more beautiful to them, it all becomes that much easier.

One of the biggest steps is allowing yourself to become vulnerable around other people who are also hiding away in fear and shame. Mirrie paints the clearest picture of how letting go of our insecurities not only releases us from our own chains but also gives others the perspective to see that theirs can be released too. The gift that keeps on giving.

It's one thing to read an inspirational book which touches your heart in a way which inspires you into sincere action. It's another to see the honest, sometimes messy, proof being lived out by someone you love with your heart and soul. That's why I knew this book would change lives and have a massive impact on the world – it is not just words. It's action.

Also, when a book includes a prescription of 'Italian Self-Love', you know you are onto a winner.

Self-love is a life-long journey, but I've learned that it's not an impossible one. It can be truly meaningful, even as you make the first, frantic, flaps of your metaphorical wings as Mirrie not-so-subtly kicks you – baby bird – out of your nest of doubts and fears that's outgrown you.

Witnessing the transformation from a badass motherfucker to an even more badass (and swearier) motherfucker has been awe-inspiring and I'm not kidding when I say that Mirrie's my Ultimate She-ro. Beyond being one of the few people who have loved me unconditionally in spite of – and maybe, because of - everything, she has shown me day in, day out, for years, that it's truly possible to love yourself during the best and the worst of times. Even when the shit-stained llamas[1] are raining down and partying so hard, they're stomping a whole new level of hell out, 'specially for you. The person I've seen her step into – herself – who was there all along, before and since she began this journey, has been incredible. She motivates and inspires me every single day – through good times and bad – and loving her messy has made it that much easier for me to love myself messy.

_____

[1] Llama: A beautiful creature that represents the unnecessary dramas in your life

If there's one thing which surpasses my pride and joy in seeing this essential book out there is that you, dear reader, are holding the honest, unfiltered, searingly raw, loving masterpiece that is her gift to you and the world. It's been years in the making for good reason and you get to experience the unfolding of that journey through the pages of this book.

Take a deep breath. Now, go enjoy your own path to discovering that you truly are Already Enough.

Acknowledgements

Firstly, thank *you, gorgeous messy reader,* for inspiring this beautiful bastard in the first place.

Massive thanks to my mum and dad who have always overbelieved in me, put up with my mess, insisted on me being myself even when the world was against it and for looking after me and the kids so many times while I was birthing this book.

My family (especially Sam whom I miss every day) for accepting the real me.

My editor Binati for her brilliance, fucking awesome power, patience and grace.

My kids, you got the dedication, don't get greedy!

My mucker Drew for teaching me to look up in trees (and hug them harder), kick the llamas out of my pool and find pictures in rocks. For bringing me baby birds, plastic flowers and everyday fucking magic. Thank you for helping me see the beauty in my dark as well as my light.

My soul partner in grime, Mel for the years of unwavering support, infinite hashtags, GIFs and memes and an extra thanks for the nights of book doulaing (and all the laughs in-between #Deeetractions)

My soul family Rachel, Michelle, Micah, Geoff, Sarah, Andrea, Shanthi, Ana Maria, Aaron (and the rest) for the proof that I didn't need to do this alone.

Thanks to the collective consciousness of the universe for never giving up on me.

Thank you to my Higher Self for inspiring me, having fun with me and using this whole process as a love letter to myself and a fucking mind-blowing expansion. Thank you for never giving up on me, allowing me to reach my highest highs and loving me through my lowest lows. Seeing your unconditional love and infinite power gives me goosebumps every day.

Finally Thank you to my Body. You carried me through this and my entire life. Never stopped protecting me, never stopped loving me. For you I give the biggest thanks of all, I'll let you have a rest before the next book now. No matter how messy you are, I'll always Love you.

Introduction...

On the last day of 2020, I was feeling very excited. We were still in lockdown but going to have a midnight BBQ and a cross-continent zoom was set up with my soul family to celebrate as many New Year's that we could manage across the world.

I just wanted to have a bit of fun, wear a sexy dress, and look hot for once. Since I left my marriage and moved onto a boat, I've been feeling more and more like a swamp thang[2] every day! As all the shops were closed due to the lockdown, I messaged a couple of ladies selling dresses near me. I didn't have much money but thought I'd do this one thing for myself. Only one lady replied, and she had a purple dress: brand new for only a fiver. The picture was a bit sketchy, but she was around the corner and could meet up straight away. Seeing that as a sign from the Universe and thanking my lucky stars, I went and picked up the dress in a rush because the kids were in the car.

I got back and felt super happy that I had a little something to make me feel special. When I got it out of the packet though, it turned out to be the ugliest, most ill-fitting, unflattering dress I'd ever seen in my life. Bright velvet purple with black lace...the first thing my kids said was, "Are you dressing up like a witch tonight mummy?"

I wanted to see the funny side of the whole situation, but I was pissed. What the fuck Big U? I was trying to be kind to myself, to show that I care about myself...what the fuck was this?
My mum started getting down dresses that would be big on me that we could pin in, but I was determined, "No if this is how the universe wanted me to see in the new year, in this ugly arsed dress, I'm going to fucking wear it."

---

[2] Swamp Thang: A mythical creature who you can imagine emerging from a swamp covered in boggy moss and seaweed all crusty and warty.

It was decided. I did my hair and makeup. I put on my dress and my dad took the photo that I ended up using on this cover. If you had told me how I would be using a photo of THAT dress on my finished book that night, I would have laughed in your face!

So why did I use it? Why am I telling you the story behind the dress?

That evening, my family couldn't stop giggling every time they looked at me in that dress. My kids found it hilarious that I wore it even though I hated it. Fuck, I couldn't stop laughing and kept spinning around like a swamp thang princess.

I sent photos of it to my friends. They pissed themselves laughing about how mad I was at the Big U. On the Zooms, everyone actually liked the stupid thing, and again it led to teasing and laughter. I had such a good night, not in spite of the dress but *because* of the dress. I used that photo of me on the cover because I'm surrounded by mess, still got my socks on and I have a big, genuine smile on my face. It is kind of the perfect picture to sum up how I try to live my life:

Imperfect.
Messy.
Fun.
Still beautiful.

I knew there would be a reason as to why I ended up in that purple monstrosity. I knew I should trust the Big U in all her mighty wisdom. As soon as I put my ego aside, I knew what it was...

Connection

Your imperfections do not define you, but they actually make you more lovable. People connect with you more when they can relate to you. If that dress had just been sexy, it would have been boring. It was because it was such a mess, that it made the night so much more fun and interesting.

When life gets messy it's easy to blame God/Big U/Anyone or just get angry. When *you* get messy it's easy to hate yourself.

We all sit around trying to find the perfect thing that we can wear, buy or change in order to make us feel enough. We believe we need to be fixed or perfect before we can love ourselves.

I disagree.

I believe we need to embrace our messes, embrace our ugly and accept ourselves fully; today... right now. I believe you are already enough without you needing to change a thing.

I believe you deserve to love yourself unconditionally and I want to show you how.

Lordy knows, if I can do it, so can you.

Self-Love changes everything.
Let's get there together.

Chapter One- What is Self-Love?

What is Self-Love?

What is Love?
Is it acceptance?
Is it approval?
Is it being seen with no fear?

Is it giving the vastness of your soul, your darkness and your light-
Knowing all of it is worthy?

Knowing worthiness is unconditional?

Is it not having to drip feed your crazy, not having to hide your demons, your shame, your beliefs, your shortcomings, your raw passion, your amazingness - your purest self?

Trusting that all to another?

Love is...

More than a feeling
More than a belief
More than an energy

Acceptance not approval

It needs to be all of that. But it can't be any of that until you have it all.

Poets have talked about Love forever trying to put its raw power into words.

People feel like love will save them- but save them from what?

To save them from themselves.

To not be alone.
To feel loveable.
To feel worthy.
To feel Enough.

How do we look upon love as being so magical, so undefinable, so powerful and life-giving but see Self-Love as so much less than that?

Unimportant.
Selfish even.

Self-love is all the things love brings
but instead of entrusting this all with someone else
It's investing the time and energy in yourself.

Fuck you don't even need your own approval- Just acceptance.
Believing and seeing your boundless BEING for who she truly is and loving her regardless-

Giving grace for your imperfections
Seeing the shiny and the dark
Seeing the ugly and the beautiful
Seeing the wobbles, the fuckups, the intensity

Loving regardless
Accepting Enoughness
Feeling your worth
Feeling vulnerable but trusting yourself anyway.

Trusting you'll stick around to learn more- that you'll cope with whatever truths come bubbling to the foreground.
Trusting you'll be kind, understanding, gentle, non-judgemental, soft and loving even after seeing all your ugly.

You are not a one-dimensional person.
You are not a peppy, happy leader with your shit together.
You are not the perfect mother
You are not a perfect friend

You are not a perfect lover

You are not perfect.
That is a given.
That is allowed.

Facing up to our humanness and still believing we are worthy of love might just be what most people are running from.

We run from this vulnerability our entire lives.
But Love is also a commitment.

We are ever changing
Ever expanding
Ever growing
Everything is energy.
Energy
Cannot
Does not
Will not

Ever stand still.

It is impossible to contain, restrain, catch or trap.

To love our own energy, we need to commit to that love daily.

Be vulnerable and raw with ourselves, nurture that rawness.
Learn, ponder, reflect
Feel that compassion, empathy and kindness.

Be tender with yourself.

Accepting yourself in the now doesn't mean that you'll never grow.
You will grow, it's impossible not to, it means loving yourself through the process.

Not focusing on an end goal but embracing the organic flow and the moment of now.

Anchoring your feet in love while your inner self is free to float, sway and be free.
Knowing your Isness[3] is the foundation of your worth- that nothing you do, think or feel can change that.

What and who you are inside, is the ONLY reason for your worthiness.
That you are Already Enough.

True love doesn't judge, criticise or belittle.
True love knows you are not the final version or the perfect outcome.

Of course, life changes.

Your skills, depth, ambition, dreams, income and happiness are all subject to change.
Some are even as fickle enough to change throughout a single day.

What stays the same is you.

Your worth
Your essence
Your energy
Your Self

You are enough. So much more than enough.

You are the ultimate power
The wild one
Boundless
Untamed
Uncut
Imperfect beautiful mess
Fucking unbelievably messy

---

3 Isness: Your "being"; The fact that you are here.

You don't need approval
You don't need fixing
You don't need someone else to tell you what a Goddamn Warrior
you are.

You just need you.
To make that commitment
To invest that time
To give energy
To give a damn

To not give up
To give freedom
To give trust

To feel
To believe
To understand
To show how much you matter

To hear you
To see you
To love you

This is more than just possible for you. This is vital for you.

And you deserve it. You are worthy of it.

Today, not tomorrow.

You deserve self-love just as you are, right now.

Chapter Two- Listening to Your Body

I thought self-hate was noble.
I thought self-hate was the only option.

Just six short years ago I literally hated everything about myself. My flabby disgusting body. My bad skin. My OCD. My depression. My anxiety. Every morning I would tear myself down, face all my ugly in the eye. I would tell myself I deserved this loathing. I was a failure. I frustrated myself. I felt like a shit mum. Too repulsive to even be seen.

I was useless.

I would lose months in a fog, sometimes not leaving my bed for days on end. I deserved the pain. The pain was the only thing I could hold on to. It was real. It wrapped me up in a protective prickly bubble. The slightest movement would hurt so bad, so I'd stay still, safe. The pain and the hate were all I'd ever known so it felt safe to be there.

Every single day was the same process. Tear down, collapse, then try and rebuild. Fail. Self- abuse. Hateful inner voice. I wanted to change everything about myself. I was obsessed with self-help books. Every day was a battle against my body and Mind.

If only I could be a better person. More successful. Get up early, exercise. Get plastic surgery. Be beautiful. Be a happy mum. If only I could be different. Someone who was steady, loveable, worthy- just not a fuck up like me.

THEN I could be proud of myself, THEN I could help other people, THEN I could let go of this hate and finally love myself.

IF ONLY
THEN

The first time I ever felt a tiny bit of love for myself was a sunny April just before my 34th birthday. I had decided to go on a health trip (again!) and paid money to join an online cleanse. I wasn't new to the detox world and enjoyed the feeling that I was "winning" against my body (almost as a form of punishment) so would normally follow the detox religiously.

This time I knew I needed the extra support, so I paid money that I didn't have for super food powders for my smoothies, and I filled my cupboards with shitloads of fruit and veg.

And yet I still couldn't stop eating junk food.
All the junk
All the sugar
All the booze
Not much of a cleanse

Normally I'd have beaten myself up over this but for the first time ever, for some unknown reason, it was like I just accepted the fact that my body couldn't cope with letting go of that crutch right now.

It was the first time I allowed myself the grace of accepting and understanding myself. This wasn't love though, this was more just a basic acceptance of how I was feeling, which was a massive leap forward for me.

You see, I was three months deep into pure grief after my miscarriage in the January. I'd spent about 6 weeks bed bound and I was finally getting out of the house again and trying to move gently forward so this cleanse was going to be my new start.

I started embracing all the information but just couldn't start the eating part of the cleanse. It confused me but I was being surprisingly accepting and easy on myself.

Saying that, though, I did feel very guilty. I felt like I was letting everybody down, especially the course leader, so I decided to try out another aspect that she had suggested.

It was just a recording of a five-minute guided meditation. I'd tried to meditate before, but my brain was way too busy, so it had just frustrated me. The guided meditation turned out to be so freakin[44] easy. All you had to do is listen!

So, the next time I tried a fifteen minute one. It was just a random one I'd found on YouTube but this one asked me to sit with my Body for just a moment and see what I felt.

My Body was really tired, I could feel an ache travelling up my spine and across my shoulders. My tummy had a dull cramp, and this was the moment that everything changed for me.

Normally I'd have felt this and said, "Stupid fucking body, I feel like crap again." Living with chronic pain means you often feel like your body's broken and constantly letting you down.

But this time something else came over me. Something much more substantial then aches and pains- suddenly my whole body was awash with sadness. Deep, painful sadness. Tears sprung up in my eyes. My body was actually filled from the core with deep breath-taking pain.

It was more than the feeling I'd been brushing aside daily- it was felt by my entire body and for the first time in my life I just wanted to pick myself up and give myself a big fat hug.

Of course she was sad, this whole time my body had been working hard to protect our baby, feeling all these hormones, changing shape and size, preparing for the future and now she was just empty, a vast nothingness in my torn and battered womb.

And I couldn't even allow her to grieve- I was still working her hard, ignoring her pains, ignoring her feelings, ignoring her cries for help. I'd literally felt no compassion for my body ever before.

———————————————————

[44] Freakin: More polite way of saying "Fucking"

I held myself and sobbed my little heart out. She'd been protecting me and loving me my entire life and I'd never once done anything to make that job easier for her. I'd never once been kind to her. The only time I'd ever tried looked after my body had been with the sole purpose of trying to look HOT and even that was torture for her.

And here I was with a body in grief and deep sadness, whose only goal was to protect and heal me and I couldn't even give her the chance to cry.

But then I realised that that if that was true for my body, then it must mean my brain had the same goal too. All the destructive crap I'd put up with from my brain- all the time I'd spent trying to change it. All those years fighting against myself and all it had ever wanted to do is protect me, the best way my brain knows how.

To protect me my brain would do anything that she believed "worked". If it's true for my body than it's true for my brain.

This was the first time I'd ever felt any compassion and empathy for myself. I could see that I was crying out for love. I desperately needed love, but not from anybody else, I needed it from me.

This was the moment that started that shift in myself, just by having and allowing myself to feel that compassion for my body, it fuelled me to start looking after myself and start accepting who I already was. I'm not saying that I've not lost/gained that compassion many times since and I still have messy/negative days (like eating tubs of ice-cream instead of addressing my emotions kind of days) but now I understand why, and those messy days are a sign that I need to love myself that little bit harder.

How Your Body & Brain Protects You

So, your body and brain have one main goal in life – to make sure YOU do not get hurt. They want to keep us alive; they want to keep us safe from fear and pain. The way we are wired is that literally everything we do is programmed to protect us.

To avoid physical pain is the top priority (i.e., to stay alive) but a close second to that is to avoid emotional pain.

From now on I will refer to your physical Body & brain as one-namely "Body" or "Her".

Although she is a part of you and obviously your brain's thoughts and belief systems are part of an "inner you", the Body's actions are more primal. She believes without logic and is wired for survival.

Our Bodies will try anything she can do to protect us from being hurt. Often sacrificing health, goals, dreams, opportunities, change, love or ANYTHING as long as it "works".

What she considers a victory is us not feeling physical or emotional pain "in that moment".

Our Bodies are not very future thinking, and she always believes that she knows better than what we do. She often believes we wouldn't be able to cope with whatever is threatening us so it's better to sacrifice your dreams/hopes and goals then it is to take a risk with our emotions or physical safety.

If the threat has actually happened, then she still needs to protect you for the fall out of that situation so it's safer for you NOT TO FEEL.

So, no matter the extent of the emotional pain that we are facing she will use all the tried and tested ways to block out that pain and not allow you to actually feel what you need to feel. Whether it's the uncomfortable feeling of having to have a conversation you don't want to have or the massive overwhelming feelings you have when you're grieving, your Body is really unsure of whether you can cope and so will try and protect you by stopping you from feeling those feelings at all costs.

This comes from a place of pure love.

Your Body loves you so much, even before you have that love for yourself.

Her love for you moves her to do everything she does! It means that she will do anything in her power to protect you from getting hurt. She loves you deeply even if you hate yourself.

This is massive.

Your Body's number one goal is to protect you. Isn't that just amazing?

Pretty much every negative habit and probably every imperfect thing you beat yourself up for can be traced back to a way your Body or brain is trying to protect you. Let's have a look at some of the ways together right now.

Feeling Your Feelings

Feeling your feelings seems like it should be the simplest thing in the world.

You got the feels[5] - you feel the feels.

But it's actually one of the most difficult things to decide to do, but in my opinion, it's one of the most crucial steps you can take on the path towards self-love.

Feeling our feelings can hurt
Feeling our feelings can be really hard
Feeling our feelings brings up more uncomfortable feelings
Feeling our feelings is a big and bold thing to do

---

[5] Feels: Feelings you may be actively avoiding.

Because our Body's love for us is so strong and she wants to protect us – remember she will do *anything* (especially if it worked before) to block, distract or drown out those feelings.

Although 9 times out of 10 the healthiest thing to do would be to feel, process, accept and work through these emotions- our Body will lovingly draw out the process and bury those feels deep down with methods that are 9 times out of 10 unhealthy, self-sabotaging or just plain dangerous.

Here are a few signs that may mean your Body is protecting you from feeling your feelings:

- Distracting yourself from being in the moment
- Busyness
- Obsessing over social media
- Gambling
- Numbing
- Being angry or dismissing someone else's feelings
- Being unable to be alone with your own thoughts
- Perfectionism
- Extremes with food (overeating/ under eating/ super controlling)
- Alcohol or drug abuse

Check
Check
Check
and Check

Oh fuuucccccckkkkk

Basically, all these actions cause us to disconnect from ourselves and to disconnect from what we are truly feeling.

Once we recognise that these negative behaviours are actually just how our Body is trying to protect us, we can begin to forgive ourselves, have compassion for her and say "thank you" to our Body for loving us so damn much.

Now we can reconnect with our feelings and change our patterns of coping but first we need to give ourselves permission to do so.

As a child we were probably (at least at some point) told to contain our emotions, hold them in, that some feelings are unacceptable to show, some emotions are too big for the situation or that there are good and bad emotions. It's SO the right time to unlearn this shit.

All feelings are valid- You are allowed to feel however you feel.

Look into your eyes in a mirror and say the words out loud: "It's OK for me to feel this way"

Give yourself permission to feel compassion and empathy for yourself. Your Body has been desperate for it for so long.

Say out loud: "I deserve to feel compassion for myself. It's safe for me to be kind"

Give yourself permission to be imperfect.
Say out loud: "I'm far from perfect and that's OK- I still choose love"

Give yourself permission to feel whatever you need to feel without judgement.

Say out loud: "There's no such thing as a bad emotion, whatever I am feeling it is valid for me to feel."

Note: In times of extreme grief or trauma numbness from emotion can be a massive gift for you from your Body. If an emotion is just too big to cope with, she will let it out in small chucks to give you the time and grace to process it. However, if you find yourself not allowing yourself to have any emotion at all for a long time than it might be time to ask for help.

Knowing what your beliefs around feelings are, can make you more aware of when you will need to feel more compassion for yourself.

Compassion:
A feeling of deep sympathy and sorrow for another who is stricken by misfortune, accompanied by a strong desire to alleviate the suffering.

Empathy:
The psychological identification with or vicarious experiencing of the feelings, thoughts, or attitudes of another.

Meditation To Help You Listen

Before I tried guided meditations, I had thought that meditation was completely unattainable for me. For one sitting quietly alone with just my thoughts terrified me. For fucks sake, I used to take my phone in the toilet just so I wouldn't have too much time to think on my own!

Of course, now I know it was the tool my Body was using to protect me but at the time I didn't know if I could cope with my thoughts. In fact, I successfully avoided grieving for my friend for about 13 years because I was afraid of what would happen if I allowed myself to feel it. That takes a shedload of control and ninja type blocking skills by the way.

I even had years of CBT therapy but still avoided dealing with any grief by using distraction, numbing and alcohol.

Sometimes I'd let a little tiny it out but often I'd feel like to let it out fully would mean I'd never be able to stop. when I finally faced up to the grief that I'd been carrying around like two heavy suitcases for all those years, it took about 6 weeks of completely falling apart before I felt like I had started healing.

Note: If you are dealing with a loss, grief or another major feeling that you have been avoiding or even facing right now it IS still possible to fully and truly love yourself (See Chap 9) but it may take longer, you may not feel ready right now but you can start the process you with extra support and understanding from the people who love you.

It was only after opening up to my grief that I'd spent so long trying to hide from, surrendering to the process, that I felt able to sit quietly just with my mind.

Before that I felt scared, trapped, frustrated and like a failure every time I tried to meditate or even just relax. The space to hear what my brain had to say felt like a very dangerous place.

Although I was actively grieving about my miscarriage when I began guided meditations, because I was consciously letting my grief flow, I no longer had that fear around meditation.

So, this chapter is all about listening to your Body- what does guided meditation even have to do with that?

Not only has meditation been proven to make you feel more relaxed and less depressed or anxious (and less pain!) but it's also an amazing tool for helping us get in touch with our Higher Self, our emotions, wants and true feelings. By disconnecting (our brain) we reconnect (with our Body).

How to start?

Make sure you've been to the loo, you're not hungry or thirsty and you are wearing comfy clothes (if any, naked meditation rocks) then sit or lay down comfortably.
Make sure your kids are being looked after (I.e., Watching DanTDM[6]) and put any distractions away (phones etc)

Because I'm often knackered from my babies and nutty kids, I often fall asleep, so I make sure I use a timer and lots of pillows!

I like to relax into position and because I feel pain in my neck and pelvis easily, I tend to lay down. I like feeling my body is fully supported with lots of pillows.

---

[6] DanTDM: Youtuber that kids have grown up with.

There are loads of different types of meditations that you can try:

- Guided

  In a guided meditation you are listening to someone else's voice so it's easy for beginners as you just have to plug your headphones in and listen. There are hundreds of guided meditations on YouTube, and they range from 5 minutes long to hours! I love Mooji.[7]

- Compassion

  Also referred to loving/kindness meditation. This is great for practising compassion for others and yourself. You can find a guide at the CHM website.

- Mindfulness / Open Monitoring

  This is where the object of the meditation is to be aware of your thoughts and feelings but observe them without attachment or judgement.

- Mantra

  This is when you repeat a single word or phrase over and over to keep your brain focused on a single task which helps keep the thinking mind busy so you will not have to ignore or silence those pesky reoccurring thoughts you may get during a silent meditation.

- Music

  Meditating with music in the background to help zone out.

- Breathing

  While meditation using this method, the object is to become aware of the sensation of your breath as it enters and leaves the nostrils.

- Apps

---

[7] Mooji: Jamaican spiritual teacher based in the UK and Portugal.

There are lots of app's that many people feel helpful. Some good ones are Headspace, Calm, Insight Timer, Audiojoy & Mindful.

Here are some problems that you may feel. These are all completely normal!

- Overthinking
  When your brain will not stop, please know (again) this is just another way she is trying to protect you. You are not failing, and it will get easier every time you meditate!

- Falling asleep
  This happens to all of us at some time. If it happens to you, try to concentrate on your breath going out, change position or just take note of how tired you are and nap.

- Vivid visions or colours
  This might mean it's time to drop your expectations and relax. If you are seeing something you don't want to see than that another way for your Body to protect you from something deep, so its suggested you stop the session and try again another time (or ask for help from professional if it's reoccurring)

- Aches pains, tingles and itches
  First figure out if they are external, and if so, change posture or stretch out. If there's nothing external that seems to be causing them it's your lovely brain trying to distract you from your true feelings again! Say thank you, feel compassion and try not to judge if pleasant or unpleasant, just feel them anyway.

Connect With Your Body

Although connecting with your Body can be toughAF[8] and brings up lots of emotions and pain you've been hiding away from, it's one of *the* most powerful tools you can use in the beginning to learn to love yourself.

But when you connect, it needs to be with compassion, empathy, patience and gratefulness.

When you truly feel what you are feeling, it has to be without judgment, and you need to let go of any "shoulds". We need to do this because that's the only way to really connect to her and listen to her.

Everyone has some pesky "shoulds" that turn up like a guilt inducing party pooper every now and again (or every time we start having fun or doing something just for us) You know the type:

"I really should be doing this instead..."
"I should have said this"
"I should be tidying up"
"I should have spent that money on bills"
"I should be able to deal with this"
"I should be a better person"

You get the drift! They are there to block out not only our feelings, but also to stop us from taking care of ourselves.

We also need to be aware that is this not a freakin' exercise to "fix" ourselves- I know as people we tend to put a high value on our skills to fix things – but think about this:

You are feeling super sad. It's about a problem in your family and you are thinking about it every minute of every day, but you are trying to hide the pain and worry from your kids and partner.

---

[8] AF: "As Fuck" ...said for emphasis.

You feel like you have the weight of the whole world on your shoulders.

A friend comes over who is completely away from the situation- there's no one else home and you know she won't judge you or your family, so you finally feel able to open up and let it all out. You can tell her how you feel, and she is listening intently, nodding and holding your hand gently. As you finish, you break down and cry. She holds you in her arms while you sob it all out.

- She hasn't said much
- She hasn't been able to take away your pain
- She hasn't been able to fix your problems

But she has listened, put herself in your shoes and you feel she understands what you are going through. She cares about you. Just by realising that pain, talking about your problem out loud and sharing your feelings- now how would you feel?

Better, cared for, stronger, lighter- LOVED.

When I talk about listening to your Body, I'm not saying you need to fix anything about yourself- you are already worthy of receiving your love and compassion. You are already enough.

We need to connect with our bodies on a deeper level- we need to actually hear what she is saying. Please understand the reason she's not been talking to you about how she truly feels is because she wants to shield you from that pain, the pain she has been carrying for you for so damn long.

All the time she's been waiting for you to be that friend, to listen to her without judgement, to hold her and reassure her that she is not alone.

And how have we paid our bodies back for this protection, for this love she is constantly giving us?

We starve her to "look good" or feed her crap to shut her up. We beat her up with our words and tell her she is not good enough.

We constantly give her unreachable goals of what she should look like, feel like, how she should react, act and BE. We expect her to change fundamental things about herself overnight with no empathy or kindness. We are constantly disappointed in her and give her hoops to jump through *just to deserve our love.*

Could this be why we are all so ill and tired all the time? Is there any doubt as to why so many of us are so depressed and overwhelmed with life? Is this why we all feel so lonely?
Can you see why you feel unworthy of love?

Can you see why feeling your feelings and breaking the cycle of self-hate is a brave and bold thing to do?

Your Body deserves your love
Your Body deserves unconditional love.

Unconditional love: Affection with no limits or conditions; complete love

The switch in your mindset to allow yourself to feel this, could take months or it could happen overnight. You may have just had that lightbulb moment right now! But it takes much more than just realising that you are worthy and that you deserve your own unconditional love- you really do need to feel and believe it.

That compassion that I will mention a million times in this book – you need to practise it, really feel it for yourself. You need to start being that non-judgemental friend for yourself. You need to listen to your Body without judgement, not ever trying to fix her but just being intent on loving her.

You may not be able to feel it at first and that's OK. Throughout this whole process I want you to have zero expectations from yourself. I want you to read this book with an open mind and in a place of kindness.

Remember: There is a huge difference between trying to love yourself while trying to be a better person...

and hating yourself for the imperfections that can't be changed, the imperfections that makes you human...

Now you might be worried that unless you are struggling and hustling to constantly better yourself, improve your finances or pushing to be a "better" person every day, then you are going to turn into a complete waster.

We do have a responsibility to correct ourselves when we commit a wrong against someone else and we will mess up often because of our imperfections. We may want to study and work hard to "better" our position in life or expand our knowledge. But we have had these "shoulds" weighing down on our heads every day of our lives. It gets drummed into us from such an early age it's hard to think of ourselves as anything but creatures who constantly have to change in order to live up to standards that have been set by someone else or perfect expectations that we have for ourselves.

If you've believed this, has it helped you to change for the better and love yourself more or does it just fuel the feelings of not being enough? Does it help that nagging self-doubt (or even self-hate) in your head?

We are creatures of change, we are creatures of growth- we create, expand, evolve and adapt. We do this every day in a positive or negative way. Each tiny decision we make will influence this change. You cannot stop this change from happing. Whatever we feel about ourselves will influence this change. The change, growth and creation of our life does not influence our worthiness for self-love, nor does it change who we are fundamentally as a person.

The object of this book is not to say love yourself and don't bother changing or growing. The message is that even if you decide to sit in your pants all day eating pot-noodles, you still deserve self-love and once you "get it", once you find that love and compassion for yourself, the changes will become organic and easy!

You won't want to sit in your pants all day because you will believe in yourself and your motivation to grow and become the best version of you will be exciting and new! In learning to love yourself, you learn to hope and expect more from life (and yourself) because you know deep in your bones it's OK if you fail. You can cope with it, handle it and love yourself regardless.

Change will happen and it will flow. Pushing yourself while beating yourself up never fucking lasts. The motivation is flawed. The motivation is forced.

Change that happens while being accepting and kind to yourself feels natural. It feels easy. It still requires self-awareness and hard work, but you are giving yourself grace as you do it, so the changes become part of who you are.

So, after so many years of not listening to your Body how do we connect with her and grow that loving, compassionate relationship with her?

Quite simply you ask her and listen to her reply.

Yes, your Body is ready to talk, but you must also be ready to listen.

I like to do this straight after meditation before I've even opened my eyes or just before I'm about to go to sleep at night.

The key is to be relaxed, without distraction and commit to giving this time (We're talking just 5-10mins or even just one minute if you're really pushed for time) completely to your Body.

Sit or lay with your Body. First be aware of what she can feel externally. Relax even further into it. As you lay there just notice any feelings that pop up. A stronger emotion may feel like it is growing all through your Body and smaller ones might come and go. You may feel physical pain in areas you hadn't noticed. Feel no judgement for these feelings and try not to think about the "why" or what you could do to "fix them". At this moment just concentrate on how your Body is feeling emotionally and practise feeling compassion & empathy for her. How kind is she to protect you from these feelings all day long? Does she feel tired? Does she feel sad? Does she feel Lonely?

Ask your Body how she truly feels- tell her it's OK to tell you, that you are safe and ready to hear her voice.

Connect with your Body.

Talk to her, tell her that you are here for her, tell her that she doesn't need to carry this all by herself anymore. Tell her that you can cope with whatever she needs to say.

Ask her what she needs. Allow any emotions to come up and come out- allow them to flow through you – just like you are holding that space for a friend.

Hold yourself. Feel how you need to feel. Ensure you talk to your Body with an extra kind voice.

She needs and deserves your love. She has been crying out for your love for so long. She's been "holding it together" alone for so long.

She just needs you to be there for her. To hold her and look after her.

Today, right in this moment, she is already enough to deserve this love.

Today, RIGHT NOW, YOU ARE ALREADY ENOUGH to deserve to love yourself.

Building Trust

Learning to trust your Body can seem like you're about to take a blind leap of faith. I mean, we've been taught not to trust our bodies from a super early age.

Taught our feelings are wrong or bad
Taught to view our bodies as faulty machines
Taught to rely on medicines because our bodies can't heal
Taught our bodies will let us down or put on weight just to spite us

We expect as we get older that our bodies will fail us and that her only worth is based on how she looks.

When we find out about the protection that she gives us it can be a really scary fact to believe, because this new information means our bodies are not letting us down.

For the most part WE HAVE BEEN LETTING THEM DOWN!

So finally, you legit[9] accept your responsibility and decide to connect with your Body. You start to treat her with kindness and respect, but inside, the opposite happens. Your inner voice gets meaner, you feel sicker, and you feel more distant from your Body than ever... what the fuck is going on?

The Storm starts
when you first decide to love yourself
and your Body sees your power
so she starts to fight
with all her might
To keep you
small.
She is afraid of you being strong enough to love her.
She is happy with you hating her
because that means
You'll stay safe.

Long story short, whatever you do that's harmful to yourself is actually proof of your Body trying to protect you because she loves you so much, she is happy to sacrifice herself to keep you safe.

---

[9] Legit: For real; The realest real

Recently I've been learning about the different stages of detox from fasting/juice feasting. Each level of the detox goes deeper the longer you fast or feast. It's like peeling an onion!

As I researched more into it, it's clear that diseases, fever and even cancer- EVERYTHING is a way for your Body to protect you! We will dig deeper into this later, but she's done all of this unconditionally and without your love. She's protected you through crappy food choices, unhealthy habits, lack of sleep, too much alcohol, hardly any water and really poor nutrition! She's desperately needed for you to listen to what she needs, but you've done everything you can to block her voice out. She has loved you through all of this unconditionally and you have let her down constantly, maybe even daily. I'm not saying this so that you feel bad, but I'm showing you that it's **her** that needs to build her trust in you, not the other way round.

- How does she know that you're really ready now?
- How does she know that you can cope with what she needs to say and will actually listen to her?
- How does she believe that you will keep her safe and then keep yourself safe?
- How does she know that you are strong enough and that you will love her and that you won't let her down like you have so many times before?

You know that you are ready to listen, but she might not be ready to talk to you at all at first. It's all about building trust. You saying that you're going to do something is very different to you doing it. Doing It well, doing it daily- truly listening and truly caring.

Saying you'll unconditionally love your Body then secretly judging what she feels or wanting to change who you are or talking back with a mean voice can cause your Body to lose trust in you. So, give her time, keep practising connecting with her even if she feels like not talking. Be kind and gentle with her, allow feelings to come up without judgement and do it daily! Find out who you are so that you can truly love yourself and your Body can have full trust in you again.

Chapter Three - Finding You

You are not lost
You are already here
Just waiting to be seen

When I love something, I fucking LOVE it. There's no middle ground here- as soon as my passion is lit, I'm jumping in fullarsed[10], obsessed like a psycho on crack. I have this overwhelming insatiable hunger to learn everything about it, it will be all I talk about, think about, research and do. There will be zero let up until I've devoured every single bit of information I can.

I often blame my OCD, but the truth is: I'm a passion junkie.

Ever since I had my first baby I was obsessed with birth, breastfeeding and all things baby related. I wanted to help other women not have the traumatic experience that I did so I trained to be a doula[11] and then I started photography concentrating mainly on maternity, breastfeeding and newborn babies.

When I wasn't photographing bumps and babies, I spent my spare time at support groups (I ran some too), hanging out with doulas or learning more about our basically fucking amazing bodies and what they go through in order to birth us into motherhood. Legit boobie[12] and baby obsessed.

During the 5-6 weeks of missed miscarriage limbo, when I wasn't sure if the baby I was carrying was growing or not- I was still working as a doula, postnatal doula and photographing pregnancies and newborns. But what once filled me with joy and passion now just felt like absolute shitcakes[13].

---

[10] Fulledarsed: The opposite of half-arsed; Doing something with your full heart and soul committed.
[11] Doula: Person who supports women in childbirth
[12] Boobie: Breast-y.
[13] Shitcakes: A metaphor for something amazing or really awful

When my Body finally let go of my little sparkle (that's what I called my babe) I just felt lost. I didn't know who I was anymore, I didn't know what would make me happy, I didn't know what I wanted to be or even do. Some days I would look at a photograph I was working on for hours without being able to start or finish. I told myself it was because my pictures were of newborn babies and it was just too hard, but in all honesty, it was all of my photography. Even images I'd taken of my own kids. All of a sudden everything that once brought me joy and made me excited about life just felt Meh, super Meh. Everything was flat.

I'd lost my sparkle in more ways than one.

But I was grieving and so that's understandable, right? We'll talk more about grief and depression later because going through tragedy definitely adds more layers to "losing yourself" and finding your love again, but so many mums I talk to express how they just feel so lost, even when they are going through the happiest time of their life- in fact this feeling of being lost and dissatisfied can happen to anyone and I think of it as a type of grief.

Life changes- it's the one thing we can depend on. Whether it's your life changing for a great reason or a terrible one- any change leaves our feet feeling unsure. Our foundations can feel disturbed.

Some people crave change, and it leaves them feeling excited for the future. For other people, change scares the crap out of them and (yes, you've guessed it) it sends their Body into full blown protection mode.

You feel the fear even on a subconscious level so to protect you from ever even wanting to change, your Body will show you that any change is equal to basically the worst feeling you can ever experience, namely Grief.

Things stay the same = Safe
Stuck = Safe
Any change (good or bad) = Unsafe

The grief we feel when things change in our life is really similar to the grief we feel when we lose someone, albeit not so soul fucking destroying and heart-breaking. We feel lost. We feel loss. We yearn for our old life, and we need to mourn it. Things that we were so sure were "our calling" or things that filled us with so much passion we're now not so sure about. It's hard to find joy in anything at all.

We are in the "time in-between knowing"

I'm lukewarm
I'm grey
Not here
Not there

Drifting on nothingness
Thin air

Of course, it's "OK" and even normal to feel this way but it's almost like we need to get to know ourselves again.
If someone asks you what you enjoy doing and you are unsure, whether you've been through a big change recently or not- you need to get to know yourself again.

It's very hard to love someone if you don't know anything about them.

It's very hard to get to know someone if they don't want you to know anything about them.

It's impossible to get to know someone without giving them time.

You need to take the time to get to know yourself again.

Right now, you may feel like you don't have time to fart let alone "re-find yourself" OR you may have so much time on your hands you feel useless and have to fill it with anything to block out your emotions. The dark playground of distraction is a bittersweet, beautiful place.

So, if you are playing there, feeling lost or not even knowing who the fuck you are anymore- please know you are not alone.

And also know the reason you feel like this is just another "tool" that your Body is using to protect you because she loves you that much.

Trouble is when you numb out the pain there is no filter, so it numbs out all the joy too.
Thank your Body for providing this protection but allow yourself the time, openness and patience to get to know what you love again.

The "time in-between knowing" is a difficult, lonely place to be. But accepting you are there, having no judgement and believing you are worthy of love and compassion even though you are lost- will make this part of your journey that much easier.

And now we will try to have fun with it- consider this part of your life to be like when you first meet someone you fancy. That "time in-between knowing" is like that early dating stage. When you first start dating it's fun, exciting and you get butterflies when you find someone who makes you smile. What would happen if you took this lost, scary feeling and instead decided to treat it like a new love interest- It's your chance to decide what you like to do, try new things and fall in love but not with Barry from Tinder, it's a chance to fall in love with you!

You can find out what makes you smile and "date" yourself. It can be fun if you decide that you are allowed to have fun with it and truly believe that even when you are lost you are still enough.

Who Are You?

I find introductions a bit messy. When I'm trying to introduce who I am in a few short sentences I have a lot of "shoulds", and guilt pop up to say hello instead!

We all have labels that either do or do not define who we are. For me I'm a step mum and birth mum (see that's starting to sound weird already) maybe even a loss mum- I can say just "mum" to 7 but then that shocks people and I feel I have to explain. I love my step kids just the same as the kids I gave birth to but I also honour the fact that my step kids (well not quite kids anymore they act older than me!) have a mum of their own and they call me Mirrie. See there's a story behind every label.

Describing "me" is even harder. We normally start out with what job we do:

I'm a Photographer, Self-Love Coach, Doula and Writer now, I guess! Although I'm not actively doulaing anymore so should I include that? I also sell my clay ladies so do I call myself an artist too?

We describe how we raise our kids- If we breastfeed or bottle-feed, home educate or the kids go to school, how our kids sleep, if we VAX or how we carry our babies etc

We describe our passions, what hobbies we have or even how we eat!

Or we describe ourselves by the problems we face.

If we are depressed, we will say "I am depressed"
If we are having money issues, we'll say "I am poor"
If we have lost someone we'll say "I am grieving"

We describe ourselves differently depending on who we are talking to, but we rarely tell anyone WHO we truly are in that moment- we just use labels that we think (or hope) they will relate to.

What are some of the labels that you believe you have? How do you describe you?

How do those labels make you feel? Do they sit well with you? Do you believe they fit who you really are?

The labels and how we describe ourselves are actually very powerful and influences our beliefs and self-worth.

The more we say it, the more we believe it.

When we use the words "I AM" to other people it sends a powerful message to our brain... and the more we say "I AM" to ourselves, the more we will believe what were actually saying. Until it ends up with you saying that label to yourself every day and you end up actually believing that's WHO YOU ARE.

If you have the time google Amy Cuddy's TED talk- "Fake it until you become it "- because while it's true saying "I AM" can make us believe negative labels about ourselves, it can also allow us to believe amazing new beliefs about ourselves too. The power to create who you truly are and who you want to be starts with something as simple as the words we use to describe ourselves.

So, in other words, the power lies within you to change your labels or for the ones you can't change- you have the power to take away their power.

For example, I have OCD. For years it felt like a shameful secret- in therapy I would describe my morning rituals as "striping myself of all my dignity and tearing myself apart before trying to put myself back together again, all before I start my day."

As I go through this Self-Love journey, I now feel like I can be open about my OCD, and I'd describe my mornings as "Walking through treacle but I know I can do it."

I'm not belittling my problems to myself; my mornings are actually much easier now! So, what's changed? Only my view of what my problems are and the voice I use inside. OCD is no longer shameful- it's just the way my brain works differently than other peoples. It's no longer a secret, a hurtful all-inclusive label that would make people judge me. It's just a part of the way I handle things that I have to live with. Because it's not such a big deal to me, it's not such a big deal to others and actually it isn't ME.

My mornings are ultimately the same, but my struggle isn't.

OCD still affects my family, but it used to play a big part in why I felt depressed sometimes and I used to wish it wasn't how my brain worked, but just by changing my words and the way I relate my story; it has changed the way I view my "condition" altogether.

I don't see my morning rituals as tearing down myself anymore and so, each morning, I don't tear myself down anymore.

What I'm trying to say is our language and the way we tell our story not only influences other people's view of us but also our own view of ourselves.

When I was having therapy, we did a lot of core belief work and my root core belief was "I'm Useless" (ta dah it only took us a million years to figure out) we spent many many hours trying to figure out "why" that was my core belief (I have very supportive parents, had high confidence while growing up and a normal, happy childhood) and we spent many years trying to change my core belief. I used to find it hard to even write down those two words. I'm useless. I remember one exercise was to write down anything that anyone told me that was against that belief and prove myself wrong. Within a few days I did have a page or two of really lovely things people had said to me.

That list made me feel good, but it didn't change my belief. Other people's words have little impact when you're hating on yourself. I also had to describe the opposite of my core belief and say it out loud to myself in the mirror.

"I'm Useful" ...how anticlimactic! I couldn't really give a crap if I was useful so why did the word "useless" mean so much to me? Why was that the word that I defaulted to every time I felt that something was going wrong?

I guess the million-dollar question is, how did I change my core deep rooted belief so that it doesn't pop up even when things go wrong?

I have changed my core belief at a cellular level.

Although the therapy and CBT was very useful in helping control my OCD and anxiety, the exercises I learnt never touched on changing my core belief. Although it was useful to understand where this belief may have come from, it never stopped the word "useless" being my default word to describe myself in my head.

If you were to ask me today if "I am useless" is my core belief I would say no. (That's powerful to admit yo[14]!) Writing the words is no longer painful because I don't believe them. But if you had asked me about 6 weeks ago when I'd lost my self-love and I was in deep depression (it happens) then the words did hold meaning for me because I'd replaced the words "I'm useless" with the words "I give up" which basically means the same fucking thing, and so that says to me changing your core belief is only possible when you love yourself.

Interestingly since writing this I've had long depressive periods without losing my self-love and the core belief "I'm useless" has not come back.

So, the difference is not only the words but the feelings behind them.

You are in control of your words.
You are in control of your beliefs

The power you are giving to these words that make up your story is based on the feelings you feel about yourself.

The problem is one can't change without the other.

If you keep using the words like useless, stupid, pointless, ugly, failure or anything else you describe yourself as to hate on yourself... and you're using them again and again every single day of your life, how on earth are you ever going to believe anything different? How on earth are you ever going to love yourself? If you change the words but make no effort to love yourself, you will never truly believe and feel into your new words/story.

---

[14] Yo: Saying You or" Yo" like the cool kids.

It's a two-way street. You need to first find the person you want to be, then you describe yourself as that person in your head (I feel like if you really want to be "that type" of person surely that means that deep down you actually are but are not living aligned with your true values or beliefs?)

So now you control your story, and your story serves you. Next you align your actions with your new beliefs and feel like the real you, all the while actively loving yourself for everything that you already are...warts and all!

Accepting who you are now and believing that you are deserving of love no matter what, is a daily practice. So, take that time to really think about who you are. If you feel lost go to the core of who you want to be. Go and try out the things you've always wanted to do, but never had the guts to or the things you couldn't justify spending the time or money on before. There really is no one who can stop you from becoming who you want to be (i.e., the true you) except you.

People can mould you or tell you who you should be but it's every little decision that you make throughout your days on earth that actually controls who you are.

We all have labels we wish we didn't have that can't be changed, but the power those labels seem to have over your life really is YOUR power on how you choose to view them and how they make you feel. They don't actually hold any power at all because you hold it all!

Accepting that the woman you are today still deserves love *without changing a thing* is an amazing step towards self-love.

Your Inner Child

Kids have this amazing ability that no matter what situation they find themselves in they will find a way to have fun.

While in that fun mode children don't care what they look like, they don't care what you think of them. They have no fear of failure or success. They don't live in the past or worry about the future because they have one goal and that's to chase JOY. They find what lights them up and they just DO.

I home educate my kids. I remember when Eli was 6. What sticks out to me is how he would always learn regardless of what was going on. He loved learning something new because it felt fun for him. He was relentless in finding out about everything! It also meant he wanted to try out a lot of things just to see if he liked them. Even at that young age I could see the difference in him and his younger brother- particularly in the area of painting and music. Eli had an expectation of how good he "should" be in these areas so the pressure he put on himself when he isn't living up to his own high standards made these subjects "boring" to him. His 3-year-old brother- having no idea or goal of what he wanted the painting to look like or how his music sounded to anyone else, loved doing these things and lost himself in pure joy while splashing paint everywhere. Eli didn't put any pressure on himself in maths though. Having no outside pressure or anyone else's opinions (or tests etc) influencing him he really loved maths, in fact he still loves it so much he will choose doing sums over going to the park (don't ask about Roblox though)!

When you were a kid, you probably had things that sparked your joy and before anyone influenced you there were things that you were drawn to doing for no purpose other than to make yourself feel happy.

As adults a lot of us lose this. Goals and expectations can take the joy out of things that used to be so much fun for us, or the fear of getting something wrong or not being perfect can make us not even try to do the thing in the first blinking place!

As adults we often hear the term "Getting in touch with your inner child" but what does that mean to you? Who is your inner child?

Some psychologists believe we learn our core beliefs by the age of five, others state it's before we are three, but almost all experts agree that our core beliefs, especially about ourselves, develop in very early childhood. Before the age of five our ability to learn through play is amazing.

It's also at this time that our need for love and acceptance is perhaps the highest it will ever be and how you were loved and nurtured determines your core beliefs, right? Wrong! In some cases, this might be right but I had the most amazing childhood with parents who accepted me and loved me unconditionally and yet I grew up with the core belief that "I am useless." The key in core beliefs is not how we felt as children but ultimately WHAT WE SAW.

You see, our parents core beliefs are passed down to us like a grand old grandfather clock, even through our DNA but we'll talk more about that later. Saying that, there's no doubt that if you were neglected or felt unloved while you were very small, it's going to be affecting how you see yourself as who you are now.

But a lot of people will poopoo this inner child talk as hippydippy[15] baloney because you're an adult now, you've changed, learnt, grown- become better!

While it's true that you are no longer a child, that little part of you still is and it's in there somewhere, full of wonder and gratitude, expecting things to be fun, and for magic to be real, and needing a whole lot of love. While we all change and grow and become focused on what we think is important in life (normally the boring shit) The part of you that was there first stays within you unchanged.

I like to think of the inner child of being the pure essence of you. The part of you that sparks up when you find yourself doing something you love. The part of you that needs fun and wants to play around. She's the part of you that's normally the first thing that feels lost when you face a very real, scary or sad adult problem. Like a child she's probably hiding until you can sort the problem out and she feels safe again. Children need safety, guidance, fun and above all else love. If you've not been giving

---

[15] Hipydippy: Airy fairy; wishy-washy

yourself these things, maybe your inner child is hiding from you right now- which leaves you with a life with no sparkle.

I love playing with clay, just making little faces. As my hands get messier and I can see a little face forming in the clay I feel my smile growing, I feel happy, satisfied and excited. For no reason other than I love doing it- when I feel that little spark in my heart, I know I'm feeding my inner child with the good stuff.

The more your inner child is fed and feels safe to show herself, the more joy and wonder you can feel again in your life now.

Your Kind Voice Vs Your Inner Bitch

There's normally only one little voice inside your head and unless you love yourself already, she's probably a bitch.

Where the fuck does that voice come from?

The voice I'm talking about is much more than just your thoughts. It's your inner consciousness. It's the voice that rationalises what's going on. Takes your feelings and makes you understand them. It's the voice that sees everything and relays it to you in a way that either hurts you or confirms the fact that it's ok, that you will cope.

When your Body is left uncared for, although her main goal is still to protect you, your Body will take on a harsh voice in order to be heard. When your Body is cared for, acknowledged and appreciated, this voice is usually taken over by the real you or "Higher Self". We need to talk about how to switch from one voice (that is highly emotional, negative, critical and irrational... not to mention very overprotective!) to a gentler, kinder voice- a voice that not only believes in you but who knows you better than you know yourself.

Firstly, Meet Your Bitch...

Most days we go through the day without really thinking about what our brain is telling us. We don't have time to think because there's just so much to do. When something goes wrong (or right) we react internally or externally. Often if we are blaming someone, it will be an external reaction but as you are reading this book, I'm guessing the blame normally falls on you. Very often this makes us have an internal reaction, in other words we give ourselves a really fucking hard time (An English bollocking[16], if you will!)

This reaction is usually beyond harsh. We are usually harder on ourselves than we'd ever be on anyone else.

This bitchy voice and the words that she uses feels so normal because it happens so many times a day, we hardly even notice. Let me say that again-

You are being so hard on yourself, often using disgusting words towards yourself and it has become NORMAL. You are not only not hearing the words because you say them so often, but your BRAIN IS BELIEVING THOSE WORDS TOO.

Hold up, heyyyyyy...[17]

Earlier I said not only when something goes wrong during the day, but also when it goes right? Yep, your inner Bitch can pipe up when things are going great too- why? Because she will tell you that you don't deserve these awesome things that are happening to you. She shuts you down to opportunities. She shuts you down to receiving love and money. She tells you to shut up and put up.

Even if you are not listening to your Inner Bitch- your brain is.

Your brain believes everything that bitch says. That's scary, right? That's why it's SO important to replace her with a kind voice who actually cares about you.

---

[16] Bollocking: English way of saying "Telling-off" but one that's so bad it feels like a kick to the genitals

[17] Heyyyyy: Song reference from the 2000's to be sung not spoken. (Dr. Dre – The Next Episode ft Snoop Dogg)

The first step to changing your inner bitch into an inner kind voice is actually by taking notice.

Uncomfortable Action:
When you have that reaction to good or bad things that happen today, actually stop and listen to what your inner voice is saying and write down at least 5 words or sentences. Listen to the language that you use. If the words are painful to write, do it on scrap paper so you can destroy it afterwards. Remember these words are not your truth, rather they are either a protection or some shit that you need to explore.

As soon as my inner voice becomes bitchy it's my first sign that I must be struggling with self-love, or I've been putting myself last. If I ignore that warning and carry on the same way my Inner bitch gets irritated, then shouty- until she's so loud she's the only damn voice I can hear.

When she gets past the shouty stage, then she's on a roll because she has no competition, there's no one to stand up to her. She is ruling your roost which means she is ruling your brain, and in turn your beliefs. That's a lot of power for one bitch to have. That's fucking way too much power!

But if your inner bitch is just a part of you, then why is she putting you down all the time? Why is she sabotaging your attempts to make a better you, to make a better life? Why is she so hateful towards...herself?

At this point you might be still feeling that it's you against her. That the awful voice is something you need to defeat. That it's a battle. That you need to get that whip out and tame her Indiana Jones style- but hold on to that thought while you read this:

You know when a child is so desperate for love and attention that their attitude is horrendous, so they call their parents spiteful names and act so destructively that it even hurts themselves? They do this because any attention (even negative) is better than no attention at all. Let that sink in.

Your Inner Bitch is Your Inner Child.

This is not about You Vs your Body.

So, your Inner Bitch is a warning sign that you are actually desperate for self-love and self-care. You need your own attention and the longer you ignore this need, the LOUDER your Bitch becomes.

The type of self-love or self-care you need will be different on how your Inner Bitch is talking to you and this is what we want to figure out. There are three main areas:

1.   *You need LOVE*

If you are neglecting your basic needs and putting everyone else first
If you washing clothes comes before washing yourself
If you are tired, cranky and feel like you haven't got "time" to have a moment for yourself
If you feel like you are barely surviving

Then Your Inner Bitch is SCREAMING at you to give yourself more love. More care. Denying yourself basic care and love is not OK. You need to go into mama mode for yourself.

2.   *You need to find Yourself*

If you loathe the way you look
If you feel overwhelmed
If you are saying "Should" in every other sentence
If you don't know what makes you happy anymore
If you are unsure about what you enjoy

Then Your Inner Bitch is SCREAMING at you for attention. You have lost yourself in a sea of everyday-ness and that's not OK! You need to focus on you to bring back the magic in your life!

3.   *You need to let go of Your Fear*

If you feel like the world is against you
If you are neglecting your passions
If you feel stuck

If you feel hopeless
If you feel like you don't deserve better

Your Inner Bitch is protecting you. She loves you SO much that she is unwilling to risk you feeling hurt or failing at something new. Your inner Bitch wants you to soar high and achieve great things, but she also wants you to be safe- super safe and SUPER SAFE = SUPER STUCK.

So, she is SCREAMING at you to freeze you into place. Being stagnant and not allowing yourself to be open and grow is not OK! You need to believe in your worth and do it afraid!

We know our Body will do anything to protect us and this is where that bitchy voice is coming from, it's an expression of protection-

For example: if you are self-sabotaging instead of going for it towards your dreams, you will be less likely to take risks and therefore there'll be no risk of change/rejection or failure and so you'll be safe from hurt.

Your Inner Bitch is the voice of a body & brain who has been unloved for too long. A Body that has been hated on and ridiculed for too many years. If you expect nothing less than perfection from your Body then she will demand it from you! There is literally only one way to stop your inner voice from being unkind and that is to practise compassion and empathy for yourself every single day. Stop that voice in her tracks and replace it with the voice from your loving Higher Self who just wants to wrap your Body up in her strong arms and say:

"I understand you are angry. It's OK, I'm here to love you and take care of you now. It's OK to be imperfect, I'll love you anyway, my love for you is unconditional. Lash out all you want; I'm not going anywhere"

A lot of people when talking about self-love will think of hippies with flowers in their hair floating around talking about love, man. Well while hippies rock (like, for real!) I see the modern-day self-love crew as rebels, warriors even! Standing in their badass wonder woman pose with unicorns shooting freakin' rainbows outta[18] their butts in the background!

Loving yourself on this little planet that floats in space is nothing short of a fearless rebellion! It goes against EVERYthing society wants us to believe, everything we have been taught about being good!

This world wants you to be a good, polite, pretty girl. Quietly unhappy in her self martyr-ism (I looked it up- it's kind of a word!). To love yourself is bold, brave and downright scary.

But to Ms Inner Bitch:
Scary = Risk
Risk = Fear

So, when you start to love on yourself (to heal her!) don't be surprised if she comes at you *all guns blazing! *
She is trying to protect you.

Have compassion & empathy towards her. She is a scared, sad little girl who has been unloved for so long.

Bullied children bully
Neglected children lash out

What do we feel for these kids who have been bullied or neglected by the person whose job it is to love them the most?

Have compassion & empathy towards yourself. You are just human. You have been trying so long to be ALL the things to ALL the people, without ever giving anything to yourself. Just stop and let that sink in.

But beware of this danger, there is a HUGE difference between compassion (awesome) and self-pity (sucky[19] victim mode).

---

[18] Outta: Gangster way of saying "Out Of"
[19] Sucky: Something that sucks ballbags; Something ba

Self-love is big and bold! It's empowering! It allows you to take back control of your thoughts and life! Self-pity is just another tool your Inner Bitch uses when self-hate isn't working. It keeps you small and in your place. Pity doesn't help anyone.

Compassion and empathy are seriously THE KEY to self-love and switching from that bitchy voice to a kind one. And self-love literally changes everything in your life for the better so there's no other word to describe it, it's truly the bomb[20] diggity!

Uncomfortable Action:

We want (read: need) to love ourselves unconditionally so that means loving ourselves regardless of any real or perceived faults or imperfections.

That means that loving yourself is possible today, without changing a thing about yourself.

So, ask yourself right now:

1. *Why is my voice being unkind- is it to protect me or am I needing love?*
2. *What am I not accepting about myself?*
3. *Am I allowing myself to be imperfect today?*
4. *What am I expecting from myself today?*
5. *Am I setting the bar too high or is it even unreachable?*
6. *Is my voice actually helping me?*

Living with an unkind voice is not only exhausting it's also un-motivational. You will not want to love yourself if you are living with a bitch in your head.

A crappy, bitchy voice will not make you change into a better person- it will make you give up.

---

[20] Bomb diggity: Something is the shit; amazing; the best thang ever

A kind, compassionate voice who is not asking you to change will inspire you to be the best person that you can be today and will love you even if you can't!

Who would you rather live with? A grumpy, unkind, unforgiving woman starved of love or a loving, kind, understanding, compassionate woman who has so much love she feels able to give it out freely?

Who would motivate you more?
Who would you warm to?
Who would you want to spend time with?

YOU are in control of your own voice! You can literally choose which one to listen to!

Your worth can not be measured by anyone or anything-
Your worth just is
And you just need to see it.

Hold up again! If my Bitch is only acting like a bitch because I've been neglecting myself, then that means this is all my own fault anyway! Maybe I deserve the things she's been saying! Why do I need to forgive her if it's all my own fault?

Imagine this: You've got a really important interview tomorrow and tonight you can't stop worrying about it. You try to sleep but you don't know how to stop your brain. All night you toss and turn, you get a really crappy night's sleep and then when the alarm goes off in the morning you want to throw it out of the window, but you are really glad it went off because without it you would have slept right through.

Would you feel guilty about not being able to sleep?
Would you blame yourself for hating the alarm clock?
Would you feel ashamed that you were tired but still woke up in time for your interview?

No! Being nervous for an interview is normal, the alarm annoyed you because you were tired, but you'd still feel great that you still rocked your interview!

So, the rough night's sleep represents your (lack of) self-love/self-care in the past. There's no need to blame yourself or feel guilty because we are not taught this stuff, we don't know how to love ourselves and may have even been taught that self-care is selfish or unkind. In this day and age, barely caring about ourselves is normal.

The alarm is your Inner Bitch; annoying, hurts your ears and you want to shut her up! But all she is doing is trying to wake you up. Wake you up to how you've been living so far and just how much you need to care more!

The job interview represents our future. Now we are awake we get to jump up, get ready and rock it, despite how much of a bad night sleep we had the night before.

So now we really have no more time or space for blame, guilt or shame, those emotions only make our Inner Bitch louder because that's the opposite of what she is trying to achieve (although boy does she go the wrong way about it!)

If you don't heal it, you'll repeat it.

We can't heal without forgiveness first and now's the time to forgive. Forgive our bitches for being such...well...bitches and forgive ourselves for what we didn't know before. Sounds simple and really it is, it takes just a few minutes but will impact your life forever!

If while trying to heal, your bitchy voice ramps it up and becomes louder, this is totally normal and actually a good sign! It means you are on the right path and she is trying to protect you from change. Thank her and tell her you can handle this, and you will feel her relax and melt away knowing your kind voice is now in control.

This next Uncomfortable Action is loosely based on Hoʻoponopono which is a Hawaiian practice to forgive and heal.

Uncomfortable Action:

Either close your eyes and visualise taking your own hands (really see your face), look into your eyes and say the following words:
OR
Look into a mirror, deep into your eyes and say the following words out loud:
(Change any words after "because" to make it more specific to you and it will be even more powerful)

"I forgive you because I did not know that all this time you were trying to protect me and show me that I needed to take care of myself better.

I'm sorry it took so long for me to listen to you and know you have been saying these hateful things because you are hurting.

Thank you for loving me so much you relentlessly try to show me I need to love myself more.
I love you unconditionally, you are loved, you are safe, and you are worthy."

As you become used to the new words and the beliefs beyond those emotions, you will see yourself grow braver and stronger. The more compassionate and empathetic you can be towards yourself during this time, the faster and more beautifully your kind inner voice will flourish.

Chapter Four - True Self-Care

Self-Care... A commitment to your Body to take care of her as much as she takes care of you.

Self-care...What we have been taught:

Most of what we are taught about self-care is what I call: "Acceptable Selfishness"

Most of it that makes it acceptable is the fact that it contributes to how we look rather than how we feel. The selfish part we're told is us spending time on ourselves or money but that it's OK or we are "worth it", but this is only for activities that are socially acceptable depending on our age. Here's a tongue in cheek review:

Preteen:
-Brush your teeth (looks)
-Take care of your hair (looks)
-Do your nails (looks)

Teenager:
-All of above
- Start exercising (health, weight, looks)
- Watch diet (health, weight, looks)
- Skin care (looks)
- Make up (looks)

Pregnancy: (Only time in society that bigness is valued as beautiful)
-Eat for two
-Treat yourself
-Rest as much as you need
-Vitamins (think of the baby)

Mothers:
-Long bubble bath with wine
-Mum's night out with wine

-Colour your hair (get rid of greys)
-Anti-aging cream

Notice a common theme here? Most acceptable acts of self-care involve making sure you look good (for someone else) or well, that's it! For women we are given a clear goal of who self-care is actually for and guess what, it isn't you. So much of our worth and value is put on our attractiveness in society, that's the only junk we are sold that we are truly "Worth it" for.

Well, I call Bullshit. Self-care is for YOU. We're talking basic human needs but also Soul Needs. The extra pockets of joy that light us up, make us feel accomplished and feel fanfuckingtastic. You deserve that every. single. day.

Filling Your Cup

"If you don't look after yourself, you'll have nothing left to give"

"You have to fill your cup first then you can give to others"
We hear these expressions enough but what does it all mean?
So, this is where our self-care and who we truly are kind of merges into one. As we saw before, as a child we should be taught the basics for caring for ourselves- the things we should be doing- the basic human necessities:

Fed
Hydrated
Clean
Rested
Safe

When you are a mum with no time, depressed, have PND or just full on hating on yourself these can be hard enough to keep up with. If we look at this list, there may be things we aren't doing for ourselves every day that we need to do just to be functioning humans. If you're struggling to do this, it would be useful to make these things a priority right now.

However, these are just the basic things we need to survive, there's so more that will help us thrive and it seems that schools and our parents forgot to teach us.

And there's an important reason they forgot, it's because kids don't need to be taught this extra stuff, they just do it instinctively.

Filling your cup. Any of the above self-care activities might fill your cup as well as filling your basic human needs but that's only if you really truly enjoy doing it.

Children fill their cups every day without being asked or told.

You can ask a child to brush their teeth but if they don't enjoy it you will have to bug them because it's a chore to them. But put them in a room filled with toys or even just cardboard boxes and children will play.

Children learn a lot through play but that's not the reason they do it. Children play because it's fun. Next time you see your kid doing something you've not asked them to do, ask them why...

"So I don't have to tidy up" Honest answer from my 6-year-old right now.
"Because it's so fun"
"I just like it"

Children play because it's fun. It brings them enjoyment, satisfaction, makes them happy. It fills their cup.

They don't need to think about the end product because they are too busy enjoying the process.

FUN: *Something that provides mirth or amusement, enjoyment or playfulness.*

This fundamental part of self-care is almost forgotten because as adults it's seen as pointless. We will go to the gym and see it as self-care (which it is) but unless you are someone who loves the gym, it won't be filling your cup.

For me soaking in a super-hot bath filled with Epsom salt, essential oils and surrounded with candles (and silence) is not part of my cleaning routine because I could jump in the shower and be clean within two minutes. It's my bliss, I enjoy it, I savour each moment- it fills my cup.

Having fun (i.e., doing something just for enjoyment) is so important when we are young, it's our main goal in everything we do.

As we grow up and our goals become serious, fun gets pushed into the background. There's no time to have fun. Fun becomes all those unhealthy ways our Body's block out our feelings. Fun is now not an amazing thing that fills our cups, nourishes our souls and makes us feel truly good about ourselves- it's now our escape from the "real world" and most of the ways we have fun is frowned upon, or downright dangerous to do it daily. So fun becomes naughty. A self-indulgence rather than a daily necessity.

To me filling my cup daily (I.e., real fun) is as vital as eating daily to fill my belly. Without it I lose my self-love and then basic self-care (needs) goes out the window too.

So, what do you do to fill your cup? What's healthy and kind to you that feels great? What's something you do that's just for the fun of it? What's the thing you do with no goals, just enjoyment? Just for you?

When I ask mothers this it seems a lot of women just don't know anymore, it's similar to when we are feeling lost, like that part of you gets blurred when you become a mama.

If you know what you enjoy that's great! Do more of it! Try new stuff- go fill your cup!

If you don't know, now is the time to find out. Try different things- have fun- make a list and ask your Body if she feels good afterwards. It doesn't have to take long, and it doesn't have to cost a lot of money, it also doesn't have to be anyone else's idea of fun but it's also fine if it is! The great thing about this vital aspect of self-care is there is no wrong way to do it!

It all starts with permission from yourself:

"Today I will allow 15 minutes just for me"

"15 minutes Mirrie, are you fucking messing with me? Fat fucking chance, I don't have time to even shit by myself let alone have 15 minutes to enjoy myself."

Dude, I hear you. I am you!

15, 30 minutes, 1 hour, 4 hours... however long you can give yourself is amazing. But if you are still in the throes of parenthood, balls deep in nappies and crying babies, please stop a minute and think of this.

The 4 Minute Miracle

Even 4 minutes a day can make a huge difference. I know that sounds completely pointless and not even worth trying for, but the commitment to chase joy, even for just a few minutes can completely change your life.

You are a living, breathing human being. Based on that fact alone you deserve 15 minutes in a 24-hour day to feel happy or to enjoy something just for you. There are 96 x 15 minutes in 24 hours, surely you can spare just one- surely you are worth 1 out of 96? But If 15 minutes seems impossible, surely you could manage 4?

You are allowed YOU TIME. You are allowed a few minutes in a day to put yourself first. You just need to give yourself permission and remove the guilt.

I ran an experimental group program a couple of years ago called: The 4 Minute Miracle Program. I had this feeling that if I could get a bunch of women to commit to just 4 minutes of self-care/ pockets of joy per day that magical things would happen. Nothing could have prepared me for what happened next. I was hoping for tiny miracles and what the women got was nothing short of life changing magic.

So here I am writing this chapter and I thought, fuck it, YOU need to know this shit too! So, here's what we did.

The 4 Minute Miracle- The Basics

It all starts with the daily commitment.

As soon as you wake up every day, I want you to declare a daily commitment to yourself while holding your hands to your heart.

Although it may feel uncomfortable or weird, this is a really important part of the whole process. It sets the tone for the rest of your day and cements your commitment to have Self-Love at the forefront of your mind. It allows us to remember to react to our actions, thoughts and feelings with compassion and understanding. Try and say the words out loud or whisper them to yourself as you gently wake up (or after the kids are done jumping on your head).

DAILY COMMITMENT

"Thank You, My Beautiful Body, for trying to protect me but I'm already safe.
It's safe to feel. It's safe to be loved.
Today I promise to believe I am Already Enough"

Daily 4 Minute Daily Activity Themes

As well as the Daily Commitment Statement, every day I want you to commit to a 4-minute activity. In the program I gave a suggested activity for each day but really, it's about getting creative with your own plans. The prompts help for those uninspiring days though, so here you are...

4 Minute Self-Love Miracle

MONDAY: REFLECTION

Get those thoughts, beliefs, feelings and hopes out of your head and out into the world! Use your 4 minutes to challenge your mindset!

4 Minute Self-Love Miracle

TUESDAY: LET GO

These 4 minutes are all about releasing control, frustration and more importantly SHOULDS! Singing, dancing, shouting. Anything goes!

4 Minute Self-Love Miracle

WEDNESDAY: GET STILL

Time to get quiet and comfortable being in your own silence. Use these 4 minutes to meditate, listen to your body with no judgement or just sit with yourself.!

4 Minute Self-Love Miracle

THURSDAY: GET OUT

Whatever the weather, Thursdays are for connecting with nature. Bare feet in the grass, soaking in the stars or even sungazing to feel the warmth in your bones.

4 Minute Self-Love Miracle

FRIDAY: CARE FOR

Fridays are all about showing your body how much you care for her. Genuine simple acts of self-care. You could give yourself a massage, drink more water or even try out EFT.

4 Minute Self-Love Miracle

SAT & SUN: JOY

Over the weekend actively look for ways to bring joy to your heart. Nourish your body, create something new, express gratitude to the people you love and most importantly carve out time to have some fun for fun's sake.

Masterclasses

We also had four masterclasses called:

Your Kind Inner Voice
Body Positivity
Self-Love
Worth

These were videos that we discussed as a group but most of that grade A shizzle[21] can be found in this book, so you're good to go!

Why does it work?

Commitment to yourself
What was the last thing that you committed to do just for yourself. I bet whatever it was it wasn't fun...or was it? *Insert creepy smile emoji here.
Making a commitment to yourself means something. It sends a strong sign to your Body that you mean business, that you are in this thang[22] for the long haul, that you ain't[23] going anywhere.

Builds trust between you and your Body
The more you honour that commitment, the more times you give yourself self-care, even when you don't feel like it or life gets in the way, the more your Body will start to trust you. You need that trust in order for her to open up to you, show you the hurt she is carrying for you. When you start seeing all the things, she is doing for you, then you start to trust her more too and you'll start to actually care for her, you'll actually give a shit about her which always helps with this kind of thing. Imagine caring for your Body, not just with the end goal of looking good, but with a genuine concern with how your Body is feeling.

---

[21] Shizzle: Like shit but with extra glitter.
[22] Thang: Saying thing with an extra twang
[23] Aint: Isn't it annoying when writers use words that mean something the same as a word that they could just say. Isn't it just?

71

Perfect reminder that you matter too
Our days are so hectic it can feel like we give give give until there's nothing left and it's still not enough. It's SO fucking easy to put yourself last again and again, especially when there doesn't seem like there's enough time in the day to look after everyone else. But you do matter. Your needs matter. Hell, your wants matter. By committing to do something that fills your cup every day, even if it's tiny, you will be reminding yourself that you are an actual human and you are allowed to have needs too.

Permission to make time every single day
Permission is a big one here. We are all waiting for someone to give us permission to feel, permission to look after ourselves or put ourselves first.

Dude, our people's permission will feel good for a moment but it's empty unless you can give yourself that permission. You are the only person that can make yourself do this. There's no knight in shining armour coming to save you and tell you to put your feet up and have a cuppa or command you to fucking meditate for a few minutes.

There's YOU.

This comes down to you. Making that time, feeling like you are valuable enough to make that time for, and not just a one off. Every day you deserve that permission, every single day you deserve to take care of yourself even in the smallest way.

Brings self-care to the forefront of your mind every morning
Saying your daily commitment as soon as you wake up in the morning sets you up for your day in a positive, more compassionate mindset. It helps you to be more mindful throughout the day. It also helps you be less stressed, more forgiving and less overwhelmed. It helps you to think of self-care during your day and be gentler with yourself. Even if you can only manage saying the daily commitment and nothing else, it's still going to have a huge impact with the way you treat yourself.

Small enough amount of time to be doable but still makes a huge difference

Four minutes is really sod all time to give yourself in the grand scheme of things but it's still an accomplishment to get it done every day because life is Cray Cray yo[24]. Knowing that just a few minutes can still impact you in a massive way is really a turn on and feels doable in your head.

Challenges your beliefs

Most of our beliefs are formed when we are kids or young adults. They become so ingrained in our subconscious that we rarely even think about them, let alone question them! When you start looking into your belief structures, especially around worthiness and actually caring about yourself, you get the opportunity to check where your beliefs come from and if they actually serve you. You disrupt your subconscious and bring them into your conscious mind, allowing you to disregard those shitty beliefs that have been holding you back and form healthy, rainbow arsed new ones that power you along into being the true you, with no guilt or shame!

If you allow yourself to do it, it can be easy!

Who am I kidding, it's not always going to be easy, but this *can* be when you let yourself get in the swing of it. We're talking a few minutes a day to make you feel good. It's pretty simple right?

So now you feel like you are allowed a small or large amount of time to enjoy something- what will it be?

If you have kids and there's no one who can help look after them, then there's things you can do together but it has to be something that's still "for you". It's one of the most powerful self-love lessons a kid can learn, seeing their parents make time for self-care and to see they value themselves enough to make their needs matter too.

---

[24] Cray cray yo: Full on crazy, yo!

Uncomfortable Action:

If you do have children- removing emotion, shame or guilt, write down what you are teaching (modelling) your kids about self-care with your current behaviour?

Knowing you can't do this wrong is such a relief.

Another Uncomfortable Action (Like a BOGOF)

Go back to a time when you had fun just for the sake of it- no other goal in mind. What did you love to do when you felt more aligned with the real you?

Why not try it again and remember what you liked about it. When did feeling happy start feeling like a chore that you had no time to do?

Why did you enjoy that activity? Does it still spark joy for you? Did you feel full and inspired?

It could be something as simple as a hot bath or as adventurous as freakin' skiing! There are no limits and no goals other than having fun.

It could involve doing something for other people (i.e., entertaining guests etc) BUT ONLY if you are doing/giving from your excess.

IE you feel inspired/alive/happy enough to give to others without resentment or any hint of "shoulds"

If you are going to be taking from your cup, you need to make sure you are filling it too. You can still help other people but right now you need to focus on helping you first. It is one of the most important things in the world to concentrate on finding out what makes your heart sing. Finding that zen without any "shoulds" or preconditioned ideas of what that should be.

Your fun/your sparkle/your happiness is your only goal, and you need to do what you need to do to find it every single day, view it as vital as water is to your body!

It's vital to love yourself and really live aligned with your true inner self.

Mindfulness

We've already spoken about how our Body uses distractions to block out any potential pain and we are living in an age where this is easier than ever.

I can literally go a whole day without actually thinking about what I'm doing. Doing this is fine and sometimes necessary if you are happy to live in "autopilot" mode (IE survival) but it's not how you live when you really want to take care of yourself- mainly because it may help you to live without pain, but it also makes you live without joy. If you numb one you numb the other.

Mindfulness:

1. Quality of state of being conscious or aware of something
2. Mental state achieved by focusing one's awareness on the present moment, while calmly acknowledging and accepting one's feelings, thoughts and bodily sensations, used as a therapeutic technique.

Did you know that even the NHS is now using Mindfulness as a therapy technique?

Mindfulness is living and being present in the now. It's accepting that you can't beat yourself up about the decisions you made yesterday when you didn't have today's knowledge. It's forgiving yourself (and others, even when they don't deserve it) for what has happened in the past, giving yourself that grace and inner peace that comes with that acceptance and forgiveness.

Mindfulness is letting go of "what might be" in the future. Trusting in Perfect Timings and that the big Universe will give you exactly what you need rather than what you want. The trust is fucking hard but a bigger thing to trust in, when it comes to the future (which is even fucking harder than trusting in the Big U) is trusting in yourself to cope. Knowing that no matter what happens YOU CAN COPE.

When it feels like the world is relentlessly shitting on you, and you feel like you just can't take anymore, it can be so easy to get sucked into the future, exploring the ways that things may happen to finally break you. It's easy to get sucked into that darkness and lose all hope. I know, I've been there very recently. But the weird thing about worrying, is the things that turn out happening are never the things that you are actually worried about. It's always something that comes out of the side lines, sweeping you off your feet, catching you unawares...But then you still cope. Even when the future holds something that threatens to rip your entire world apart, you still cope.

Anxiety and worry are another of the Body's protection mechanisms and although they are as painful as hell, they really can be seen as an act of love from your Body. It's a way for you to prepare for the worst so that whatever hits won't be such a hard blow. Trouble is they suck the joy out of the present and are normally based on shit that simply isn't true.

Mindfulness pulls you back into the now. Back into the absolute truths, so you can cope with or enjoy what's really going on around you rather than the warped view of what could be in the future.

Being present is scary for your Body though. It does mean you may have to sit with the uncomfortable feelings you have been avoiding. Distractions and time travel are oh so tempting especially when you are unaligned or feeling unhappy with your current situation.

So how can we use mindfulness as a tool for self-care?

It's about caring for yourself right now.

When we bring ourselves back to the present moment and connect with our senses it helps us connect with our Body.

It takes away the worries or stresses to do with the past. Most of which can't be changed anyway. It takes away the future possibilities that are usually fucking catastrophic. You can allow feelings, emotions and fears to rise from within your Body, acknowledge them without judgement and release them. You can find out what your Body needs in this moment and actually care enough to try and fulfil those needs.

Through your senses you can connect with the earth, nature or the sea. It can also help with overwhelm as you focus just on what's happening around you right now. It helps you connect with your children or loves on a deeper level.

The more you practise mindfulness the closer it brings you to gratitude, for both yourself and for other people. It's an amazing act of self-care because it both rests your brain and allows the Body to feel.

Change Your Life with Gratitude

Everything is energy, Have I said that before? Shit, I seem to say this to myself every day. Each type of energy that you put out has a way of finding its way back to you.

I'm a big believer in the Law of Attraction, but most of the mainstream teachings of it out there are far too simplistic. There's plenty of rich negative people out there, bastards with too much power who you know isn't putting positive energy out into the world. There's also lots of good people who seem to get shafted again and again. But manifestation and attraction are a type of energy and while I think it's counterproductive to believe if you have a shitty day, you're going to attract more shit, I do believe the vibrations of our energy affects both our inner and outer world experiences.

Also, the mainstream teachings are mostly focused on cars and money, but I believe manifestation so much more than that, it's allowing your inner child to be free to believe this world is full of limitless possibilities and that you are worthy of what you truly desire, deep in your heart.

The vibration of lack

Especially now, it's understandable if all you can see is lack, it seems to be the default belief for most of us.

Feeling lack or dissatisfaction is hard and heavy and also makes it hard to love anyone- let alone yourself. It doesn't motivate you to do anything but fester in your own "not enoughness" The negative voice comes in because if you are unhappy with your lot in life you now have three choices:

1. Blame someone else
2. Blame yourself
3. Change your situation

Of course, the easiest choice is to blame someone else (If it's not your fault then you have zero responsibility, right?) but that doesn't then get rid of the two other choices and they'll both be niggling away at your brain. That niggle will almost always lead to uncomfortable feelings or even some tasty, unlocked trauma and will send your Body into panic mode so she will try to cut in to protect you by blocking out or distracting you from those feelings or seemingly impossible decisions.

She will use any of the tactics to do that especially the ones she knows have worked in the past. So if you are having a mardy busy day, she will put you in autopilot mode because you've just got "to get through it" and if you aren't busy - you will start eating or obsessing over social media, basically you'll do anything so that you can stay in a place of anger or dissatisfaction without having to feel any other real feelings.

When you are full of gratitude, your Body feels light, it's hard to feel unhappy or angry because you are feeling so content with life and your heart feels full.

You feel like you must have made good choices to be in this position or even that you must be a good person to be receiving this much love. Of course, you don't even need to have everything going right in your life to be in a place of gratitude, your whole world can be going to shit, and you can still feel super grateful for the little that you have.

In that place little things that would normally annoy you or stress you out don't seem like that big of a deal. So what if your house is messy, it's warm, it's your home, it's protecting you from the snow outside and it can be tidied up, it's no biggie. Little things that add up into big stresses can be broken down and seem possible to sort out because next to all the things you are grateful for, the daily stresses do just seem small and are not worth breaking your mood for.

This is a high vibrational state and while in it, it's easier to give love to others and yourself. Gratitude gives you more compassion for both your kids and you too- it makes you more understanding. Good things seem plentiful and seem to just flow to you.

But nothing has changed in your actual life- the only difference at first is your own mindset. The way you are looking at things and the way you process your situation. This mindset first shapes your inside view and then that spills out, affecting your reality positively.

The trouble is when you are in a super ungrateful vibe, it's really hard to get yourself out of it and if you know you "should" be feeling grateful but feel unable to, then you feel guilt and shame, which are the biggest de-motivators and causes of self-hate ever...so what to do?

First start small with your mindfulness and "This Moments Truth"

Bring yourself away from the blocks and distractions. Think about and write down your moment's truth. Close your eyes and take some deep breaths.

There might be some things that need to change in your life, maybe you've been putting up with shit for too long. But you don't need to change your life this instant, so right at this moment just try to choose to see one tiny thing that you can be grateful for. It might be that although your kids are going nuts, they might be smiling. They might recall this very moment when they are older, as a really happy memory. They won't remember the mess or the shouting (hopefully). They'll remember feeling free, wild, safe and loved. That definitely sounds like a beautiful thing to be grateful for.

Or think of just one thing- one tiny thing that you have that makes you happy or a person who really cares about you, makes your life sweeter and brighter.

It can be really small or insignificant but if it makes you smile or feel glad, then it's yours, turn your attention to it-
It's OK to feel shitty now and again but it's not OK to use that anger against yourself, especially if your goal is self-love.

The Rapid Gratitude Game...

I actually love playing this game with the kids because they come up with cute random things, but you can play it on your own too. You start off with one person saying one tiny thing that they are grateful for, then taking it in turns, the next person has to shout out one thing but as quickly as they can, and you just keep going until someone hesitates or says something so silly you all start laughing.

If you are playing it on your own, you could just try to write down as many things as possible in one minute. The shift from lack to gratitude is rapid and long lasting because you're literally forcing your brain to look for the good as quickly as possible and it really helps kids get in a good place too.

Hold these tiny thankful things inside your heart. Close your eyes and concentrate on the warm, lighter feeling in your Body. The tiny moment of gratitude wants to change your day. It wants to soften your heart- it wants you to know there's so much goodness in your life when you choose to see it- when you turn your head and heart towards it.

Chase that tiny grateful feeling and hold it tightly, add to it, find one more thing. Feel the warmth grow, not EVERYTHING in your life is bad.

Remember when you are feeling like there's no good - deep down you will be blaming yourself for it and it's impossible to love yourself when you are feeling shame or hate towards yourself.

Uncomfortable Action:

Fill in the blanks...

I honour my negative feelings and feel compassion for myself for feeling this way. It's OK to feel this way. I am so grateful for .... it makes me happy to know I can .... I am thankful for......

By concentrating on the tiniest bit of good you will not only see more and more good but you'll be attracting more goodness into your life.

Do it without shame or judgement.

Honour all your feels even the negative ones.

You don't have to feel positive and grateful all the time, but give yourself extra kindness when you don't because you're going to need it.

We don't want to squish feelings down or ignore them, we need to acknowledge, release and honour them.

The goal of all this is to remind you if you're feeling good or bad, it's always beneficial to find things to be grateful for. Sometimes it's easy to forget.

The tiniest moment of gratitude can change your whole day.

Chapter Five – Sweet Alignment

Who the Fuck am I to teach you about Alignment?

ME THE GIRL WHO FAILS

Me the girl who feels weak
Me the girl who doubts herself
Me the girl just winging it

Who am I?
Who am I to know this?

Who am I but a naked, vulnerable human-being, once cocksure
Now so often afraid

The scary place of power
The scary place of visibility
The scary place of Infinite Possibilities

Infinite Possibility of failure
Infinite Possibility of success
Infinite Possibility of change

All scarier than the last

Who am I but a girl who has lived through and
Is living through it
Committed to learning more
Every single day?

Learning who I am
Learning why it matters
Learning that I'm human

I am allowed to fail
You are allowed to fail.
I am allowed to succeed
You are allowed to succeed

Zero expectations
Absolute trust
Who am I?
Who are you?

Are we all just winging it?
Do you know who you are?
The absolute power you have inside of you?

Everything but
Everything is energy
Pure energy

Including me
Including you

What is Alignment?

Alignment covers:
Your beliefs
Your actions
Your intentions
Your energy
Your Higher Self

People feel that shit
YOU FEEL THAT SHIT
That's why Alignment matters so much.
Once you align your outside world (I.e., your actions and surroundings)
With your inside world (Beliefs that serve you)

You find you
The real you

You connect with your Higher Self
You see yourself as she sees you

Powerful
Loveable
Worthy

Magic happens.

People are drawn to you. The right people.
Life unfolds magically around you.
Life feels so much lighter, easier and more fun.

Inside of you is Source energy.
The energy that creates worlds.

The spirit inside of you is a part of the consciousness of all living
things. Deep down inside your bones there is a strength that's
immeasurable, infinite and unfailing.

Your strength, your intuition, your passion and love.

A self filled with pure love
Zero expectations
Solid worth
The person who can see beyond sight
The person who is secure without needing external security

Your spirit
Your soul
Your Higher Self
Unafraid
Unbound
Powerful
Strong
Sure.

This immense power is our true selves, our inner self, our Higher
Self. With unwavering, rock solid foundations of trust, worth and
strength.

The part of you that observes your thoughts, knows your beauty,
counteracts those human doubts and loves you unconditionally.

Call it God, the Universe, your Higher Self or your Soul, what you call it has no significance, you just need to acknowledge that it's there. Deep inside yourself. It may feel distant to you right now. The worries and stresses of life may be weighing down on you, fogging up the waters. But the first step is just to know it's there, or the first step might even be the wanting to believe that it's there.

Source energy. Beyond human. Pure love.

Your Body knows it's there. It scares the shit out of your Body. She sees the power and the limitless possibilities but all it spells out to her is risk. Like if you become conscious of just how supported, powerful and limitless you are, think of the trouble you are likely to get yourself in.

Imagine where you'd be if you knew without a doubt that you were worthy, limitless, loveable, sure of yourself, self-aware, safe, with an infinite source of power and support you can tap into at any time? Imagine the dreams you would chase, the experiences you'd have, the changes you'd make?
Imagine the risks you would take.

Ah change, change is scary right? Body fears change because change always means risk. So, she tries to hide your true power. She makes you doubt your strength, your worth, your very reason for being. She does all this in love but sometimes she can be a real bitch about it.

Alignment is firstly acknowledging your Higher Self. Then it's connecting with her, getting to know her, getting to love her, getting to trust her. Once the trust is in place it's about allowing your Body to play catch up.

Your Higher Self has a whole set of beliefs that feel good to you. They feel good because these beliefs serve you, they are for your highest good, they carry you towards your soul's purpose. They feel good because they *are* good. They allow you to feel worthy just by being YOU.

All of you
Your dark and your light
The real you

No hiding
No asking
No pretending

Just you as you are.
These beliefs are good for you because they are you.

When you are born earthside the battle for your beliefs begins. We're taught a bunch of beliefs and behavioural patterns that are passed down to us from our parents. They had them passed to them from their parents, and them from theirs. Generations worth of deeply ingrained beliefs and expectations are thrust upon us, and as children we are not taught to trust our gut or listen to what's inside because there's always someone older, wiser, bigger, someone who knows better than us. Parents, siblings, teachers, society, religion...

Every day at our softest most malleable age/state we are exposed to hundreds of ideas, beliefs and obligations that are thrust upon us and these facts and beliefs become normal, our base standard. We don't even question them. So, we've ended up with layers and layers of other people's beliefs and expectations covering our own. Our inner wisdom is often ignored and not valued like academic knowledge or even street smarts. The views and opinions of our Higher Self become muddy. Often, she is ignored, shut down and not even acknowledged to be real.

But your true beliefs and the powerful urge to follow them stays there. Because those true beliefs, the ones at the very core of you, are there for a reason. They are there to serve you. What happens when you have deep rooted beliefs that don't serve you? Your Higher Self will start shouting out. Life will seem a lot harder because you're going against the grain of your true path. You may feel miserable because you are doing things for other people's approval rather than your own. You may become depressed or hopeless, in a job you hate, a marriage you hate or in a Body you hate.

You are misaligned.

This is super sneaky because you'll think that you're doing everything "right". Your belief system, by the time you are an adult, is strong. Core beliefs can seem infinitely deeply rooted in everything you are. So, you have all these things that you genuinely believe, and you're trying to be "good" or "successful" and you may even have amazing successes, but you feel unfulfilled. You are not happy. You think you know who you are and what you believe, and you have all these stories about yourself, but you still feel empty.

Your feelings are your first indicator of how aligned or misaligned you actually are.

Feelings of satisfaction, joy, abundance, gratitude, appreciation, love and bliss are a pretty amazing indicator that your beliefs and actions are in alignment with your Higher Self. It's like she is in agreement that you are going the right way, and that agreement feels so good.

Feelings of lack, depression, anger, hopelessness, apathy, distrust, unease and hate are a definite indicator that you are misaligned with your true self, your true beliefs.

Even when you are feeling these about someone else, it's likely that you're mirroring your own feelings or fears about yourself. Having the self-awareness to honour these emotions (because as we talked about before, there's no such thing as a bad emotion) but to not get drawn into them is the ultimate fucking blessing in life. To not create stories, but rather to know that these are just an indicator that your beliefs, actions or thoughts are not aligning with your Higher Self. Mainly that you are feeling from your Body's viewpoint and not seeing the situation through your Higher Self's eyes. She is basically disagreeing with you. She sees the whole picture and has compassion, empathy and grace beyond measure. She is fully ready to support you, move mountains for you and help unfold your life in the sweetest of ways. She knows you deserve all this and more.

Your Body deserves for you to acknowledge all feelings and not to push negative ones down because it feels uncomfortable. All feelings deserve to be felt and your human self needs you to process all emotions. Seeing yourself with compassion means you can investigate these uncomfortable feelings and see where you are coming out of alignment. What beliefs are you holding on to that don't align with your Higher Self?

This is actually easier than it sounds...so why does it feel so difficult to do?

What Are People Going to Think?

When I first investigated my beliefs I realised that, although I had an amazing childhood, I wanted to parent my children differently from how I had been raised. I wanted to home school. I didn't want to use punishments. I wanted to let my children decide when they stopped co-sleeping. I ended up breastfeeding until they self-weaned.

All these were little things that felt huge. My parents could have seen this as a threat or a reason to feel like I saw their way of doing things as "wrong". I was changing generations' worth of parenting behaviour. I risked them getting upset or even angry at me. Luckily my parents are legit amazing and supportive, so they went along with everything like fucking champs, but I know lots of people who faced serious backlash and criticism when they wanted to do things differently.

When I left my marriage, I risked (and felt) like people saw me as selfish, flippant about my vows and many people who I thought loved me cut me out of their lives. When I left my lifelong religion, people who I saw as family rejected me, disapproved of who I became and eventually stopped hanging out with me.

It was scary to make these huge changes in my life but so very necessary in aligning with who I really am and actually being truly happy.

Beliefs are often like glue that hold us in certain communities. They help us belong. Changing beliefs and acting on your true beliefs, even if it serves you and you are much happier, can bring some heartache. It can be scary. You may feel ostracised or even rejected.

People may think you are acting superior, like you're now too good for their beliefs or they may see you as selfish or say you are acting like a different person.
It is not your responsibility to explain yourself to ANYONE.
It is not your responsibility to explain yourself to ANYONE.

If you've spent your life making other people happy, these people won't like it when you change your behaviour and start making yourself happy. Of course, they were happier when you were bending over backwards and killing yourself to try and make them happy.

Learning that it's not my responsibility to make anyone else in this world happy has been one of the most life changing lessons I've ever learnt. No one actually needs to understand you or accept your new beliefs. The only responsibility you have is to yourself. To your own happiness. To your own alignment.

Normally if you come across negative reactions to your alignment it is that person mirroring their own misalignment. Mirroring their own unhappiness. It's like they are thinking "I have to do all this shit I'm unhappy with, why are they getting a free pass?"

You questioning your own beliefs makes the people close to you question theirs. Some people are ready for this, and others are not. It's hard to stay objective but the sooner you realise that your only responsibility is to yourself, the sooner you can live freely.

If the risk of rocking the boat is so high, why would anyone actually want to do it?

We are an entire universe wrapped in skin. Our consciousness is connected with each other, and we are still unique, powerful beings. Our human experiences shape us, expands our consciousness, but often makes us feel smaller than we actually are.

The chances of being you, born at this point of time, in this body, with your personality and your life circumstances are basically as close to zero as you can get. The number was thought to be a 1 in a 40 trillion chance but upon further inspection Dr Ali Binazir has figured out it's more like one in 10 to the 2,685,000th power.

The number is kind of just a fun brainfuck because it's zero. Zero chance of you existing right now. Yet here you are.

Can you imagine that for just a moment? Do you think you defied all of those odds just so you could live out your days being a watered-down version of yourself? To work some shitty job, to spend your days making every tosser[25] out there happy while you feel miserable and unsatisfied? Fuck that! You have the very stars dancing in your bones and the force that creates worlds sourcing through your veins. You came here to experience life. There was no fear involved, no expectations apart from using this FULL human experience to help you to expand both your consciousness and the whole Universe! To feel everything...every range of emotion from the deepest sorrow to the brightest joy and everything in-between. You came here to shine.

Regardless of your religion or beliefs of "why" we are here or the purpose of your life, I think we can all agree that it would be a bitter waste to live out your days without getting to know your true self, your true soul purpose, to not know what lights your soul on fire, to not taste the pure deliciousness of feeling

---

[25] Tosser: Another word for wanker, a fool.

absolute certainty, the fullness of your power, fully supported, pure unconditional self-love.

And that's not even the best bit! When you get rid of the beliefs and expectations that don't serve you and you figure out the ones that do, then align your inspired action while trusting your Higher Self to guide you... Oh, now we are cooking with fire, baby! Life starts being magical. We start to attract similar people into our life. All of a sudden you see just how worthy and deserving you are of all the good that life has to offer. Your feelings matter. You are as important as everyone else. You see other peoples' worth so much easier too. In fact, you start to notice all the little things throughout the day that are so magical, and you appreciate them more.

Life is now full of gratitude and even when you experience shitty moments you know that they are just moving you towards more clarity, more alignment. Suddenly, strangers are kinder to you. You feel inspired, you notice the perfect timing of everything that is happening around you and you feel steadier, like your wellness is anchored no matter what life brings you.

Unconditional living.

The Trust, trust, surrender saying will now make perfect sense as everything will feel easier. Life is good. Even when it's not it still is. You trust your gut, you love your humanness, you love yourself...even if everything still feels messy, even if you are failing, even if you've rocked the boat and people are saying you've changed. Fuck yes, you've changed. You are living up to the miracle that you are. You are putting your wants and needs ahead of the people who didn't give a shit about you in the first place.

Spoiler alert: if they truly care about you, they will be SO incredibly happy to see you blossom in this way. Someone who truly loves you will be excited and thrilled to see you at your full power, shining your brightest...they won't be threatened or afraid you will leave...that's a beautiful, sometimes painful, lesson in doing all of this.

You are being you.
You are happy being you.
You love you.

Doesn't that sound worth rocking the boat for? Risking a few
butt-hurt feelings for? Are you ready for the magic that's about
to unfold? But how? Where do you even begin?

Easy Alignment

Investigate Core Beliefs

Let's jump straight in.

Uncomfortable Action:
*Without overthinking and with zero judgement, write down a
short summary of your beliefs for each of the following...*

1. *Spiritual*
2. *Your Body*
3. *Your Worthiness*
4. *Goals*
5. *Morals*
6. *Diet*
7. *Values*
8. *Ethics*
9. *Money*
10. *Beliefs*

Do these beliefs still serve me?
Are these beliefs mine or somebody else's?
Are these beliefs absolute truth?
Can they be questioned?

Feelings

What is my gut reaction to each of these beliefs?
What feelings come up when you read back through your
beliefs?

Which of these beliefs do I feel to the very core of me?

Your Actions

Uncomfortable Action:

Write down your current actions in each of the areas of beliefs.

In which areas do you feel the most Powerful? (I.e. True belief matches strongly with current actions)

In which areas do you feel the weakest? (I.e. Misalignment of beliefs with current actions)

So, the formula for easy alignment is as follows:
Belief
Feeling
Action
Alignment
First up we need to explore our beliefs, make sure they serve us, are true to who we are and are there because WE need it in our life rather than based on another person's "Should".

Next, the belief needs to be more than just words. We need to *feel into* the belief. Make it deeper than just a way of living or thinking.

Naturally next comes action. The actions and decisions that we make every day. When what we DO matches up to who we feel we ARE and what we BELIEVE...

BOOM!!! Now you're in alignment, you beautiful MOFO!

Tiny Little Decisions

Every day you make hundreds of decisions that are either keeping you aligned with your core beliefs or going against them. Every single decision you make is tiny. Some will feel huge, some may have massive repercussions, some may affect other people more than we want them to, but, in essence, every single decision you make is tiny.

When you choose to make it, you have limited options in front of you and deep down, when you take away all of the outcomes and all of the Expectations, deep down you know which one is "right" for you.

Whether it's deciding to have a doughnut and coffee for breakfast instead of an healthier option, choosing to wear knickers or a thong, choosing to start a business or go to school; all these decisions affect other people either a tiny bit or massively, but the actual decision that lays with you is tiny. Even when it doesn't feel like it. We make hundreds, if not thousands, of decisions every single day and most of these decisions don't actually have much of an impact *at that moment* but these decisions when added up over the course of days or months or years have a MASSIVE impact on you.

You can choose to write a book and once you decide to, it feels huge in your head but in essence you've just decided to do something, you can choose not to do it too! After you've chosen to do it, writing a book means every single day you have to choose to write. You have to give yourself the time, you have to give yourself the mental capacity, you have to give yourself the grace but ultimately, it's just a tiny decision to write. Then as time goes by you create a book. So those tiny decisions added up every day to create something amazing; potentially life changing!

Your initial decision feels huge because of the energy that you put behind it.

So, the more commitment, the more desire that you have for that decision to actually succeed and the more energy you've put behind that decision, the bigger it will feel to you!

That decision doesn't feel like anything to anyone yet, apart from you.

In essence it is quite tiny (it doesn't feel tiny, but it is) and then it's the commitment of making tiny decisions to support the initial decision that makes BIG things happen!

Your desire - aligned with your true beliefs - will be big or small to you, depending on the energy that you put behind it. The more energy that you put behind it and the more committed you are, the more tiny decisions you make every day to support that first decision.
That leads to more impact and more confidence TO BE SEEN and the more everybody else SEES your energy, the more that energy is infectious!

When you take away
-Expectations
-Outcomes
-Fear
You already know the "Right Decision" for you.

Whether we are talking about personal or business decisions, I think it's fair to say that without a goal in mind while you are making these tiny decisions, it's like you're pissing into the wind!

So, we want to choose alignment in our beliefs with every tiny decision that we make, but we also want them to have a direction. We want to know where we want to be and allow the tiny decisions to slowly add up and make a HUGE impact on our goals.

Energy - Commitment - Desire

During the next few weeks try to commit to ONE GOAL. This needs to be something that scares you. Pushes you past your comfort zone but ultimately is achievable. It needs to be in alignment with your TRUE beliefs, FEEL GOOD, have actions that you can commit to daily, and your tiny decisions need to support you in this goal.

My One Goal...

What Do I Want?
What is my Soul Dream?
What do I really want to spend my days doing?
What do I really want to achieve?

Write Fast - Forget Fear - Forget Limits

Who Am I?

Explore who you've aspired to be in the past and which beliefs or actions have supported or sabotaged that person. Think about the beliefs you have about yourself right now, and if they serve you or put you down.

Who I want to be is truly who I am inside, when my True Beliefs Align with my Inspired Actions

Biggest Misalignment

Now go back over the observations you've written with these uncomfortable actions. When you look at your beliefs, actions and decisions...in your gut which feels like the biggest misalignment in your life?

What niggles you the most? What causes you the most pain or guilt?

Choose two tiny things you can do THIS week to make you more aligned in this area. Each tiny thing you do to step back into alignment with yourself causes a ripple effect in your life and will be SO worth it.

Alignment Magic

You can't unknow this. Once you've tasted the sweetness of alignment you will KNOW when you slip out of it, which you will every now and again because that's a human thing to do. Once you know it you will KNOW, and you will feel the contrast of being misaligned and that shizzle does not feel good. The amazing thing is though, that you can get back into alignment at any point of your life and in any circumstance. That sweet spot will sit there waiting for you. That sweet spot is in abundance, it sits in a place of complete freedom. It waits for you because it knows that this is where you are meant to be and, good Lordy, it feels *so good* when you get back there.

Feeling alignment is one of the most satisfying feelings because it is unconditional to the life that is actually going on around you. This way of living, where you're not just reacting to everyone else, or your external circumstances, means you have this deep satisfaction and feeling of steady hope deep inside of yourself that needs no external validation. You still feel all of your emotions and allow your Body to feel "negative" emotions when she needs to, but you easily find your way back to the good feelings after processing the not so good. That feeling of flying high and loving life is your guideline for how aligned you truly are. Trouble is, we're so used to living a conditional life where we expect our feelings to come from what our experiences are, that we often ignore how we feel or just don't care enough about it to notice when we are slipping into misalignment.

Everyday Magic

When I was just 15, I had a pretty bad vaginal prolapse while in America and I was told by a doctor it was unlikely that I'd ever be able to have children but because I was so young, it would be better to investigate it when I got older. That niggle stayed in the back of my mind. Obviously as a child I'd pretended to be a mama. I longed for someone to heap all this love I had on. Although at 15 I'd never thought about whether I wanted children or not, I knew I wanted the choice. That throwaway comment by a doctor who didn't actually know me stayed with me for many years and influenced my decisions.

Although I didn't have the immediate "want" of having a baby, the thought that I "probably couldn't" made me rebel against that desire so I would tell people I never wanted children. When I started dating, I would tell my partners I'd probably never want children and probably couldn't anyway. As I was in a religion that didn't allow sex before marriage, and had the view that you should only date if you were serious about marrying that person (and also valued creating a family above anything else), this little niggle changed things in such young relationships. It became a stubborn sticking point with me. Almost a way to test the other person's feelings for me.

When I found myself falling for a guy who already had three children, my close friends and family were worried about me. Being a step mum is hard. You won't be their mum. They might reject you. Life will be so hard. But I didn't see it that way. I got on with the kids so well. I loved them before I even started going out with their dad. I never ever saw myself as replacing their mum. They had a mum who loved them completely. I knew I'd never be their mum. But they were the cherry on top of the cake. I loved their dad and would be with him regardless, but they were a seriously happy bonus. They brought SO much fun and happiness every time I saw them.

Honestly, I was happy. They were (and are) amazing children and I just felt honoured to play a small part in their life.

I was obsessed with puppies though. I never felt the longing for a baby, but animals were a different matter. Puppies, chickens, even baby pigs...I wanted ALL the baby animals.

After about five years of marriage, I had a small operation to do with my pelvis and the doctor (again, what felt like a throwaway comment) told me everything was normal with my reproductive system, and everything was working normally. He started talking about something else and I just sat there in shock.

"You mean I can have children? I was told it was unlikely."

"Oh yeah, everything is fine, you can if you want to."

I remember almost falling back into my pillow. Like I was a thousand times lighter.

You can if you want to.

Ten years or more of this little niggle of "what if?"
Ten years or more of being scared to want, being scared to desire.
Ten years or more of pushing down this pain and disappointment.

You can if you want to. Obviously, I did want to because it happened within weeks. Five years of never using protection, then without even trying bam! I'm preggo within a month.

Nothing changed in my Body. All that changed was the belief in my head. The doubt gone. The resistance gone. The possibilities open. I now believed it was possible.

You can too, if you want to.

As soon as you believe anything, it becomes possible.

This goes from your belief in your Body to heal, to your belief in yourself that you can have, do and be anything that you desire.

You are creating this amazing life with the support of the collective consciousness all around you, and alignment with self-love is the key to unlock it all.

Back in the Summer I brought the boys across the country to see their dad and unexpectedly I ended up in my beautiful bell tent alone for the weekend. My vibe was already beautifully high and everything was unfolding so deliciously. I naively thought that this was going to be my last chance to finish my book. THIS weekend was THE weekend.

But dropping off the boys was so abrupt and unexpected that I got to the campsite shaking.

As I put up my tent, I was angry, hurt and sobbing. A lady passed by with her dog right at my most vulnerable moment and asked me if I was OK. I wasn't. She gently spoke to me and told me her own story of being a single mum. Her dog was so playful and gave me lots of cuddles and she invited me down to her camper that night for a drink.

Now, on a side note, I'd had my tent up in a field near my boat for nearly the whole summer and my mum had given me this canopy (tarp). My dad had gotten poles because I wanted to cover the jetty with it but, because it's always windy down the ferry, they were too flimsy, so I took them back to the shop. So, I just had the canopy sitting there. Every time I looked at it, I thought "I really need some poles" but couldn't afford any. I just had to let go of the idea that I'd be able to use it this year.

On Epiphany Day[26], Mel was in the boat and I was in the tent, but I wanted a coffee so walked back across the jetty. There laying in the mud, right next to my boat was a long strong pole. It must have come in with the tide! Big U had delivered me a pole! I ran in to get Mel to film my hungover arse climbing over my jetty, into the mud to get this pole but it was surprisingly easy! Straight away I grabbed the canopy and ran down to my tent to try it out. Because it was some sort of strong fishing pole it had a hook thingy at one end and so was perfect for the canopy. It was so satisfying sitting under it, especially because of the fun way the universe had delivered this pole to me. It would have been perfect if I had had just one more pole. So, every morning I checked around my boat after the tide just in case the universe wanted to gift me another pole.

When I was frantically packing to take the boys, I looked at the canopy and thought about this big old pole in the car and decided against taking it. But something made me just grab the canopy as we were leaving, just another just in case.

So anyway, back to me alone in my tent. The lady left when she saw that I'd calmed down and I finished putting the tent up and making it all pretty inside. I had a blow-up king-size sofa bed,

---

[26] This was an epic day that changed the course of my life. The day was full of mind fucking blowing epiphanies and rapid expansion.

loads of blankets and fairy lights and I was back in a place of gratitude. I had zero money, but I went to a shop and decided to buy myself some real food and treats. I set myself up with a glass of wine and opened up my laptop. That was when I realised just how shit chapter 5 was. I had no idea what the fuck I was going to do with it. It was so disjointed talking about food, niggles, depression and so much other stuff. I felt stuck. I decided to switch my vibe up and tried to get into fun mode Mirrie.

At that point the lady was walking past again, she's admiring my tent setup (All of which was manifested in the most beautiful ways too) and says:

"I know this is random, but would you want any poles?"
"Tent poles?" I asked
"Yes, I was going to throw them away, but something made me keep them just in case."
"I would love them. Yes please!"

She goes off to get them and low and behold she brings back two strong tall poles that break down into three sections. They are a bit battered but exactly what I had been needing for my canopy.

Later that night I went down for a beer and there was a group of young 'uns celebrating a birthday who invited us both to join them. We all ended up partying till the early hours, under the stars around the fire, talking about life, the Universe, travel, love and everything in-between. I basically had to crawl back to my tent. I got my laptop out and sighed at my chapter 5. I shut my laptop instantly and thought about my poles, how kind people are, the unlikelihood of meeting these sweet fun people and sunk into a deep sleep feeling really grateful.

The next morning, I had one word standing out to me.

ALIGNMENT

I talk about alignment all the time, wrote an entire course about it, LIVE it every day and that's when it hit me that there wasn't a chapter about Alignment in my book. How could this even be possible?

I looked at chapter 5 again and just like that woman with all the maths equations around her head on that GIF...the chapter sections started shifting around in my head. A feeling of purpose and clarity washed over me, and it all felt so satisfying and delicious. Ah, sweet Alignment. Ah, Chapter 5 was going to be so satisfying.

When the famous five, as I called them, had packed up their car and were leaving the campsite it was chucking it down raining and I was sat under my canopy with my glass of wine writing about the amazing possibilities of the Universe. That rain was so incredibly satisfying because I was sat there, so grateful to be dry, just looking at my poles in smug deliciousness. As they passed by, I put my laptop down to wave them off and they wound down the windows, their fists in the air, all chanting "Chapter five, chapter five, chapter five!"

My tears welled up and with a warm feeling in my belly and a grin across my face I thanked the Universe for all the beautiful signs that she showed me to prove how supported I really am. Little did I know what was coming before me. The extreme contrasts of highs and lows. The fear and excitement. The love and loss. The expansion, the trust, the letting go, the inspired action, the adventure, the absolute mundane, Having the best year of my life and reaching what felt like the lowest point of my life.

All leading me to this point. On a beach in Newquay. My favourite place in the world. Despite what seemed like impossible odds of me being here after 20 years of longing and wishing. Here I am. Stars truly aligned and just in the most fun way.

And here I am.
I've lived all this.
I Learned all this.

Prioritised my Alignment, trusted in my Higher Self and it seems like it's all led me here to finish this chapter in full knowing that what I'm writing is my truth.

That all things are possible.

All things.
That you are fully fully supported.
Completely loved.
Completely guided.

That your Higher Self knows you.
Wants to show you in all the fun little ways that what you want matters.

How you feel matters.
How you see your world matters.
How you see your worth matters.
How much you matter.

She has such beautiful love to give you. Such a kind voice to soothe you. All the answers to all your questions and will time everything in such a delicious way for you.

The closer you align and the more you allow yourself to be guided the more every day magic will pop up in little and big ways.

One day I hope I'll meet you and I can tell you about the crystal caves, the baby bird, the gluten free cake, the magic tree, the flower penis, the snail rock, the scratch card, Ruby and about a million other moments of everyday magic that I've had since I made the decision that my alignment, my niggles and my self-love matters. I can't wait to hear yours.

The more you trust in perfect timings, the more fun you have and the more love you feel... the more gratitude you will feel. It will be so much sweeter to love yourself when you can see yourself through the eyes of source. When you can experience life through the eyes of your Higher Self. When you see the things you have wanted for so long actually turn up in your reality.

As it happened the big pole that the universe gifted me in the tide was the very pole I needed to guide in my very own boat (that I bought when I had 33p in the bank) into a place where everyone said it would be impossible to live. My own home. Did the Universe already have the plan in place for my boat when she gifted me the pole? It sure feels that way.

The things that you will manifest by being in alignment are fun, but what's even sweeter is seeing that you are having a hand in creating them, feeling into your emotions and being able to enjoy the unfolding of what you are creating every day. Because after all, life isn't about getting there, it's about the journey and the journey to alignment is one of the sweetest unfolding you'll ever feel.

Fuck knows you deserve it.

Chapter Six - Tomorrow's You

The YOU of tomorrow is all of You.
It's your Body.
It's your Mind.
It's your mental health.
It's your physical health.
It's your joy.
It's your sadness.
It's everything about you...in the tomorrow.

Everything that you do today will affect your tomorrow.

Do you care enough about Tomorrow's you?

Do You Care About How You Feel?

In order to be able to care about how you feel, you have to actually care about you. Your Higher Self wants you to feel good.

Think about someone you love very, very much.

You love seeing them happy. You love seeing them in their full power: expressing themselves fully, enjoying life, feeling bliss, full of love.

There's something very beautiful about seeing a child in awe, in a moment of pure bliss, gratitude and appreciation. Kids seem to be able to get to that point much easier than adults. They have no resistance to the joy, less "should's", less awareness of any shit or drama going on around them. They live in the moment fully open to feeling whatever the moment brings them.

It brings us huge joy to see someone just blissfully enjoying life, especially when it's someone you care about, someone you truly love.

Your Higher Self is pure love.

This energy and power inside of you already loves you unconditionally. In the purest most beautiful sense of the word.

Of course, she is going to want you to be happy, feel good, experience bliss - she loves you!

She wants to see you stand in your full power.
She wants you to be beyond happy, the happiest you've ever been, grateful, joyful, playful, expansive...she cares about you.

Do you care about you?
Do you care about how you feel?
Is this something you've explored before?
Is happiness, gratitude, satisfaction, bliss and fun important to you?

Do you prioritise these feelings in your daily life?
Does how you feel actually matter to you?

You can't control how other people feel, even if you love them so much. Even if you could give them everything they want in life, even if you change how you act, how you speak, who you are...you cannot make anyone else happy, nor is it your responsibility to do so.
Actually, THIS has been the biggest lesson that I've learnt in the past year...not that I can't make *everyone* happy but that I can't make ANYONE happy.

Of course my actions have the power to influence someone else's happiness. I can be kind, give gifts, advice and love but it's not up to me how the other person responds to it. Only they are in the position to decide how to respond to life. Only they decide how to react to situations.

Kids are another classic example of this. Being fully in the moment and honouring their feelings without masking can go both ways. I used to say my only job as a parent is to keep my kids healthy and happy. I was wrong. You can take a kid to Disney World, and they still have a meltdown. You can buy them presents, spend 13 hours making a cake, hire a bouncy castle, throw a big party and there they are sitting in the middle of all this and then start crying because they're so sad. As adults this can be so bloody frustrating but actually it's quite a beautiful thing.

You see, as an adult you can be on the most gorgeous island in the sun and still have a shitty argument about nothing. You can be at a party and still feel very alone or sad. We are human and even when we are in the most lovely or happiest of situations our emotions can still leak out. Often, when we feel like we "should" be happy, that's when past hurt or trauma we haven't dealt with rears its ugly head. It seems that when life gets shitty, we react to the conditions and feel shitty but when life gets good, we might find it uncomfortable.

It's not that we are not grateful, it's just that most of us (especially those with worthiness issues) have a kind of "Happiness cap". A certain level of happiness that feels comfortable to us but anything over that and it can feel too much. We can feel like we don't deserve to feel this good, we might be afraid of what other people may think of us, afraid it will make us stand out from the crowd, afraid of being judged or that we need to prepare ourselves for everything going to shit so we bring ourselves down before life can.

Children are just as human as adults and have just as real emotions. The difference with kids though is they give less shits about social correctness, so they let out ALL their emotions as they happen completely unapologetically. It's not that they are ungrateful for the presents or the holiday or whatever, it's that the emotion they are feeling at that very moment matters the most to them. For the most part they are acting unconditionally to their circumstances. If they want to be happy, even at a funeral, they will be. If they want to be sad, even at the Christmas meal you've spent hours preparing, oh they will be. It's not that they don't care about the way it impacts other people, they're just not aware of it. They live very much in the moment and how they feel in that moment really matters to them.

And while it makes sense to teach a child that their actions and words can hurt other people or frustrate their parents, giving that child the responsibility of anyone else's feelings is overkill. Because then you are teaching them to put down their emotions, mask or that their feels are completely inconvenient or "wrong".

It's likely that this may have happened to you. Were you taught that making other people happy was more important than your own happiness?

You can give anyone everything you have, and they could still be unhappy.

And that's OK. It's not your job to please them. Adult or child. Our only responsibility is towards ourselves.

Be kind to all, but never take on that thankless job of feeling like you have to save someone, make them happy or make them proud. Those feelings will come regardless, if that person truly loves you.

But you do have a responsibility to yourself. You need to care about how you feel. You need to use those emotions to gauge how aligned you are with your Higher Self. You need to care enough about yourself to have that kind inner voice, to take risks when you need to, to realign, rock the boat, do the things that light up your soul. That's your responsibility - to be the truest self you can be in that moment. To know whatever you are feeling is OK. To choose to love yourself unconditionally and show that love every single day.

This is not some toxic "always positive" bullshit either.

There's going to be times when you feel misaligned, maybe even when you feel like completely giving up. That's OK too. Your responsibility to yourself isn't just rainbows and lights shooting out of your peachy arse. It's accepting (and loving) both the dark and the light.

It's not your responsibility to capture the beauty for other people
To describe the experience
Put away your phone
Your only responsibility is to
Be
To Experience
Appreciate the beauty for yourself
To allow it to mould you
Shape you
Expand you

Grow, move and really live
Enjoy the fuck out of each and every moment

See all of this through your true eyes
Interact with nature

Allow it all
While you set your vibration
to joy, satisfaction and unconditional love

Just start each day with the knowledge that your feelings matter today. That how you respond to what happens in this day, and how aligned you are, actually matter to you. That in itself is life-changing.

Making how you feel a priority without giving yourself unrealistic expectations on what the day should bring or trying to control it. Knowing this doesn't have to be "the best day of your life", but enjoying the fuck out of every best moment as they happen, while honouring, accepting and processing ALL of your emotions, staying in the moment and standing firm in your power. This will change your life. Full stop.

But in order to do that you do actually have to give a shit about yourself. Through the good AND the bad. Through the high emotions and the low. The light and the dark.

And so, let's have a little dance in the shadows...

SURVIVAL MODE

Over the past couple of years, I've been both soaring in thriving mode and clawing at life in survival mode.

While it's obviously a beautiful thing to feel like you are soaring, to be fully aligned and to have everything working out, it can feel like a slap in the face when it's not. You can get mad at yourself and mad at the world because in survival mode, everything just feels hard and out of whack. It feels like the Universe is testing you and it's so frustrating.

But we need the dark just as much as we need the light. It's hard to feel aligned in survival mode because this is usually at the very time that we are disconnected from our Higher Self. It's harder to trust the Universe, your own infinite source of power and even your Higher Self when it feels like your whole world is going to shit. During these moments in life your Body takes over. She will allow you to feel the bare minimum. She believes she is fighting for your survival.

In 2020, for a good few months, I was in survival mode. I was just getting used to living on a tiny (but cosy) boat with my three kids and little dog. I was definitely not at my healthiest. I had been bleeding (as in a period, shark week, riding the crimson wave) for over three months straight. I was under fucking immense pressures since the breakdown of my marriage and that's not even adding in the effects of lockdown and the Rona. I wasn't eating well (or at all). I was not sleeping enough (or at all). I wasn't drinking any water or juicing. I didn't have the head space to meditate. I was boozing it up and smoking a lot. You get my drift? After a day of looking after my boys, herding mine and everyone else's llamas and generally dodging my emotions, I'd drag myself to the end of the day and would only then realise I had not eaten or looked after myself in any conceivable way the whole day; but at that point, I was too tired to move, to think, to adult. Another day had passed and tomorrow I knew it would be time to do it all over again. So I cut corners, drinking too much coffee, and survived by distracting myself by giggling at memes at night instead of actually sleeping.

A phrase that has become my favourite during this Rona shitstorm is "Needs must when the devil's driving" which seems to fit me perfectly. Needs must. When you are in survival mode, looking after yourself is *fucking hard*. Being on my own and caring for so many people is hard. I knew it would be. I just wasn't banking on all the other pressures choking me at the same time. In spite of all my struggles, I knew how life has this way of moulding you through these rough old times and making sure you are sticking to your alignment and beliefs even when you barely feel like you're able to stand.

It felt like a test. But it wasn't a test.

It's never a test.

Remember YOU are a part of the big Universe. You are a part of this collective consciousness that has the power to guide you, love you and teach you.

Yes, life throws up all kinds of shit at you but ultimately you are helping create the shit in the first place.

You are a co-creator of your reality. But maybe not in the way you currently believe.

Other people will have an impact in your life. People you may love more than life itself may let you down. At times your very faith in humanity may have you rocked to your very core. Tragedy happens, illness happens, life happens. Yes, you have a lot of power in your veins, but you do not control other people. You don't create everyone else's reality. Thank fuck, eh? You can drop all of that responsibility right here, right now. You can impact their reality, just as they can yours, but ultimately, it's up to each one of us to choose what sort of impact others can have on us.

You know what I'm going to say next, right? All of these things happen that are outside of your control, but you can control how you react to them. You can control how they affect your beliefs about yourself. You can control how they affect your alignment.

How you process your feelings around them. How kind you are to yourself while you process.

You are creating your experience and how you decide to react to the gloriously diverse world around you.

You are a co-creator. But you are creating with your Higher Self. It is your alignment with her that has the true impact. It's your relationship to her that matters more than anything. What you create is completely dependent on that higher version of yourself and how much you allow yourself to be what you've already created vibrationally. When your energy and beliefs match that of your higher being, you can feel it so powerfully. You just "know" what to do, where to go and also how to react to the shit you can't control. You see all the good in people, in the world and in nature because you are looking at your life through the eyes of source. Through your true eyes. She sees it all through pure love. The most unconditional love you'll ever feel. That's why it feels SO good. Alignment is basically your human self agreeing with your Higher Self.

It can never be a test because your Higher Self never judges you. She sees your worth without you ever having to prove it. She sees you as the amazing being that you are. She accepts you just as you are right now...survival mode or soaring high. She has no need to test you. Life has no need to test you. The only person who can test you is you.

Your soul wants to expand. That expansion hits differently when you are going through hell to when you're flying on bliss. But it's all expansion and all needed. You came here to feel everything. The whole spectrum of the human experience. Although when you're at the bottom of that deep dark hole, misaligned and hopeless, it may feel like there's no way out...there always is. And there's no need to rain shit on yourself when you are feeling that way, because without darkness there could be no light. Everything is needed. Once you realise this, the dark times can become shorter. You don't need to be so hard on yourself OR the Universe. Life isn't doing it to us, to punish or test us, we are creating life in perfect timing to what we need to grow, live, appreciate and realign.

The more you feel, the more you feel. It's a beautiful guidance system from Big U, and proves that we are fully supported, never being tested.

At the start of this whole journey my goal was to find unconditional love for myself. Going down that rabbit hole made me realise just how conditional our love for everyone is. So, then the goal became unconditional love full stop.

Now as I go deeper and deeper my goal has evolved towards unconditional living. Alignment, satisfaction and love regardless of my current life conditions.

Unconditional living means not living your life just reacting to what life throws at you but consciously caring enough about how you feel to keep the alignment and flow going no matter what is happening and understanding the value of the perfect timing of all that you are living right now.

Unconditional living means how people react to you has no effect on how you feel about yourself. Whatever llamas are going on around you, you still stand firm in your worthiness, firm in your knowing of your true self, your true magnificent power.

Remember, with 100% freedom comes 100% responsibility. We get to create our reality but our whole existence is based on contrast, and so even when we find ourselves stable in what already is and living unconditionally, life still keeps presenting contrast to help us grow, learn and practise. Like I said before, coming out of alignment is part of being human. It helps us see just how delicious being in alignment actually is. It helps us clarify what is truly important to us and just how important it is to unconditionally love yourself.

It also helps us to grow, learn and expand. Anchors ourselves to the foundation of our power and the wholeness of who we are. You don't need llamas and struggle to grow but they sure as fuck help speed up the learning if we are willing to let go of our ego, stop blaming everyone else, take responsibility for how we feel and actually give a fuck about ourselves.

Connecting with your Higher Self, even loving yourself, while things are good and breezy is easy (*well easier*). Doing it when you are down in the shitter is nothing short of legendary.

Survival mode is hard. Well, duh, you are literally fighting for your life.

I feel like I've just emerged from losing a couple of weeks to my depression. When in the thick of it, it feels like you're at the bottom of a deep dark hole looking, searching, for a glimmer of light, a glimmer of hope. It's a timeless place where minutes can feel like eternity but days morph into each other like mere seconds have passed.

For me, this time, it started with feeling very emotional, little things starting me off. Then a deep sadness that very quickly turned into anger. Injustice, anger, even rage is so much easier to deal with than hopelessness or depression. If I had caught it there then maybe I could have turned it around very quickly but once you get into that place, it's very hard to *want* to make yourself feel better. It's very hard to live (and love) unconditionally when you get the rage. Every little thing that goes on around you fuels the fire.

I figured out that the anger was a protection from my Body because she felt like I couldn't handle the sadness. I held on to the fact that tomorrow was a new day. But tomorrow brought with it a disconnection, a disillusion, that all-encompassing apathy and hopelessness. I got frustrated at myself so many times. I tried to meditate, I tried to write. I sat with my laptop at my feet trying to guilt myself into working. It sat shut the entire time, causing me to feel frustration and disappointment with myself. In a weird kind of way, it felt good to feel that towards myself because at least I was feeling *something*.

But the distaste was not a good feeling in itself. Why? It was an indication to me that my Body was feeling something that my Higher Self disagreed with. As a source of pure love, your Higher Self is full of compassion for you. She would never agree that it would be helpful for you to feel anything but pure love and compassion for yourself.

But in the realms of darkness when you have lost your light it feels impossible to see yourself through Source's eyes. It's like your eyes become very human and your Body is fully in control and fully in "protective" mode. Your Body loves you unconditionally but her fears for you clouds that love so she does what she knows will best protect you from actually feeling, even if it hurts you in the process. A lesser evil situation, if you will.

Then, you get very focused on the hard, and softness feels a world away. You get lost in the shadows and you forget what light feels like on your face. Everything seems harder and it is. You feel totally alone.

While you read this, I want you to remember how this book is not out to *fix* you. Even if you are in survival mode and cannot look after yourself properly, you still deserve your own love and compassion. Give yourself a little grace. Allow the words to sink in but do not allow any shame or for your inner bitch to pipe up.

I feel like I'm popping out of my black hole, fuck knows how long I will stay in the light this time. It feels like an awakening. Like I can finally see the mess and carnage the black hole has caused this time around. I feel like "I'm" back again but where the fuck did I go? Honestly? Now that I'm out, being in there seems just so weird, like why couldn't I just see what was happening? What did I do wrong? What is wrong with me?

The intense desire to plan out my meals, schedule in meditation, do anything to fix me. To not go down that hole again no matter what. The thing is, I feel that when I'm on the edge, I'm peering in. It's not a conscious decision to jump in. I can do everything in my power to protect myself but sometimes it happens anyway.

The feeling of "fixing" yourself really just contributes to the shame and disgust you feel when you are down in that hole. There is nothing to fix. The shame, disgust, regret, frustration...all of it is wasted energy. It doesn't inspire you to "do better", it doesn't motivate you to change anything. It just sends you deeper into that dark hole, further away from the light, further away from actually caring enough about yourself to just give yourself that time and compassion to heal. Really heal.

Mental Health

Mindset plays a significant role in how we look after ourselves, how our days go and how we can turn our thoughts around to focus on all the positives around us instead of the shit.

Unfortunately, a lot of people get mindset health mixed up with brain health. For instance, they will tell someone with depression to be more positive or more grateful. When you are experiencing the blues, in a shitty mood or you are literally just being self-indulgent, wallowing in your own llamas (we all do it!), then of course mindset can change your whole day, even your life.

If you have a mental illness, mental disability, mental disorder...although gratitude and all that good stuff helps, it is not a cure all. In fact, most of these disorders (if that's what you want to call it) can't be cured at all. They can be helped, they can be lived with, they can even fade into the background, but they remain a part of our brain makeup, the way it works.

We are in Brain health territory now. As you become more connected with your mind and Body, you will notice that it is easier to tell if you are just having a bad mindset day (because we still get them) or if your brain is actually not well.

Although there's loads of work going on to raise awareness for mental health, there's still a stigma attached to it.

Simple things like changing plans or feeling judgement from your peers are also topped with really big things like being careful what you tell your doctor or people in authority in case they don't actually understand your condition. Feeling like you need to hide the extent of your "illness" from people at work, or family calling you lazy etc.

When you can see someone's illness or disability, it's obviously a lot easier to empathise with it. Really, mental health has only just started to be talked about. Only 30 years ago a lot of these conditions were not even recognised let alone understood.

What a lot of people don't understand is that when your brain is actually ill, you are just as ill as a physically ill person.

When things get bad, you easily slip into survival mode, sometimes still pushing yourself to be *normal* because the guilt that these types of illnesses can cause is colossal.

So, if you are right there in survival mode, and you are finding it hard to bring yourself out of bed to make a cuppa or even go to the toilet, please remember this, give yourself some grace.

Allow your brain time to rest and heal.

Just as you would not expect someone who just had their arm mauled off by a bear to put on a smile and hoover the floor just in case someone pops round, you do not need to expect yourself to be able to put on a smile and just get on with everything. When you are ill, you need to listen to your Body.

It is okay to not be a ray of sunshine every *fucking* day.
It is okay to feel too ill to do everything you had planned in a day.
It is okay to leave the housework in order to nap.
It is okay to give the kids their TV time for an extra hour or so that you can rest.

Take the pressure off. You have a lifetime to live. Today is just today. Some days are for healing. Sometimes, being kind to yourself is just surviving one task at a time. Do what it takes to survive while trying to do whatever it is that makes you feel a tiny bit better.

Your mental health matters just as much as your physical health (arguably more) but it's so much easier to ignore, until it isn't.

Again, put yourself in the situation of just having survived a bear attack (love bears really) and now you are walking around blood gushing out of your arm. What's the first thing you would do? Stop the bleeding. ASAP. Why? Because you know you would die if you didn't. Looking after yourself is now a no-brainer because it's become a matter of life and death.

You wouldn't stop off at a friend's Body Shop (other brands are available) party because you were worried about upsetting her feelings. No! You'd do what it takes to survive. Later even when the initial urgency is over, you'd still expect to take months or even years adjusting and healing from the attack. You may get angry or frustrated by the injustice of what you were going through, but you and everyone around you would understand you need time to heal.

The only real difference between this example of when your brain gets really ill (apart from the bloody obvious) is expectations. Both your own and others.

Now you know that your only real responsibility is to yourself, you can allow the belief that other people's expectations have a bearing on your worth to just melt away.

You do not need to fulfil or entertain other people's expectations. Nor do you need to justify why you are no longer doing so, to yourself or them.

Your own expectations? These you may need to process. The more you can drop the happier you'll be. Because your Higher Self has zero expectations for you so the closer you get to that type of love the closer, you'll be to that source inside of you.

Just as your expectations would need to change in order for you to empathise with your Body if you were suddenly missing a limb, so they do now as you understand more fully and process your brain health.

First you have to do what it is you need to do in order to survive. Next you have to do what it is you need to do in order to heal.

Then you have to do what it is you need to do in order to align and love.

Although I've explained it like it has an order and timescale, it doesn't. Healing is never linear. You will have ebbs and flows. You can have no set timescales, deadlines or expectations. Sometimes the survival, healing, alignment, love, hate, frustration and compassion will seem to merge into one another as you are taken for a dark rollercoaster ride. Catching the briefest moments of light before pummelling down the dark hole again before you've barely had a moment to catch your breath.

You may feel completely alone in your struggles.
But you are never really alone because you always have YOU.

Most people will scoff at this statement, or it will bring little comfort to them because they have come to detest the person they believe themselves to be.

But you are so much more than what you believe yourself to be.
You are so much more than what you believe yourself to be.

Even if you love yourself, you are still so much more than what you believe yourself to be.

The "you" inside of you is infinite.

Time has no meaning to her.

Take all the time you need because she understands you need grace, energy and to actually fucking care about yourself to allow yourself to reach into the light at the end of that hole, to allow the light to crack through and give you hope to carry on while you heal, to allow for you to see both the dark and light in you and love yourself regardless, just as she does.

Tomorrow's You

Even when you're not in survival mode it is still easy to slip out of alignment or mistrust your Higher Self's guidance system. Being human means this might happen often. It's like your brain gets in the way. Just as Self-Love is a daily commitment so is being in alignment. The two go beautifully hand in hand. Once you feel the sweet thrill of living unconditionally in alignment, quite honestly nothing else will compare. You will not settle for less.

If you had zero responsibilities, lived on an island with swimming pigs, sipping cocktails and smoking weed all day this shit would be easy (just dropped my life goals), but you are an adult. There are things you have to do. Work that needs to be done, llamas to herd, children to feed. Most of this "stuff" we fill our life with feels like a chore. Days can feel burdensome, we are often stressed, in overwhelm or feel like there's too many people to please, that we can never measure up. Slipping out of alignment happens. Other people's expectations happen. Our own expectations happen. Shit happens.

Taking the time to explore your beliefs, care about how you feel, or chase fun can feel like an impossibility when faced with "real life".

What are you supposed to do? What are you supposed to change?

You simply have to love yourself. When you love yourself, everything changes. That said, in order to love yourself, some things will need to change first.

I'm not talking about changing you as a person; but you may need to change your view of what you are allowed to do and your expectations and beliefs about yourself.

If you want to see your Body as something to be cherished and looked after, your whole attitude towards her has to change and actions will have to speak louder than words.

To change your inner voice to a kinder voice, to change the way you love yourself, your actions need to be in line with your new feelings and thoughts towards yourself. You don't have to beat yourself up if you still fall short in the self-care department, we do that enough, daily. You must instead still look after yourself with a forgiving attitude. You need to remember you don't need to love yourself perfectly in every way but that you may have to shift some of your priorities in order to love yourself imperfectly in any way that you can in that moment.

We fill up our days with just so much *stuff* to do that feels so important but most of it is boring shit, or not enjoyable, or duties, or for other people.... just stupid boring shit filling our days, stressing us out and making us feel guilty and unfulfilled. Some days it can feel like we've just spent the whole time chasing our own arse.

We make all this small stuff feel so big and important like the world might actually implode if we don't make it to work in time or that life won't be worth living if we don't have time to pick up bread before dropping little Lucy to ballet.

Most of the time it's us chasing high expectations of others or unrealistic expectations of ourselves and it just makes everything so "human".

When you are living like this it's misaligned because you are not giving yourself any time or opportunity to connect with your Higher Self. No time to just be. No time to connect with nature, do something lovely for yourself, get creative or just enjoy the moment. There needs to be a shift. This is the important shit you came earth-side to do. Loving yourself needs to be a priority.

If you're putting yourself last, life feels relentless and hard because you are relying purely on your own strength and often your inner voice gets more and more harsh because you are cutting yourself off from that pure love source energy.

To truly love yourself it's so much easier when you can see yourself the way your Higher Self sees you and take a step back from the pressures and expectations of your day-to-day life.

Really, when you find yourself in that place of being stressed about tiny little things or life feeling jagged or relentless, it's a sure sign you have popped out of alignment. This is when I make alignment, self-care and vibrational work my top priority.

This is how I decided to come up with this simple strategy.

Basically, I ask myself a question before deciding if what I am about to do is actually good for me or not.

That question simply is:

"Is this kind to tomorrow's Mirrie?"

"If I *do* this...
don't do this
eat this
finish this
leave this
feel this

...then tomorrow, will I look back and be glad?

In other words:

Am I being kind to tomorrow's me?

If the answer is no but you don't care about yourself, the answer won't matter because tomorrow you can just suck it up. When you don't love yourself, you don't give a shit about the you of tomorrow.

Honestly, I have been known to say, "This is tomorrow's Mirrie's problem." See how I dismissed myself? The thing is, when you don't give a shit, it is easy to dismiss your future self. Why would you care about tomorrow's you when you don't give a shit about today's you?

Everything that you do today will affect you tomorrow.

Something you should know about me: I am known as the procrastination queen. I keep playing with the instant gratification monkey every fucking day.

Procrastination seeps into everyday life easily. "I will do it later." Housework, work-work, and everything else in between gets piled up until it all feels like you got to climb Mount Everest in a bikini. It all just seems too much. This procrastination habit is really unfair to tomorrow's you because you know it's going to put stupid amounts of pressure on the you-of-the-future. But if you are a true procrastinator, you will know that this is just the way your brain works and another beautiful way it's trying to protect you. It may feel like you are being kind to yourself in the moment, but you need to reflect and figure out if you are *actually* being kind. Think of this like the brain health versus mindset health debate.

Are you genuinely being kind to yourself in this moment, or are you putting something off because you just don't care enough about how you are going to feel tomorrow when the deadline looms over your head?

Are you feeling ill? Are you putting your own needs last? Are you seeking that instant gratification to feel good right now, knowing that really you are just playing in the devil's playground? Are you just not looking after yourself because you don't give a shit anymore?

The only question it boils down to is are you doing/not doing this with love for yourself or in spite of yourself?

Only you know the true answers. Only you know the difference deep in your gut.

In life, we can blame other people for our situations. We can blame lack of time for not doing what we want to do. We can blame anything on anyone but looking after tomorrow's you is your sole responsibility. Other people can make it difficult for us to care for our own self. Our situations can actively affect our day to day living but really, as a grown arse adult, it is up to you to prioritise your needs as well as the needs of your kids (if you have kids) and decide how you spend your time and how you can make things easier for yourself tomorrow.

Live by the moment. What you decide in that moment will affect what you have to do or feel in the future. All your tiny decisions add together. Each tiny decision matters. At this point in time, this may sound like a fucking nightmare. I get it.

But it is the truth. You know for sure if you stay up all night watching Netflix, the next day will be harder, and you will feel shitty. At the end of the day, it's all about getting in a mindset of what can you do now to make things easier for tomorrow's you.

Now the questions arise:

How can you show that you care about tomorrow's you?
Do you care about tomorrow's you?
If not, is it time that you did?

The way you look after tomorrow's you is in the every day. You could wash up earlier. You could make sure you drink more water or even give yourself some self-loving by chasing a dream or idea that you've had niggling at you. You could *fill your cup*. Do whatever is kind and healthy to do with your Body or mind. It will have a positive effect on both your health and mood the next day.

You need to decide the impact of how you will feel tomorrow compared to how you are feeling today. Start with being kind to tomorrow's you. Just having that thought of, "Am I being kind to tomorrow's me?", will have a huge impact on the decisions you make in that moment.

What Have You Been Putting Off?

Let me tell you how I felt the evening I accidentally announced the date I was going to release my book. Not just that evening but every day since then.

Shit scared. Scared shitless. A whole barrel of shitty fear.

It had nothing to do with the fear of failure or even the fear of success. I was not afraid of people reading it or what they would think of me, or if they would judge me. I have had this book niggling my brain for the whole time while going through an accidental home birth, losing my brother, a hundred-day juice feast, losing my self-love, surviving the first lockdown, ending my marriage, being homeless, living on a boat, going through another hundred lockdowns, leaving 2020, bouts of deep depression, finding my self-love daily, soaring high, buying my own boat and even more, all of that, so what did it take for me to finish writing this beautiful bastard that you are currently reading?

I have had just about every fear you can think of surrounding me. My Body has been in full blown protection mode to stop me from finishing this book.

But no, it was not any of those things that made me want to curl into a foetal position and rock the night away. It was the fear of actually writing the damn thing.

The reason why this has taken me so long has been the very real fear of *facing up to my emotions.*

I am talking about unspoken, underlying emotions here, the deep shizzle. I have been exploring all my dark, as well as my light and I know what is coming up in the next few chapters. I know what I need to edit and explain. I know that I'm going to have to go in deep in order to do my stories justice. I am doing it because I know that by telling my story and letting you know what a mess I can be, it will allow you to give yourself permission to do the same.

It will give you the hope and the courage to face your own dark side, which is something we all have and yet we are still worthy of love regardless. I want to show you, by my examples of my own life, how if I can do it and survive, you can too.

I used to think "If I can be such a fuck up and still love myself, anyone can." But now I see all the fuck ups, all the llamas and all the frustrations I have about myself, are just a perfect unfolding of both my love for myself and my life. To not love myself despite these things but to see all my humanness and wrap myself in a loving hug knowing that without them I wouldn't be me. The perfectly imperfect me, that I've fallen in love with. I lay all this out so you can see if I'm still worthy with all this mess YOU must be too.

I know I will cope. I know it will be healing. I know my Body has been carrying this trauma for me for way too long now. She deserves for me to acknowledge and feel some of these feels. But Lordy; it is fucking scary. Every fibre in my being is screaming, "No, you can't do it". My Body is giving me every excuse under the sun as to why it's OK to put it off until I am ready; until I am strong enough.

Guess what? As soon as I decide I am strong enough, that is when I become strong enough. I *am* strong enough.

Before I decided to agree with my Body; not to face the fear and allow the niggle to rule my life, I allowed the niggle to influence how I saw myself. I wrote this message to a friend late one night which explains how I was seeing myself. You now get a peek at the type of llama levels my friends had to put up with...

"I have nothing left to give tonight. Do you know why I can't move my pillow to the other side and sleep the other way?

Cause I don't know.

Maybe it's because I don't like change.
It scares the shit outta me.

I mean, the other way is more comfortable, and I can see the TV easier.
Maybe I'll try it tonight
But I know I won't.

Maybe it's the same reason I resisted watching the moon video.
Maybe it's the same reason I still drink too much.
Maybe it's the same reason I want everyone to know I'm a fuckup.
Maybe I'll never change.
And always change.

Maybe it's the same reason I've resisted speaking out about shit that matters to me.

Maybe I'm scared.
Scared of change.

Good or bad.

Maybe it's the same reason I told you I don't deserve you, even when I was the happiest I'd ever been.

Maybe it's the same reason I can't finish my book.
Can't finish creating my business.
Can't finish anything.

Maybe it's the same reason I resist soaring.
Being my best me.
Accepting a compliment.

Maybe it's why I feel stuck all the time,
Can't grieve for my brother.
Can't move from the past.

Maybe it's the same reason why I love the comfortable,
I love the easy, but I can't stay there.
Maybe I feel like I don't deserve it.

Maybe it's the same reason I don't feel at all.

Maybe it's the same reason I believe my own labels, create my own cages, and accept my own punishments.
Maybe I just wanna feel safe.
Better the devil you know, eh?

Oh, look at that.
It's a poem.
I do have something left in me tonight."

When you ignore your soul prompts, it makes you feel like shit.

What if I had listened to my fears forever? Allowed her to protect me? Believed I was not strong enough? What would have happened? Firstly, I would still be running from my emotions like the wind and secondly, you would not be here right now, reading this book, soaking in the wisdom being channelled through me in my own unique sweary voice.

The niggles are a strong indication that your Body is protecting you from something big. It is your choice to run or face up to them and play with where they might take you. But guess what? Nearly all niggles are important, and following them not only creates magic, but can also be a huge act of self-care.

Every fucker out there has that corner in their brain where there is a list of things that niggle at what needs to get done. Usually, it's the things that are for the kids or people you love that will emerge first and make it on your to-do list which will mean they might actually get done. The other stuff is normally for you, and will therefore remain as niggles that you say you will do "when you have time." But you know how that time rarely comes unless it is a medical emergency and forced upon you, unless you start viewing your needs as important as the needs of others around you.

There are two types of niggles that normally end up in this no man's land in your brain, and the more they niggle, the more you tell yourself that you are not important enough to carve out the time for them.

The two types are:

"Shoulds" – these are your self-care niggles. They include:
"Should I ask a doctor about that?"
"I should see a dentist."
"I should ring up this person about this problem I am having."

"Woulds" – these are your love, fun, passion, and soul-care niggles. They include:
"I would love to write a book."
"I would love to try that pottery course."
"I would love to have a girls' night out."

The "*Should*" Niggles that stick around are just shit you need to do because your health is important. This is a different "Should" then the ones we are used to coming from other people. This is real self-care, try to get these "Should" niggles handled immediately.

Coming to the "*Would*" niggles; I often think how the "would" niggles are the ones brimming with potential magic. Now imagine me dressed as a ye' old gold digger saying, "There be magic in them there niggles."

These are the ones that are actually nudges from the Universe. They may not make much sense or seem completely unimportant, but they always lead to something bigger.

If the "would" niggle passes, it was just one idea to lead you to somewhere magic, and you'll get another. But when it lingers, you know that it is a niggle worth listening to right now. But too often, these niggles get neatly packaged away with a bow and stored under the "when I have time" tab in our brain. Our subconscious gets a strong message when we don't act on these niggles and what your Body hears is:

I'll do it...

"When I am important enough."

"When my needs matter."
"When I can justify giving myself what I give to others."

Why are we putting them off?

If you are actively searching for something to heal you or move you forwards, just look at your niggles, the things you are putting off; therein lies your magic answer. The truth is, these are your gut feelings, your intuitions, your souls' prompts, and you are sending the message that you are not enough to listen or act on them. Your answers are already within you. You simply need to do what you are putting off.

Alright Mirrie, simmer down. I know, I know it sounds harsh especially coming from me, but I trust in perfect timings, and you need to be ready to hear this before you are ready to act on it.

When I started my new self-love group on Facebook, the first week, I asked the question, "What have you been putting off?" but people said, "Hey, I thought this group was going to be about self-love." So, I asked again, "In regard to you and your health, what have you been putting off and why?" I decided to answer first to put everyone else at ease, "I have been putting off making an appointment at the dentist because I don't have the time to go by myself." The truth was, going to a dentist was something I was scared of. I knew I had to go because my tooth had been hurting but I also knew how stressed I had been. So, I had been putting it off for years. Avoiding the stress and the pain meant I was being kind to myself in the moment but what about tomorrow's Mirrie? Was it kind to her? No; of course not. I was being a knobber[27], not facing my fears. I was not being kind to my Body and I knew how that was just going to lead to more pain or something worse.

After reading my confession, one lovely lady replied and said that her niggle was that she needed to see a doctor but said she did

---

[27] Knobber: An affectionate term for literal dickhead; idiot

not have the time, *really*. She was so busy with work and the kids, she felt she could not let anybody down and so she had not been able to see a doctor for a while. I sweetly and kindly pointed out that what she was really saying was, "Screw my health; I am not important enough to make or take the time to go to the doctor's. That this/ that/ everyone else is more important than me and my health." She may have replied with, "Well fuck me!" I cannot remember for sure but what I do remember is that she realised how it was a fear of changing plans and everyone being disappointed in her which had kept her from making the appointment. That fear had been more important than actually sorting her health niggle out.

What you have been putting off is a direct reflection on how important you believe it to be.

Is your health important?
Your sanity?
Your goals?
What do you need to feel good?

Once upon a time, I bought luxury spa day vouchers. Do you know it took me a year to use them? How important was I viewing my alone time back then? Making time to do what you have been putting off not only shows other people how much you value yourself, but it also shows YOU how much you value your own self. It is a reminder to put yourself at top of the priority queue or if not at the very top, at least to be in the running.

Remember the Niggles. There's magic in those niggles. Your niggles are there to serve a purpose. Whatever you think about them, if you put them off, they will burrow inside your brain and won't go away. The magic only happens when you choose to act upon it. Not only is it an act of love and courage but it's a message. Your needs are just as important as everybody else's are. It is important to remember this. Take the time and look at what you have been putting off and make sure you do something about it today, even if it is just one tiny step.

Your niggles are your Higher Self's voice. Now's the time to listen to her. She wants to guide you and you truly are worthy enough to make the time to follow your niggles.

Following your niggles, giving a shit about how you feel and caring about Tomorrow's You will inspire you to act like you love yourself TODAY.

Whether today is a day for survival, for healing or for following those glorious fun niggles, the fact always stands, you are still deserving of that kind inner voice. Flying high or at the lowest of your lows, you are still deserving of your self-love.

This one question will genuinely change your life:

Am I being kind to tomorrow's me?

Chapter Seven – Your Worth

You are worthy.

These are just words. Words that may spark an idea for you that maybe, just maybe you are. Words that may make you stop and think, make you question your beliefs, make you hope that you are, but they are, in essence, just words.

If you search on social media for these words, you'll find hundreds and thousands of videos, meditations and songs telling you the same thing.

You are worthy.
Capable of anything.
Be kind to yourself.
Love yourself.

So easily dismissible.
So easy to hear and think:
"Yeah, but not me"
So easy to ignore.
So easy to skip.

Until you believe it, until you can feel it, these words will be worthless to you. You will dismiss every person; you will dismiss every word.

Those words mean nothing until you can say them to yourself.

Those words mean nothing until you feel it in your heart.

Those words mean nothing until you believe it fully and allow that belief to move the way you live.

The way you treat yourself.
The way you show love towards yourself.

But words can't change the way you see yourself until you decide to see yourself in your full power, your full beauty, your full potential, your full badass, unicorn riding, fucking free, magic YOUNESS.

Only you can tell yourself you are worthy.
Only you can feel worthy.

Only you can know it so strongly that it runs through your bones and ripples into all that you are and all that you do.

Words from anyone else will never be able to do that.
Words are just words...
Until they're your own.

What is Worthy?

Worthy of what?
Worthy to be happy?
Worthy of respect?
Worthy of satisfaction?
Worthy of success?
Worthy of lots of money?
Worthy to be comfortable?
Worthy of your desires?
Worthy to be loveable?
Worthy to live?
Worthy of love?
Worthy enough to love yourself?

Seeing your worth and loving yourself are essentially two different things. But seeing your full worth and loving yourself fully go hand in hand.

Most people can see their worth in one or two areas of their life, for example in their job. They're good at what they do and must be worthy because someone pays them to do it. But this rarely filters into other areas of their life.

There are so many people out there who do not feel enough, who do not feel worthy...but what are we actually chasing this feeling for?

Most humans are measuring their worth against something. Even if we feel like we don't, subconsciously we've learnt to gauge our worth on some external ruler and most of the time it's so ingrained into our deep core beliefs that we don't even know we're doing it.

If it's something almost all of us do, it must be normal, right?

No, I don't believe it's normal or serves us. I think it's fucking dangerous and one of the biggest reasons why people don't love themselves or ever feel enough.
Depending on how deep the belief goes and the attention you give to it, equals what impact and level of control it has over you.

Your unconscious brain makes decisions up to 10 seconds before you are consciously making them. When you're deciding whether or not to fuck your diet and choose a greasy burger instead of a salad, your Body knows what you've decided even before you do.

That's why it's so important to discover your unconscious beliefs and check to see if they are still serving you.

Unconscious beliefs are like an old, abandoned house.

You peer into a window, wiping away the muck with your sleeve. Inside there is still furniture, trinkets and ornaments but because they have been untouched for years they are layered thick with dust. You need to actually go in and move stuff around to disrupt the dust or it would just stay that way forever.

So, every so often (as you feel strong enough), go in and disrupt that dust. It may hurt and be scary at first to shift some of that shit, but you need to check that your beliefs are actually serving you and if they're what you want to believe.

If they aren't, you can always clean them up! But, unless you are in a place of living completely unconditionally, you can't do that until you get to know what is influencing you in the first place.

Let's go through some shizzle that you may be using to measure your worth against and see if we can shake up some of the dust.

Think about your beliefs and values that you wrote about when exploring your alignment in chapter 5 and feel free to jump to the areas that apply most to you.

Worth - Your Money

I love mindset shit about money. I've very nearly left it out of this chapter, because my relationship with money has been so dire for so long and I thought it really hasn't got anything to do with self-love...or has it?

There are many well-respected life coaches out there that state "YOUR BANK BALANCE IS A REFLECTION OF YOUR SELF-WORTH".

Guess what? I completely disagree. I've met a lot of self-loathing people with a more than healthy bank balance. But I've also met self-loving people who are as poor as fuck. Your bank balance is already old news, just a reflection of where your beliefs have been, not of what they are right this beautiful moment. Old news people, old fucking news.

It's basically nuts that there are people out there trying to teach about self-worth and making it about the money that you have, or more like the money you don't have. But so many people use money to measure their worth and it's a dangerous game. An even more dangerous game is measuring your worth against your debt.

As we touched on before, money is such a sensitive subject and there's so much shame attached to it...Shame if you have too much, shame if you have too little. People see money as a measure of success, worth, how good they're doing in their lives, how well they can provide, how good a parent they are...the list goes on, and that's without even touching the subject of shame surrounding debt.

Debt can make us hide, feel worthless, stupid and completely block any hints of hope that our money situation will get better in the future.

All of this contributes to negative – even hateful – self-talk and sometimes even suicide. When it gets to the point that people feel like there's no way out, it feels like you are chained inside a black hole.

Basing your self-worth on money just takes all of your power away.

Even if you believe you've got more than enough money, you may be so scared to lose what you own or the momentum of it coming in, that the money holds power over you because you're still locked into the belief that without it you wouldn't have the same worth.

Considering we're talking about a piece of paper, there's lots of subconscious deep beliefs that we hold about money, especially ones which come from our parents as we grow up.

There's also lots of beliefs that come from our own judgments of others that we heap upon even more harshly against ourselves.

But are those beliefs serving us? Do those beliefs make us feel worthy with or without money? Do they keep us in lack, hold us in fear and stop us from following our dreams?
When we measure our worth against debt, money, success or even our quality of life, it's a fickle game.

Your money doesn't reflect your self-worth. It may reflect the self-worth you had in the past but not what you "should" be feeling now.

What is money anyway?

Money is a blank slate. Basically, it's a reflection of our emotions surrounding it. If a greedy person has a lot of money, the energy behind that money is greed...which is need and lack.

If a kind person has money, the energy is one of kindness, gratitude and giving. Money being evil is wrong. Money being good is wrong. Money is the energy of whatever it's being used for, by the person behind the spending of it. Having money doesn't make you good or bad, just like being in debt doesn't make you good or bad either. Whatever energy, intentions and beliefs you have about money is what money reflects back to you.

Money is not a living, breathing force. It's a tool. A tool which allows you a lot of freedom and can be a cause of stress, but it's not a measure of you as a person. Looking at money in its most simple terms, it's the value of gratitude.

If someone gives you something, even if they are not expecting it, you want to give back in some way. The same as if someone does something for you, you want to compensate them.

You're not always repaying them in money, sometimes it's in gratitude, excitement, a simple thanks or a service.
Sometimes they do expect repayment and it is money. As long as you and they feel that the transaction/exchange is fair, you're both happy and both feel grateful.

Any feelings of "ickiness" or resentment is only felt if the exchange wasn't "fair" or is linked to your own beliefs about money/value.

So, money is pure energy…pure, blank energy, just waiting for you to choose which energy to feed it. That means the beliefs and energy you give money shape the beliefs you have and how you *feel* about money. For example, if you were told your whole life that "money doesn't grow on trees", "money equals hard work" etc., you may give money the energy of desperation, lack or limits on how you get to receive it.

Lack mindset leads to debt and resenting money, resenting paying bills and feeling not enough.

Resenting getting paid – not enough.
Resenting not having enough money - not enough.

Resenting yourself – not enough.
Resentment leads to anger and jealousy to other people who seem to have it easier than you.

All of these emotions are based around a "should".

What you feel you should be earning, the car you should be driving, the sort of life you should be providing for your family, the presents you should be buying for Xmas, the meal out you should be able to afford, the debt you should be able to pay off...

Ultimately if there are money shoulds bearing down on you and making you feel unworthy, unlucky or not enough, then you are measuring your worth based on your money situation and how close you feel you are to those "Money Shoulds".

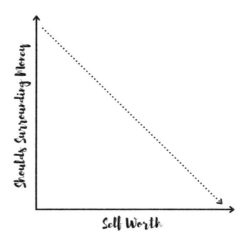

If you are basing your worth on anything, say for example your weight, the size of your penis, how popular you are...the chart looks the same. The further you get from the "shoulds", the lower your self-worth feels.

Your money "shoulds" are based on your subconscious and conscious beliefs. Take the time to disrupt that dust, investigate them and decide if they are serving you and simply get rid of the ones that don't.

YOUR MONEY DOES NOT EQUATE TO YOUR WORTH.

You are worth more than a piece of paper, a number or a status. Let's keep going to find out why.

Worth – Your Mess

Everyone has at least one part of their life which feels "messy".

- Home
- Bedroom
- Car
- Relationship
- Mind
- Heart
- Health
- Body
- Skin

Or *ahem* all of the above.

Wherever your mess lies, there will always be one or more areas in your life that feel messy...maybe even all. The reason I can say without a doubt that everyone will have one or more, is because mess is human.

Mess is a becoming.

Even the most "perfect" people have hidden messes. When something feels messy, everything feels up in the air. There are no solid plans, solutions or even brain space to figure shit out. When you base your worth on your mess, you're basing it on your imperfections.

The problem with measuring your worth on your mess is that most of the time, you are far more gracious towards other people's mess than you are of your own. We happily accept other people's messiness. We even assume they'll have some mess at some time but feel it's totally unacceptable for us to have our own. Seeing our own mess can be scary because we have to face up to our own shortcomings, our imperfections, our limitations, our mentality.

Humans tend to have this need to *fix* situations, and often much prefer to focus on fixing someone else's mess than even just look at their own.

In fact, some people base their own worth on their ability to fix other people's mess, but we are not here to fix anything. No one needs fixing, not even you.

External messes show up in your physical world.
Internal messes are to do with your mindset, mental health and internal dialogue.
Relationship messes cover your partner, children, family and friends.
Work messes may be to do with your purpose, goals or money situation.

There are hundreds more possible messy situations that could show up in your life.

When an area in your life feels uncluttered, you are clear on what to do, it feels good to you, straightforward, you feel like you are headed in the right direction, confident and it's easy to have high self-worth in that situation.

Clarity.

But when an area feels cluttered it's exactly the opposite, it feels messy, unclear, gives you a bad feeling and you feel completely unsure of yourself. It's easy to feel low self-worth and overwhelmed.

Confusion.

That's without even touching on the guilt or shoulds you are beating yourself up with for getting in such a mess.

Do you feel guilty for your humanness?

Our messes even become so normal to us that we can hardly see them. The job to fix them is so big that it seems impossible and so we just accept and put up with the mess forever. But whether our messes are internal, external or someone else's fault, it can be easy to base or measure our worth against them. Also, because messy is, well, *messy*, it means we constantly see ourselves as falling short of the expectations we set for ourselves and it can rob us of our joy completely.

Let's look at some areas. You know that worth needs to be based on just your "is-ness" but that doesn't mean you are powerless against your mess.

You can't base your worth on your mess because no matter what mess you fix, there will always be more ready to show up. Human existence demands it! When your worth just *is*, as we will see later, then you can look at the mess with fresh eyes and feel strong enough to face it, so it doesn't make you feel miserable.

If you can see your mess for what it is...just a lack of clarity, the beginning of your next expansion. You becoming more and stepping into a powerful place of knowing what you want, by now knowing what you *don't*, then you will realise nothing needs fixing. Mess is a part of life. Mess is a part of you.

If you can't see that, then it can become a vicious cycle.

If you are basing your worth on mess, then your worth is moveable, and you feel worthless and out of control.

If you feel unworthy, you then feel useless and unable to deal with the mess, which leads to feeling unworthy to have or do more anyway, which equals more mess.

If you base your worth on just the fact that you are existing, you will still have mess and messy situations but you'll *know* that you have the power and ability to change or not put up with them. The mess will inspire the next step in your journey.

Let's look closer at these areas and see how many more times I can say "mess".

I'm going to start with one that so many women say affects their self-worth, and even their day-to-day lives. Who am I kidding? When I lived in a house it affected *my* self-worth, my day-to-day life, who I invited around and even whether I went out or not. I told myself money would fix it, moving house, decorating, buying a new rug – but the truth is my home was messy. Beyond messy. There were parts I didn't even let my husband see. "The Pit" – my bedroom. Clothes piled high, clothes *everywhere*. Toys everywhere. Parts of the oven that would never get clean – it affected my depression, even my abundance.

I unconsciously measured my worth on my home and it affected how I saw myself as a wife, as a mother, as a person. I used to measure my worth against my physical mess and it was a miserable existence. There are so many people out there who have slightly messy homes or hoard things, but when you have deep depression for *years*, that shit gets out of control.

I did what I could when I could so the basics got done, but I found it hard to be consistent, so the bigger jobs piled up and there was no order to the madness.

Also, because we had the fire, lots of stuff in our house was mis-matched. We were both crap at decorating and bringing in little money while ill so a lot of the time the house felt tatty, and it made me feel poor. A "cleaner" home made me feel lighter and better about myself.

Before self-love I hated my home, hated being in it, just wanted to move. A friend said: "Your home is trying to teach you something. I bet once you've learned it, you'll be able to move."

BUT WHAT WAS THE LESSON?

I drove myself mad trying to figure it out. If I could just move, I'd be happy right? A fresh start, a new place, I'd keep it clean and feel so good about myself.

When I saw coaches on Instagram or Pinterest – with their white walls and bedding, beautiful artwork in their perfect beautiful homes it just made me feel so small.

How do they do it?

I tried – I tidied up the whole house, got a new (to us) sofa, painted (shabbily) the walls, but kids with messy hands up the walls, dog hair, permanent markers, someone drops spaghetti...and fuck white blankets, life just feels comfier with my *Ben-10* duvet.

In my mind's eye I could see my new home. The conservatory faced the sea, it was bright with white walls, comfy corner sofas with blankets and fluffy pillows. Toys had their place, there was no clothes drying on the damn radiators. There were plants everywhere that weren't dying, crystals, art... It felt light, it felt happy, it felt like *home*.

Coming out of that vision into my messy reality kind of killed my heart, especially when I believed that's what other people had (mostly due to social media) and due to my "health problems", "mental health" and "money", It just seemed like an impossible goal. It made me feel less than enough, because my reality didn't match my ideal. It made me feel like I was letting myself, my family and especially my kids down.

Here's the kicker... THE HOUSE YOU ARE IN IS THE HOME YOU MADE IT. Read that out loud.

Oh, I know you don't want to hear that, I still don't want to hear that, but it's the raw truth.

The next person who moves into your home may have come from somewhere smaller or in a horrible area. Think about how grateful they may be, they could be creating their perfect home from where you're living right now. Yes, there are other outside forces, but it's truly possible that *you* could create a safe, light, happy space.

You're not creating the home you want, instead YOU ARE CREATING A FEELING.

But because your self-worth is connected to your mess, you feel overwhelmed and disempowered and unmotivated. This goes for your home, your car or any physical thing, if you base your worth on it.

Right now, I live on a tiny boat with my three boys. There are leaks everywhere, everything is mismatched, I only have three forks, you can only flush the toilet when the tide is in. When I left my marriage, I basically left everything in that house too. But my boat is my space. I chose the bed covers (rainbows), window stickers (more rainbows,) I fixed the leaks and the locks and the toilet. I saved up the money for little blue fairy lights which hang from every window. I treated myself to an egg blue fluffy blanket but could only afford one so it's treasured. I made my space cosy because it represents my freedom. Of course, it gets messy- think of the amount of goddamn toys I have to try and fit in here! But she is sitting in the most beautiful, wild part of my favourite place in the world and I'm so incredibly grateful for her.

DISCONNECT YOUR WORTH FROM YOUR MESS.
BELIEVE IT'S POSSIBLE.
CHANGE ONE THING.
MAKE IT FUN!

The same goes for any area of your life that feels messy. You are not actually chasing the thing that would feel less messy. The perfect relationship, the perfect home, the perfect body do not exist and that's not actually what you want. You crave the feeling that comes from your belief of what these things will mean for you.

Clarity...
Goodness...
Ease...
Worthiness...
All these things are already yours.

They are not tied to a thing or a person.

Your mess doesn't reflect your worthiness or where you are right now. Just a choice that you've already made, not the one you can choose to make right now.

But, one foot in front of the other. You may not be able to do a complete makeover of your home or be able to maintain what your vision of your perfect home is. That's really OK if you decide it to be. After you disconnect any worthiness from your mess you will feel a weight of relief around it, which will make all this shizzle so much easier.

I know for me, if things are tidy my brain feels tidied. Things feel calmer. I've not forgotten about my vision of the home I want and I'm that much closer to it. I'm creating my home with every decision I make; with every tiny step I decide to take. My mess is simply my mess and although it's easy to slip into the mindset of being frustrated with myself for it, I no longer need to feel controlled by it. That is what comes from the freedom of loving yourself unconditionally and knowing your worth is not based on your mess.

Worth - Your Relationships

Traditional relationships?
They all suck ball bags. Do not recommend.
Joking...
Kinda[28].

While not all relationships suck (TWSS) basing your worth on your relationship certainly will. By measuring your worth against someone else's opinion of you, someone else's idea of who you should be or how you should act, you are literally handing your power over to that person on a plate. Your worth will be up and down like a hoebag's knick knacks[29]. Can you really rely on

---

[28] Kinda: Kinda like" kind of" but more halfarsed
[29] Hoebag's knickknacks: promiscuous person's knickers; undergarments

someone else's mood to determine how worthy you feel on any given day?

Even if that person knows, accepts and loves you fully. Even if that person respects your boundaries, gives you space to be who you are or has only reasonable expectations of you. That person is still imperfect. That person still has their own hopes and desires. By handing them control over your worth, you are opening yourself up to one fucking rocky ride. What happens if they bounce? What happens if they cheat? What happens if they end up hating you?

If your worth is steady and rooted in your "Isness" (more on this at the end of this chapter), you will cope. You will get hurt but you will move on. But if your worth is in their hands...now shit gets messy.

I'm not saying that you can't trust anyone or that you need to be closed off to guard yourself. Real relationships can be a beautiful, lifelong commitment to each other, but what I am saying is that you can't rely on anyone else to save or fix you. Knowing your worth isn't based on anyone else on this earth apart from the person who knows you best (YOU) means you can go into (or continue) your relationship with equal power, mutual respect and without the need to carry each other. Your worth is your own responsibility, you don't get to pass that on to anyone else, no matter how much they love you.

While someone you love is giving you all of their attention and giving you validation of who you are or what you are doing, it feels so delicious that it can be so easy to fall into needing that in order to feel good. The issue with making your worth conditional to someone else's actions, attention or opinions is that humans are pretty fickle and often are basing their own worth, mood or views on conditions outside of themselves. This might mean that when you get a hold of your own worth and start breaking free of that need for validation, it might piss off the people who are used to you being dependent on them or it might be the start of the relationship you've always dreamed about.

Yesterday we were on a family walk and my youngest son was skipping along singing a song that he knows always gets me emotional and full of gratitude. He kept asking me "*Are you crying mama? I want you to cry happy tears*". I showed him a little tear in my eye, and he looked very pleased with himself and held my hand, still skipping along.

"*I love you so much.*"
I squeezed his hand and felt so incredibly lucky in that moment.

But then he wanted to walk along the steep bit of the hill, at first it was fine, and we kept holding hands but after a few minutes he started leaning down the hill while he was walking, putting all the pressure of his full body weight on my arm. I kept asking him to stop but he was in his own happy little world enjoying the sun and the apparent danger, but my arm was getting tired, and it was starting to get annoying.

Then he kept doing this weird thing where he was pulling so hard it was like he was trying to paraglide down the hill while still holding my hand. It kept jolting me and I felt his hand slip from mine. Instinctively I pulled him off the hill and stopped walking.

"*You've got to stop doing that because if I let go of your hand, you'd fall down the hill, Indie," I said.*
"*Why would you let go?*"
"*I wouldn't let go on purpose, but my arm is getting tired, if you want to walk on the hill, you can, just let go of my hand first and then you'll know how to keep yourself safe, but if you want to hold my hand stay up here.*"

He let go of my hand and in the true nature of his name, he Indiana Jones-style went halfway down the hill, skipping on the dangerous route instead of being with me on the easy path.

Now I would give my life to keep my child safe, obviously I love him with my very soul, but I knew he would be more sure footed if he wasn't relying on the strength of my bingo wings.

I wanted him to be fully responsible not only for choosing his own path but also for his own safety.

Now this was a tiny hill, and I knew if he fell while skipping along it, it would be a tiny fall into soft grass. However, if he had fallen while pulling on my arm, with his full body weight, momentum would have made the fall faster and sudden and might have really hurt him. I watched him skip away from me, confident in my love but also confident in his own strength and decisions and my Body felt the relief.

It's very much the same in relationships.

You love each other fiercely. You want the other person to be safe, you'd probably risk your life for the other person but if one person is taking all the responsibility for the other's wellbeing, if one person is taking all the weighty strain of being responsible for the others happiness or even their sense of worth, it becomes tiring and really annoying...no matter how much you love that person.

A lot of traditional relationships are very conditional. It's 100% commitment till you dieeee no matter what the other person throws at you. We grow up seeing this type of love in movies where they make the other person's love the only reason for their happiness, how they feel is conditional on how they get treated, the worthiness of the main character normally rests on them being loved or saved and this has filtered into our views of actual love.

Basing your worth on someone else's love or appreciation is just like skipping on a big hill with all of the weight of your happiness, worth and security hanging off the arm of the other person. It can feel good for a short time, but it means all of your power is in the fate of their hands and whether they mean to or not, if that hand slips or their arm gets tired, you'll go tumbling down the hill.

How much better is it to be sure footed, choose your own path, with each of you taking responsibility for knowing your own worth and happily skipping along with each other, each of you in your full power.

When you get two people (or more) who live in that state of unconditional worthiness and unconditional love for themselves and each other...regardless of what the other person says, thinks or even how they act, while loving each other, respecting each other's boundaries, loving seeing the other person in their full power and chasing the fun of life....that relationship will not suck. That relationship will be expansive, beautiful and life giving...maybe with a little suck on a Friday night if you're feeling spicy.

Worth - Your Mind and Body Health

Our physical health or mental health feeling messy can happen to anyone at any time. We need to make sure our expectations aren't unrealistic. If you expect perfection from your Body or mind, you are in for a slap-in-the-face wakeup call at some point in the future. If you are basing your worth on high expectations, it's going to get messy.

AGAIN, TAKE BACK THE POWER.

Without fixing anything, can you see your value? You are allowed to love yourself regardless.

Your worth can't be measured by your health, but the results of how you feel about yourself can be seen. Do you spend money on your health? Do you give yourself (or your mind) days off? Do you show your Body the respect she deserves for *her* needs and wants?

View your Body as a Garden

She has very simple needs:
Very simple needs, to help her function...
- Nutrition
- Water
- Sleep/rest

- Emotions processed
- Connection

Very simple wants, to make her happy…
- Sunshine
- Outdoors
- Passion
- Alignment
- Freedom

Are you respecting her needs or are they always coming in last place? Do you see your Body as a garden to tend to, give love to and nurture? Or a broken machine to work until more broken and then just find a quick fix?

You need to have…
TIME & GRACE
ACCEPTANCE & GRATITUDE
COMPASSION & LOVE

Work *with your imperfections or limitations*, not against.

Your Body is always doing her best. She is imperfect too and if you base your worth on how she works or how she looks, you are setting yourself up for a crash and burn situation as you get older.

More than that, your Body loves you and if you believe that to be true, it means your brain loves you too. For your entire life, the way your Body and brain has responded to life is just a reflection of what they know works in order to protect you. All of our brains and bodies work differently and there are no set boxes to tick or "shoulds" to strive towards when it comes to your own.

Take this moment to really appreciate your Body. Your physical and mental health. Think about all that you can do, think about all that you've been through together. Think about the traumas and emotions you've buried down, seemingly not strong enough to deal with…your Body has carried all of that for you. Heavy emotions, other people's judgements, your own unrealistic expectations. Your Body takes all of that on and lovingly protects you from it.

But of course, she has human limitations. You are so much more than your Body, but she is still a part of you. Basing your worth on what she can or can't do (both body and mind) means that your worth will fluctuate depending on how YOU see your body or mental health. This spreads out to whether you allow others to influence you, to what your own shoulds and expectations are at any given moment, how others see you and how capable you feel.

Judgy
Judgy
Judgy

Feel how heavy that sounds.

Where does love and acceptance fit into this measure of worthiness?

Every day our bodies change.
At any moment our mood or mental health can change.

For a strong foundation of worth you have to let go of the idea that your physical body or the way your brain works has any bearing on your worthiness. In fact, once you do this, not only will you have more grace, acceptance and appreciation for the way your body and brain works, you'll also love yourself even more for it. Not regardless of it.

Your humanness and imperfections are just another slice of the YOU pie and, fuck me, it's all delicious.

Worth - Your Past

Measuring your worth against your past, especially if your childhood was traumatic, is on two levels problematic. Firstly, a lot of the time the past was not in your power. Second...YOU CAN'T CHANGE IT.

So if your past is your measuring stick, it's impossible for you to feel any more worthy than you do right now. But not all is lost! You can change your measuring stick! You also have the power to change the way you perceive your past.

Often, we have a set view of how things happened in the past and we leave no wiggle room. The past becomes so ingrained in our brains, the account of it is like hard facts. We forget other people have different perspectives, that there was a bigger picture or even that we are allowed to change our feelings surrounding those events, while still honouring the ones we felt while it was happening.

It's like we anchor our past into our actual identities, forgetting that we are allowed to explore our past with fresh eyes and separate who we are now from what happened to us then.

Childhood Experiences

Even if you had an amazing childhood, no one really makes it through unscathed. Being raised by imperfect humans who were facing experiences both good and bad, means that no childhood is perfect. Even when we focus on the goodness that was in our life while growing up there are still parts of it that, if we allow them, could affect the way we see our worth.

Remember when it comes to childhood trauma the child is never at fault. No child should ever have to feel less than fully worthy and fully, fully loved. Although you may feel guilt and shame, please, please remember you were the innocent one in all of this and whatever you would say to a child now if they had the same experience, you need to say to yourself. You need to heal that child within and realise that if you base your worth on the way someone treated you as a child, and you were not treated correctly with unconditional love or without expectation, you will be measuring that worth on a very uneven stick.

It is so completely unfair to yourself to measure ANY of your worth based on childhood experiences when it was completely out of your control. When you think about it, it's again handing over your power to another person's mood, mental health, issues and compassion. And that person may not even be in your life anymore so it's even more wack[30] because you have zero control to change the past or to change the way that person treats you or treated you.

If you had a bad childhood, you may feel cheated or even grief towards your past, and while it is totally normal to feel this way and you can honour how shitty it was, only you hold the strength and power to change the view of your worth now. By giving yourself extra kindness, compassion and empathy, you can heal or at the very least, accept that you do not need to measure your worth against anything other than the fact that you deserve to be on this earth and have a happy life.

There are facts surrounding the events and then how our undeveloped brain coped with them or processed the emotions they created. If not dealt with yet, we may still have the "childlike" understanding of these events and emotions and so our *Body* will want to protect us so much more. This is deep inner work and revisiting these unconscious beliefs with your adult brain may help make sense of why you feel the way you do.

Also, the knowledge that you now have, that your worth is not based on any of these emotions or any of your childhood experiences takes away any *need* to explore these events or the thought that you need to fix yourself. There is never any need to fix yourself, even if the events have left you feeling broken. You are not broken. You are allowed to feel however you feel. Now when you process these thoughts or feelings it will only be for you. An act of self-love. The process will now be pressure free and come organically.

You can now let go of all the bullshit that was 100% on other people's shoulders. Heal your inner child and know that your past does not nor never will determine your worth. The power is now 100% in your hands. You decide where to go from here. That is your freedom.

---

[30] Wack: Just ridiculously ridiculous

Heal your soul or not. It does not affect your worthiness.

Adult Experiences

Adult experiences differ from childhood ones. Often, we were more in control or feel like we should have been. Let's look at your experience with fresh eyes.

How did you view the experience then, has your views around it changed over the years? If you did something to other people – how did it affect them?

We need to look at the solid facts of the event and then dissect how we coped with/viewed it, with the information and knowledge we had at the time. There is no reason to beat yourself up for something you didn't know then that you do now and remember, it's *never too late to change how you perceive something.*

FORGIVENESS – looking into our past with understanding leads to a need to forgive; either other people or ourselves. Feelings connected to the past when not processed get stored with the Body – I've spoken about this before, remember?

Feelings need to be acknowledged, validated and expressed. Only then are they healed.

So, processing starts in the brain.

Event happens –

"What is this event?
How does it affect me?
What does this mean about me?"
BUT – before that, while the event is happening, the emotions are created by the Body. Feelings of hurt, anger and pain stir up in the Body as masses of energy. They trigger the brain and tell her something important is happening.

Brain then starts the processing of emotions... OK, I'm feeling the pain, I feel angry, why does this hurt?

At this point, most of us were told our whole life:
"*Don't overreact*"
"*Calm down*"
"*Don't be so emotional*"
"*Stop crying*"
"*Don't be a baby*"

Also, the hurt feels uncomfortable. We may have been told that anger is "bad", so the anger feels "wrong". This is the point where the brain goes:

"WOAH! HOLD UP! This feels all wrong and the pain is horrible, and our girl can't cope with this – she doesn't want to deal with it – she doesn't want to think about it right now, let's distract her, quick!"

The Body's all pumped up with emotion. All these emotions screaming around in your Body and then she gets the message that you're not strong enough to deal with them. That she needs to push them down, shut them up, shut up. Basically, your Body feels the emotions aren't as important as you *not feeling*. That your Body is not as important so it's time to shove it down. Distract you so you don't need to feel it. This is her way of protecting you.

But emotions are energy – they are real in your Body and all they need is to be understood and validated so your Body can let them go. The longer they're held onto, the longer they stagnate. They manifest in other ways. They must come out somehow, though, whether it's through illness, disease, depression, skin problems, mood swings or sometimes even worse.

How you've dealt with these emotions in the past will be having a direct effect on your health and maybe even how you measure your worth today. And that's without even talking about the effects of what you *use* to distract yourself...which is often as destructive as the emotions themselves.

We need to embrace these repressed emotions from past events – especially the ones which make us feel unworthy.

We've already learnt about "victim mode" – now is the time to step into our power. But you don't need to do it all at once!

"Thank you, Body, for trying to protect me, but I'm already safe. I'm safe to feel this way."

Acknowledge: "This event in my past made me feel ___ and unworthy..."

Validate: "I felt that way because..."

Express: "Even though I feel ____, I still love ____ (and am worthy of love)"

Heal: "I forgive myself for doing/thinking/feeling that way. I forgive my *anger/hurt*. I forgive myself for the wasted years or energy that it took to avoid this feeling.
You do not have to forgive all and feel all and heal all *today*. Start small – feel your power and that's the most important step, to know you don't have to handle it all today – but you *could*.

You can handle anything that comes up for you. You are bigger than your emotions. You are stronger than your Body – you do know best. You are *worthy* of looking after your Body. Do not accept that your view of past events is the be all and end all of what truly happened.

Now you've expressed and healed some emotions surrounding these events, look at the memory without emotion involved, like as though you were a bystander – look at the facts only. What really happened? What do you know for fact? What bits did you assume?

It's like "this moment's truth" but for the past. Talk to yourself about the event with empathy, like you would if you were speaking to a child. Or if a best friend was talking to you about something that happened to them. What positives are there in the situation? What did you learn? Even if the event was totally your fault there's still a lesson hidden in the regret.

Forgive...
Forgive...
Forgive.
For your peace.

Now, start from today. Events in the past are now in the past. It's up to you if you allow them to influence your actions in the future, or even today! It is up to you to choose not to measure your worth against them. Again, the knowledge that you now have that your worth is not dependent on anything in your past can free you in the choices you make today. Your true power is always in this moment. This is the moment you can choose to release the past and create a beautiful future.

Worth - Your Weight

There isn't much more of an emotive subject as weight.

There are a lot of people out there, "big" and "small", and I mean a *lot*, who are actively measuring their worth by the number they see on the scales.

It was at my biggest weight that I learnt to love my Body and appreciate her. After I started losing weight fast –people saw me and couldn't believe it:

"You look so tiny!"
"You look so good!"
"You've lost so much weight!"
"You're like a new woman!"

It felt so good in the moment, but what did that mean about the way I looked before? *Why* does it feel so good to hear that? What percentage of my worth am I measuring against my weight?

It's so easy to believe part of your worthiness – especially as a woman – is dependent on your weight or on how your Body looks. We grow up with this all around us.

Sex is a *currency*.

Attractiveness is a *goal*.

If you are basing your worth on losing weight, unfortunately once you lose the weight you thought would make you perfect and worthy, the goalposts MOVE.

Expectations about your Body are at an all-time high. You're expecting perfection and if losing weight isn't done with love then you can easily end up resenting your Body. After you lose the weight, you may still have wobbly bits. All I was after was to have a flat tummy again. I lost 50lbs yet still have a preggo belly. I wanted instant results – I had no grace for how my Body was healing, I felt like I had no time to lose. So, the weight was gone but the belly was still there.... if I had used that as a measurement for my worth, despite all the hard work I'd done, my worth would have been in the shitter, wouldn't it!

In fact, a lot of people (me included) report feeling more insecure about their bodies after losing weight! You have a picture of perfection in your mind and your Body can never quite match up. It felt to me that I had to relearn to love my Body. Rediscover her. My perception around my Body had to change too.

Remember in wanting to look different you are chasing a feeling. Unless the weight loss is purely for health reasons, most people think that if they lose weight they will look better and that in turn will make them feel better about themselves. So, in that case, they are chasing a feeling. Most of our desires are just for that purpose, to feel happier, accomplished or satisfied. That's normal human behaviour but if some or all of your worth is tied to how you or others perceive how you look, it's unlikely that feeling will ever be satisfied. You can get moments of satisfaction or validation but even I remember fitting into smaller and smaller clothes but not *feeling* any smaller. I mean the whole fact about a woman's Body being smaller is more attractive is really fucked up, but that's for another book!

What I'm saying is the way you view your Body is an inside job. While losing weight for gaining other people's validation of your attractiveness may feel good in the moment, without the inner work of changing the way you perceive yourself, your loving Body and your worth, the feeling you are chasing will not come.

160

It can only come from you alone. You can change your attractiveness in any moment without changing a thing. There isn't anything sexier than a person who stands in their own power, fully knowing their worth and loving the fuck out of life.

In fact, if you ever happen to look in a mirror and see just a glimpse of how beautiful, sexy AND worthy your Higher Self sees you, it will honestly take your breath away and you would just KNOW. You would understand then why no-one else's opinion of your weight, or anything else for that matter, actually is worth a shit at all. Why only how *you* and your Higher Self sees you makes any difference in how you actually feel.

You are worthy at any size.
You are worthy at any weight.
You are worthy with or without wobbly bits.
You are worthy while losing weight or gaining it.

Once you start loving on your Body for all that she has done and is doing, your focus on this subject will be forever changed, and you'll know your worth at any size because you will *feel* it.

Worth - Other People's Judgements

If you are basing your worth on someone else's judgement, you have a measurement of guesswork. Half of any judgement is what *you think* people are judging you about, which is very much to do with reflecting your own judgements or fears on other people and yourself. Other people are but a mirror to your very soul!

Basing your worth on other people's judgements is normally about caring what other people think of you. This may be because you are not yet secure enough in your own worth and you're seeking external validation, or it could be because you want to feel like you belong, and fear being rejected. These are both very human reasons, and we are human and we *do* care what other people think, so it's OK to feel this way sometimes. But if we are constantly measuring our worth on what other people think of us, things can get messy fast. Again, we have to remember that when we feel like we are being judged, half is what they're thinking and the other half is what we perceive ourselves about what we think they are thinking – of course we don't know what they're thinking unless they tell us, which rarely happens unless you know a lot of opinionated or mouthy people. So, it's mostly just a story that we make up that we think they are thinking.

We also have to remember that we are but a mirror for other people so even if you are right and they are judging you, it's probably just a reflection of their fears, judgements on themselves and issues with their own view of their worth.

With such high expectations placed on us, the pressure to conform and not be true to your real self is sometimes overwhelming. Also, expecting perfection from ourselves is such a "norm". We believe if we don't hold high expectations for ourselves then we'll stagnate.

Most of us are secretly proud of being a perfectionist – it's seen as being driven, hard-working, never satisfied and rarely seen as destructive. Can you be "enough"? If you're not constantly bettering yourself, your Body, your mind, your finances...what happens if you stop? What are you worth then? If you are not "seen" as successful, beautiful or smashing life, will it mean you are not these things?

Again, this is all about how you perceive yourself.
Again, this is an inside job.

Everyone gets judged and judges.
Judging other people normally has a way of biting you on the arse.

It's fine to detach and let other people's view on you be just what it is – an opinion. When you detach then you can just smile and tell them it's OK. If you take on or measure your worth based on what or how other people see you, then your worth will be ever moving up and down – there's no stability to other people's opinions. They can be swayed like the wind. Plus, it's not your responsibility to justify or explain anything to anyone else. Their opinion of you is their responsibility. If they love you, they'll be expecting that your intentions are good and reflective enough to know their judgements are just mirrors for themselves.

We need to have rock solid confidence in our worth, to know it's like an immovable anchor attached to our self-love, no matter what anyone else thinks of us.

You need to make your feelings matter.
You need to make what you think about yourself matter.
You need to make your alignment with your Higher Self matter.
You need to make sure our fears and judgements are acknowledged, lovingly healed and released.
Genuinely not giving a shit what other people think of you is a beyond freeing feeling. It's life changing. It's pure, real self-confidence. Detaching your worth from other people's opinions will be the kindest thing you will ever do for yourself.

Imagine the life you could create, the happiness you can feel, the dreams you can live. It's already yours. You are already worthy to feel rock solid confidence in who you are and what you feel.

And if you slip up and find yourself caring about what someone else thinks? You aren't perfect and you are still human, so forgive yourself, have a kind inner voice and know your worth regardless.

Worth - Addiction

One of the biggest reasons people see themselves as worthless or unworthy is because they feel powerless against their addictions.

This filters through so many areas of what we've already discussed.

Drinking
Drugs
Gambling
Distracting

Social media
Shopping
Food
All of it.

If you are addicted. If you feel like you can't stop doing it.
It's all because you already care.

You care about how you feel. You want to feel better. You feel misaligned with who you truly are. You feel like there's a hole that needs filling, that something is missing from your life, you are looking for that feeling of escape. That feeling of unconditional love.

Whether you feel like you've had a demon on your shoulder for years or just days, disagreeing with the way source feels about you never feels good.

Body does whatever she can to stop you from having to face up to what you feel whenever it feels uncomfortable or wrong. It feels uncomfortable and wrong for a reason...because it is. Your Higher Self only ever sees you as whole, powerful and right where you need to be. She gives you love unconditionally, supports and guides you. But sometimes, due to being human and due to all the other reasons in this chapter, we can feel not enough. Feeling on your own, worthless or unloved is beyond shitty. It's no wonder then why your Body wants to protect you from this.

Of course, she is going to use ways that protect you that she knows has worked before. She will use the same things over and over again.

Can you see why it's so easy to become addicted to negative behaviours? It's because they work. Until they don't. They allow you to escape, numb and to distract. Until they don't.

They help you feel better.
Even when it's a shitty better.
Cravings for anything is not a sign of weakness, it's a sign that your Body is choosing love. Even if it's killing our physical body,

her love for you is so strong that her desire for you to not feel pain in the short term overrides her own health in the long term.

All this means is that you are already loved. It means you are loved by Body and your Higher Self. It means that you already care enough about yourself to try and feel a bit better. It also means you are just using the wrong or harmful tools in order to try and improve your situation. Even when you know that in the long term it causes a clusterfuck, in the short term it works.

Wrong tools or not, it is a sign that you are already on your journey to self-love.

You already give a shit about how you feel and that's a giant step in the journey.

You are worthy with the addiction.
You are worthy without the addiction.

Most people who try to get over an addiction will relapse at one or more points. In fact, they are called "in recovery".

The word recovery means: "a return to a normal state of health, mind, or strength"

What is normal by this world's standards?

To hold a steady job? Take care of your family? Contribute to society?
Many people do this as addicts.

What if a normal state of health, mind or strength meant feeling loved, feeling happy and feeling worthy?
Would it be easier to let go of the addiction?

I know that the Body's reliance on some of these substances or the chemicals released in the brain can feel completely overpowering and the withdrawals are real. But saying, for example, "once an alcoholic always a recovering alcoholic" and having the expectation that you will always be struggling for recovery...is that actually true?

If our worthiness is based on an addiction, it means that once we feel like we are not addicted we will see our worth as going up. But most of the time we are given these labels and told it's something we will struggle with for the rest of our life. We are told once addicted it's part of who we are. We end up anchoring our struggle with our actual identity.

Do you believe your Higher Self is struggling with the same addiction?
Do you see her as a recovering addict?
Do you think that's the way she sees you?

Does she see you as powerless?
Does she see you as a victim of a disease?
Does she see you as an unworthy person while you are addicted or while you are recovering?

It may be controversial to say, but fuck no she doesn't.

She never looks back.
She is always seeing you as your powerful self.
She is always seeing you in your beautiful glory.
She always knows your strength.
She always knows your worth.

You are worthy.
With addiction.
Without addiction.
With recovery.
Without recovery.
Worthy always.

Addiction is a very human concept. You can be addicted to something, and it feels good but as soon as that addiction stops being fun it takes over your life. It takes away your power. That's when, if addiction is a part of your measure of worth, you can feel completely unworthy. At that point, you've become completely disconnected from source, you feel fully human, it takes away your peace, your gratitude for everyday magic, it takes away joy, expansion and even hope.

You have become disconnected from the unconditional love of source and feel unworthy of that love.

But that doesn't mean that that love has gone anywhere.

Your Higher Self is still there.
With her attention on you.
Loving you.
Seeing your power.
No matter how bad it has gotten.
No matter how disconnected or unworthy you feel.
She sees you as who you are.

The very moment you see yourself as who you truly are and decide you are worthy; you open yourself back up to that.

Your worthiness is still there.

It is not based on your addiction or your actions surrounding it. Seeing your addiction with love means it doesn't have to be the devil on your shoulder or a part of who you are, and it certainly never needs to be how you measure your worth.

What Is Isness?

What are you without anything? Take away everything: looks, wealth, career, labels, beliefs, even knowledge. Who does that make you? You are a human being and so much more. What if your worth was based just on your being?

How do we calculate a newborn baby's worth?

Is it:
How much they sleep?
Their eye colour?
How long they can hold their head up for?
Amount of shits per day?

Basing a newborn's worth on their actions or abilities is dumbarse[31], right? A baby's worth just is. It's based on their "Isness". It's there regardless of anything.
A life is a life and it's precious and pure.

Our self-worth starts as a given: it just is, from day one. What you do with your life, how you grow (or don't) doesn't actually affect your worth because it's the same if you are 1 day old or 100 years old.

Your self-worth is based on your being. Your Isness.

Contrary to what you are told, taught or even believe, your worth continues to be based on your being until the day you die. In fact, your being is made up of pure energy and energy never dies, it just shifts forms, so your worth is actually infinite.

Whatever you are basing your worth on right now is just an illusion inside your mind. When you allow yourself to see the true measurement of your self-worth it looks more like this:

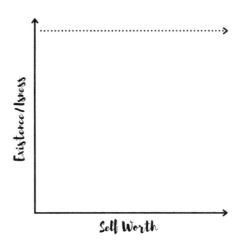

_____

[31] Dumbarse: As intelligent as a dumb person's butt

Notice there is no need to increase your self-worth or bring it down when you truly see your self-worth relating to your existence or Isness...It just simply is, and everyone's worth is already set to the perfect amount.

Self-worth based on being, is never boastful because you'll also be basing other people's worth on their being too, so there's never any reason to look down on anyone.

But also, while it's awesome to admire other people's qualities, talents or success, with this true view of worth you never need to feel inferior to anyone else or put them on a pedestal either. We are all just equal spirits, in folds of skin, winging it through life.

When you base your worth on your being and not your done, doing or shoulds, you can then look at your messy parts of your life as what they are rather than what they might mean about you as a person and a measurement of your worth.

Once you see your worth for the solid, sound, unmovable foundation of what it is, you will then know your worthiness of it all.

All of which life has to offer you.
Which is anything you want to be, do or have.

Once you get a glimpse of how your Higher Self sees you...
Sees the real you...
Sees the all of you.
Your Body.
Your mind.
Your spirit.
Your decisions.
Your dreams.
Your desires.
Your life.
Even your fuckups.

It's just a glorious unfolding of your human being becoming, expanding and really living. And it's all good. It's all worthy.

It's all you.

You are worthy.

Once you feel that worth, you can never unfeel it.

You may still wobble. You may have momentary doubts. You may
be imperfect. But you are still worthy.

Worthy regardless.
Worthy because of.
Worthy.
Worthy.
Worthy.

Your worth is.
Your worth always has been.
Your worth always will be.

You are worthy to be worthy.

Chapter Eight - Love How You Look

This is a Biggy.
This is my nemesis.
This is my gift to other people but very rarely to myself.

Right now, I have 90% unapologetic acceptance of the way I look...ish[32]. There are days when I feel like I am a legit "Swamp Thang" and there's days that I feel like a beautiful mermaid...with semi hairy legs.

There are certain parts of myself I have to actively love on. Like my squishy belly that stayed squishy even when I got back to my pre children weight. My chubby knees, my adult acne (what the fuck is that about?) and of course the list could go on. I'm human. I have to use gratitude to bring me back from hate or exasperation when I look pregnant for weeks just because I've sniffed some bread.

But I do have love. I love so many things about how I look. Even though I'm getting older, wrinklier and chubby in places that will be chubby forever more. I appreciate my Body. I accept and love her. I enjoy her. I can see my beauty even with all my flaws. It's the imperfect parts that I love the most. It took a lot in order for me to get to this point. Once upon a time, I wanted plastic surgery, and lots of it.

Have you ever heard of "pure OCD"? Well, this blessing and curse of how my brain works could be a whole chapter in of itself but long story short...

 I'm vain.
Obsessively vain.
Ish.

If you know me well, you probably don't think that about me.

———————————————————

[32] Ish: Nearly but not quite.

For one, I don't often act like I care about what I look like. In fact, I often look like a hot mess! But deep down I care. Deep down I more than care. I have a long ritual in the morning (which is obsessive of course) and it affects my mood, my confidence and sometimes even what I choose to do on a normal day.

This, of course, isn't vanity as in conceit. I'm more than realistic about my attractiveness levels. It isn't really even a caring about what other people think: I'll often wear my onesie in public. It's really difficult to explain what it is. I guess it's because of an expectation of perfection from myself that I'm terrified of other people realising that I don't match up to... or even come close to.

Maybe other people finding out the truth of how fucked up my Body is compared to the ideals I hold or me facing up to that reality on the daily.

And I used to be hideous to myself every single day about the way I looked. It takes a commitment to love and appreciate your Body and disregard those standards that do not serve you and are totally unrealistic.

Really it has to go hand in hand with having a kind voice about the way you look and embracing it and **loving** how you look even if it's not in line with your own standards of beauty.
I know my standards of beauty for everyone else are completely fluid and are often based on who they are because that is what shines through for me.

I can honestly say I see beauty in each and every person that I care about and not just because I'm a Horndog[33]. I see them through Source's eyes: all that they are and what they mean to me radiates through their face.

I hold them up to no standard really because all shapes and sizes are beautiful to me. Sure, some people are more attractive to me than others (especially where beards are involved) but that

---

[33] Horndog: Horny, insatiable, sexually charged animal of a person.

doesn't mean that I judge (or at least I try not to!) or treat anybody differently based on the way they look.

The standards of beauty for myself however were somewhat different. Fucking harsh actually, you could say.

I'd learnt those standards from Society and as much as I tell myself that they are "wrong" it doesn't help when those standards are basically expecting perfection. Standards are just another word for beliefs, and we can only change our beliefs when we consciously decide to do so. So where did I start?

Body Positivity Starts with Body Acceptance...

There is no money in you loving yourself.
There is no money in you loving what you see in the mirror.

We are taught our whole lives that we are not good enough or that there's always something we need to change in order for us to be good enough or even lovable. This can be dressed up with many sexy terms, "beach Body ready", "self-improvement", "being worth it", but however they (or we) try to dress it up, the meaning stays the same without change (I.E. BUYING THIS) we are not worthy of self-love today.

In fact, I'll go one step further...for most, Self-Love is actually a step too far. It's something that feels like it can't ever be achieved. It's some unattainable unicorn goal that's too high for us mere mortals to reach for.

So, the beauty industry knows they need to sell smaller packages: Body confidence, independence, self-growth, bagging a man, making other women jealous, looking good on social media...

These things, we are told, are attainable. But still not today. It takes hard work and more change... and usually more products.

Acceptance however doesn't really get a look in.

Acceptance is lazy.
Acceptance is unmotivated.
Acceptance is undriven.
Acceptance is unambitious.
Acceptance is settling.
Acceptance is aiming too low.

Surely Acceptance couldn't ever be a good thing?

As humans, we have this beautiful ability to grow. And as we learn and grow, change naturally happens - it's a beautiful process and as unstoppable as the sea!

We are imperfect and every one of us has points that we fail on, stuff that we can better about ourselves, that we can learn more about and then grow beautifully.

BUT THIS IS THE POINT THAT WE ARE MISSING OUT ON...

Change in itself is not a bad thing. Striving for change without self-acceptance in place, is hard. It's gruelling. It's an unhappy place to be because we won't be happy or express love for ourselves until we "get there", until we change, until we are close to perfect.

Change with self-acceptance already in place is completely different. That possibility to grow, expand and create is already within us. When we concentrate on self-love, acceptance and seeing how deserving of love we already are *right now*, the changes that need to happen to align us with our Higher Selves will happen organically.

That change, determination, motivation and ambition will be as natural as night and day.

Inspired action.

It will be freeing, easy and so natural! Change will feel good because you will already have that kind voice inside you that knows everything is already enough, even if you fail, change your mind or what you are working on goes to shit.

Not only is Self-Love achievable, but it's completely within your grasp.

I like to think of acceptance as a stepping-stone to positivity and then to self-love. It's your first step on an amazing journey.

Body Acceptance

Many women start in a place of hate when it comes to their bodies. Asking a woman to name one thing that they love about their Body will normally get an awkward response, you can see the struggle. Switch to asking them what they hate about themselves and you see almost relief on their faces. Most can rattle off a whole list and some will even enjoy it.

With summer around the corner as I write, we'll now be bombarded with images, adverts and social media posts about being "bikini ready", "summer ready", "before and afters", magic pills, miracle diets and so, so, so much more.

To accept your Body how your Body is right now *today* may feel impossible - maybe even a little fucking rebellious!

Body acceptance can be really hard especially after so many years of being in the mindset that you constantly have to improve your Body (or hide parts away) in order for you to be attractive, to be healthy or even to show your Body in public.

Accepting your Body doesn't mean you'll never want to lose weight, workout or eat healthy. It just means that you recognise that you are allowed to feel beautiful, eat like you love yourself, wear whatever the fuck you want to wear, do whatever the fuck you want to do (swimming, anyone?) and enjoy your Body TODAY.

It also means that you'll know that you deserve love regardless of what your Body looks like. Your Body works so hard for you every day. If you can't show her some love, *at the very least*, could you show her some appreciation and acceptance?

Mind Acceptance

To fully accept our Body, we must also accept our mind.

We all have quirks, personality traits and annoying habits that we'd like to get rid of or change. We all think, say and do things that prove (to us and everyone else) that we are imperfect every day.

We are imperfect beings, and we know that everyone on this planet right now is imperfect. So why do we beat ourselves up about this? Why do we pour hate on ourselves for being imperfect and fight our imperfections so ungracefully? If we were to write out our inner voice onto paper when we are being harsh to ourselves for mostly shitty things that we can't even change, the words and names we call ourselves would be disgusting. It would be hard to write and harder to read.

And yet we say those words to our beautiful, vulnerable mind.

Every. Damn. Day.

When you add mental illness into the mix that voice can become unbearable.
What do we see in the media, society, social media...even in self-help books/shows, the very places that are trying to help us?

Self-help = Change yourself
Therapy = Change yourself
Media = Change yourself

Be more positive, more confident, less fearful, less dependent, less anxious.

This is all great advice but again it's teaching us that we NEED to change in order to be lovable.

"Be more, be less" is not promoting change with acceptance first. Which means we feel like we can't love ourselves or accept the way our minds work until the change is done.

And as we learnt before the change is NEVER done. We are constantly changing and growing so we need to do this WHILE loving ourselves.

There's no time to wait until after, because there is no after.

Every single negative thing your mind is getting you to do or telling you is because she is trying to protect you.

Every single thing.

Your mind (whether you have mental health issues or not) loves you and has two main goals: 1) To protect you from physical harm (danger or death) 2) To protect you from mental harm (hurt or emotional pain) and she will do whatever it takes to protect you from these two things simply because she loves you so much.

To do this she will use distraction, busyness, blocking and addiction. She will even seem to be feeding you horrible thoughts about how you look, if that's a method of protection that has worked in the past.

She protects you because she loves you.

Accepting this can literally be life changing:

"I'm doing/blocking/eating/saying this because my Body & mind are trying to protect me. I can now forgive myself for this because I know it's my mind's way of showing love and it worked (i.e., protected me from hurt) in the past."

Your brain may work differently to other peoples. The ways she is trying to protect you may be frustrating - but know she is doing it through love.

She loves you and is actively trying to protect you today. Can you accept her and show her understanding rather than hate?

Body Positivity

Once you've accepted ALL of you unapologetically and you have gratitude, appreciation and compassion for your Body the next logical step is that you'll start feeling proud and positive about her.

The thing is people will still judge. But this is where it's all a mindset thang. We all care about what other people think, as much as we pretend that we don't, deep down it's been programmed into us for survival to care. The thing is, to truly love the way you look you need to stop accepting other people's standards and opinions as your own. Just like when someone pays you a compliment and you instantly don't believe them (stop doing that shit, next time just soak in that ego shine). How come we don't do that when someone gives us an insult or a judgy-pants comment? Why is our natural default to believe/internalise the bad and reject the good?

This is true even when it's coming from ourselves.

Anyone (no matter how close you are or how well they know you) can have an opinion on what they think about what you are wearing, what they think that you should be doing or how you look...without it becoming your truth.

You get to choose your own truth. You get to decide to listen to that criticism or that advice and then you get to decide how you respond or act.

Your Body positivity is your own. How you show it depends on you. Your boundaries are your own. Your dress sense, your personality, your story and your view about your own Body IS YOUR OWN.

You have sole responsibility for your positivity.
You have sole responsibility for your inner voice.

Other people can influence it or say things to harm it, but when push comes to shove, it's your sole responsibility to decide how that will affect the way you view your Body.

A few months after I gave birth, I decided to wear a bikini. Once we were on the beach everyone decided to go to a little posh pub near the beach. I only had a sarong with me, so I was faced with a choice. Go to the pub with my squishy belly on show or miss out on the fun. I went to the pub. I carried myself with pride. I was scared but feeling brave.

Not one sod in there blinked an eyelid. Not one single soul gave a shit about my stretch marks or wobble. Well, maybe they did but I was just having too much fun to notice.

This is an inside job.

There will always be reasons why you feel like you want to hold yourself back. The question you need to ask yourself is: am I making myself more comfortable or am I hiding away to make *other people* more comfortable? Am I avoiding conflict to protect myself, or if I truly accepted myself, would their words even matter to me?

Body positivity has to do with so much more than just the way you look. It's feeling worthy enough to be seen, to exist without apology and to fill up the space that your glorious Higher Self deserves.

To do that though, your Body needs to know that you are safe. That she doesn't need to protect you and that she has your unconditional love and acceptance.

Unconditional and unapologetic.

Unapologetic Acceptance

When I was young, I was a size 8 and had zero boobs but I had a nice big bum that everybody went on about *before* it was trendy. When I was living in America (at about age 15) I remember overhearing a guy I liked say: *"Miriam? Yeah, nice Body but shame about the face."*

That stuck with me because at that time I knew I had a nice Body (which was different to when I was at school and teased all the time about my chunky, manly Body) so I was feeling like a hottie, but, trouble is, I still had really bad acne.

Although I knew I liked my face, it was often like "World War 3", but it was my face battling against itself. Scarring, zits and bleeding bits. Also because of my OCD I did things every day that made it look even worse before I'd left the house.

Although I felt attractive and happy about the way I looked, I still had this hang up that it was my body that made me attractive because my face didn't live up to my standards.

What a sexy bastard that guy was, eh? Words can hurt and can stick around us for years, especially when we internalise those words and turn them into our own beliefs.

When I got married at about 24 and stopped partying so hard every night, I put on a bit of weight and all of a sudden I didn't have my body to save me. So I was left thinking: was I even attractive anymore?

Little did I know, after having 3 kids, I'd look back at pictures of my younger self and think I looked amazing! Isn't that always the way?

But back then I had the worst view of how I looked, and zero self-love, so putting on a bit of weight and going up a few sizes was a big deal for me. I remember watching Extreme Makeover again and again.

Do you remember Extreme Makeover?

It was a TV show where they took a woman or man, who was so depressed and disgusted with themselves they were hardly living, and "transformed" them. The show not only gave them haircuts, new makeup and new clothes but they actually took them to plastic surgeons.

They'd get their face done, often get veneers, have lipo[34], boob jobs, bum lift: they'd have it ALL done and then they had to lose weight before getting to reveal themselves to their friends and family. The family then were, of course, crying and clapping when they saw the "new" Person like it was the happiest moment of their life.

After the reveal party the show would switch to the before and after pictures like a completely different person had emerged. Then the person would gush about how much it's changed their life and how happy they are with their new body, and that now they can find a way to learn to love themselves and do whatever they always dreamt they wanted to do, that they obviously must have felt unable to do before, because they thought they were too butt ugly or whatever.

I should say at this point I was working a few jobs at the same time because I was trying to build a children's farm. I was keeping my own pigs but still had hair extensions down to my butt, I wanted to look perfect. In one of the jobs the office was next to a plastic surgery company where you could travel abroad to get surgery done on the cheap.

The owner used to look me up and down and say: "*Miriam, you don't need to put up with these tiny titties you know, we can do a payment plan and I will give you a staff discount. Why put up with these tiny titties? I help you make them nice and round. You don't need to be walking around with tiny titties.... seriously...we get you liposuction while we're there too, just say the word.*"

---

[34] Lipo: Liposuction

Like, cheers love.

I was already feeling shitty about how my Body looked and now my Body was failing me physically again. Although I was no longer housebound, I was in severe pain all day and on so much medication to try and control the pain, but they didn't control it. There were a lot of days when I couldn't work, I couldn't do anything, and I was just stuck in bed. This was also roughly about a year after the fire that I'd lost everything in, so I hardly had any material possessions that were my own and I was pretty depressed and traumatised by the whole thing.

I was watching so much Extreme Makeover when I was ill that I started to believe that the only way I'd be able to love myself is if they could sort me out. Like, I actually thought that was my only option. I applied for the show, and I had a whole list of surgery that I knew that they could do. I would look in a mirror, up and down, listing all of the things I hated about my appearance that I wanted surgery to sort out.

From a boob job to sorting out my fat knees.

It seems completely fucking nuts now, but I dreamed about my reveal and finally feeling good about myself, with everyone being amazed at how beautiful I was. I even wondered if it would heal my OCD!

At this point of my life, I'd spent about 10 years taking tablets for my acne that the doctor had warned me could damage my liver and kidneys. In fact, I had to have liver and kidney tests once every year to make sure there wasn't irreversible damage caused by these tablets! But honestly, I felt like it was worth it because having clear skin was more important to me than the organs in my body.

Can you imagine how my life would be so different now if I had gone through with any surgery?

All the lessons I wouldn't have learned?

I wonder if I would have found peace with my body the way I have now, or if I would have just found more things I "needed" surgery for?

After I had my first baby, I started looking at my body in a more positive way, especially from breastfeeding, but my belly and the extra weight I was carrying still really annoyed me. Also, because I couldn't take the tablets anymore my skin was really bad, so it made me feel less of a person and I looked like I was always tired or ill.

After my miscarriage, when I finally started to love myself and my Body just the way she was, I had been studying beauty photography for about a year and I took some pictures of myself. This was probably about a month after having my miscarriage. I felt really good about the photos so I decided to put them into a beauty photography group. One lady obviously didn't realise that the model was fucking me and said that, as the photographer, I should have asked the lady to cover those flabby arms. Instantly I wanted to defend my Body, but my first self-conscious thought was to cringe, agree with her and hate my arms forever. But, I replied to her and told her that my arms were strong; I used them to scoop up my babies and hold them tight at night when they are afraid. I did not need to cover them up.
I could finally see my arms for what they are: loving, amazing and a part of me. So that comment just slid off my shoulders and had no effect on my confidence - it was easy to dismiss the bitch. Not salty at all, eh?

That then made me realise about my legs, how they've always been strong and carried me even when I was in pain. Those chubby knees have served me well.

My boobs are basically life-giving, they help my babies thrive. They may be small, but they fed my babies for 10 solid years and produced more milk than small cattle.

Here's a little somethin' somethin'[35] that I wrote while I was pregnant with Indie. I actually look at that time as being one of the strongest points in my mindset and self-love. Notice that even when you have self-love, it's a daily commitment to keep it. That kind inner voice is not always your default voice. It takes real work to bring yourself back to gratitude and compassion. So, over to YesterMirrie…

"So, as I write this, I'm pregnant and it seems like I'm going through a test to love myself even when my acne is worse than it's ever been. This pregnancy has been hard, my brain has been in constant battle.

I've had severe acne and terrible scarring. Now I'm gaining weight like there's no tomorrow, I constantly want to eat, and I keep saying to myself you're getting so fat. I've been in so much pain so I can't walk far.

A friend tagged me in her new profile picture, she looked amazing, and I didn't even look like me. It felt so weird to not be able to control how other people view me.

The other day I went swimming and I looked at my Body in the full-length mirror, my eyes went straight to my thick thighs. I've always hated my legs growing up, especially my knees! I remember my brother calling my legs tree trunks.

My thighs were chunkier than ever.

My belly was huge and stretched out, red angry scars spilling across the tight skin, my boobs still tiny, my arms still flabby, my hair in a state, face red raw with no makeup on. Normally this would be when my inner bitch would kick in but as my tired eyes met my tired sparkling eyes in that mirror, I smiled …

I actually smiled!

_____

[35] Somethin' somethin': Something something but cheekier

I smiled at my Body like an old friend. She IS my old friend and we've been through a lot together– especially this last year she's actually been through hell.

We did what we had to do to survive and now she is growing a whole new being – how could I not love her? How can I not look at her in awe as two excited children hug her in the mirror, and one kicks in her belly? How can I not see her amazing beauty and power when I see beyond what's in the mirror?

She's not perfect but if I strip away the expectations that society has given us, to believe women have to always be sexy and our value is skin deep, if I strip that away then she's pretty damn well close to perfection.
And my Body is sexy
and bubbly
and fun

Strong enough to swim
Sexy enough to turn heads
Happy enough to run or hobble while playing with the kids
Powerful enough to power through when she's feeling broken and lost
Soft enough to cry at movies and be moved to tears by some stranger laughing with her kids.
Vulnerable enough to admit when she's scared
Brave enough to need others and yet
Independent enough to love herself completely.

She's already enough... that woman in the mirror

*She's my old friend and I **see** her.*

I see her for who she is and what she's been through and what her beautiful Body is working towards.

I see her
I hear her
I love her
I am her"

Gentle tears roll.

What made the switch inside my head go from harsh Body judgement to unconditional self-love?

Gratitude
Acceptance
Compassion
More gratitude

I'm alive to live
Not for anyone else's pleasure

Not to fulfil anyone else's idea of sexy
Not to have all of my value wrapped up in how I look

Not to miss out on life because I'm scared of being seen
Not to miss out on life because I'm scared of being judged

Not to miss out on having fun with my kids because other people's opinions matter more than my own.

Not to apologise for even existing

I decide how I see myself
You decide how you see yourself

You can decide to see yourself as fucking amazing
A mermaid
A goddess
A swamp thang
An imperfect but still fucking awesome, beautiful human being

You decide
Apologies are not needed

Unconditional, unapologetic acceptance to express yourself as the infinite, loving, creative free spirit that you are. Letting that spirit shine through in all her power and beauty.

Being Seen

Four times in my life I have felt such disbelief, such intense shock, such encompassing grief that it caused me to physically vomit. Three times where phone calls concerning the death or impending death of people I had intense love for.

The other time? Well, that was an epiphany that hit me so incredibly hard it changed my life. That's the time I'm going to tell you about right now.

You are probably thinking this was the moment I realised I loved myself, but no, I'm talking about a day just a week ago, over five years since I made the commitment to love myself every single day.

"Good luck with the baby!"

It was an innocent comment, I hope.

So, I was working behind the bar at a private party. I had decided to dress the part with an outfit in my head, but distractions happened, and I ended up having to wear this tiny Bodycon (aka skin-tight) dress that basically left nothing to the imagination. It was the first time me & my love were working together and I knew we were both up for lots of fun. The party was really busy and really fun. In fact, we were bought so many drinks we ended up getting invited onto the dance floor at the end of the night and they were treating us like part of their family.

I was in the flow, full of love watching my partner and I working so well together, having fun and having shiny eyes for each other. I felt full of confidence, full of love, full of life.
After the party was winding down, as she was leaving, one of the ladies shouted out:

"Good luck with the baby!"

I stood there in disbelief.

Now I'd been drinking, dancing and generally being a teenage rebel in full view of everyone. It was obvious that I wasn't pregnant.

Why did she say that?

I looked down and saw my small round flabby belly. In that moment my view of myself changed. All night I'd been catching glances of myself in the mirror. I was looking good. Wild, windswept hair. Tanned golden skin, barely any makeup, but that glow that only being in love can achieve.

Yes, I was a tiny bit aware of my belly but being in a skin-tight stripy dress after coming back from having babies, and being the skinniest I'd been in 20 years, I was forgiving of that little podge.

But in that instant, after that one comment, I saw myself completely differently...

All of a sudden, all I could only see was my protruding belly.

I felt fat.
Ugly.
Deflated.

I laughed it off of course and rationalised it in my head. It didn't affect the rest of my night because I refused to make it important enough to ruin my mood. But while I was laying in bed that night it was still playing on my mind.

Maybe she was jealous and wanted to bring me down a peg or two, maybe she genuinely thought I was pregnant and was trying to be kind, maybe someone else was pregnant and she got me mixed up with them, maybe she just wanted to let me know she thought I was fat.

The reason she said it didn't actually matter to me. What she thought about my body didn't actually matter to me. The fact that other people heard what she said to me didn't actually matter to me. I genuinely did not give a fuck about what any of those people thought about me or how my body looked. So why was I, in the middle of the night, wide awake thinking about this and feeling mortified.

Yes, mortified. That was the only word I could come up with powerful enough to describe how it felt.

I was embarrassed, ashamed, and feeling a little sick. Alone in the dark it's very easy for that inner bitch to pipe up and I noticed my usually kind inner voice getting harsher with myself. Why did I wear that dress? I always feel self-conscious when I wear it...I know you can see my belly when I wear it, I should have worn something else, something more flattering, I should have taken the time to get ready properly.

Why did I care?
Why did I care?
Why did I care so much?

When people have made passing comments about my bingo wings, my nips or my legs I literally don't give a fuck and would never change the way I dress because of their comments. I did used to, though. Long t-shirts to cover my arms, never wore shorts, didn't wear dresses. Fuck that shit.

Now I wear whatever makes me feel comfortable and good. I couldn't get my head around how I'd come so far but yet this one comment literally sent me back to that place again!

After a blissful morning I sat down to write in my little magic book and the question was still niggling me:

If you don't give a shit how other people see you, why do you still give a shit?

Now I know how my Higher Self sees me. She is in awe and wonder about my beauty. She sees my entire beauty, everything I was, everything I am and everything I am becoming. She revels in who I truly am, both on the inside and out. I've said it before, when you catch just a glimpse of how your Higher Self sees you, it will take your breath away...NO matter what your hair, skin or belly looks like.

An eternal appreciative gaze is upon you. She sees you as beyond beautiful and so incredibly gorgeous. Imperfections melt away and morph into perfections.

My gal Hicksy (Abraham Hicks) says that negative emotions are an indicator that you are seeing something differently than your Higher Self. That you are disagreeing with your Higher Self.

Misalignment.
Your Higher Self always sees the full picture, knows your worthiness and that things are always working out for you. You already know this.

You read the chapter about alignment, you now give a shit about how you feel, you now unconditionally care about how you feel and feel committed to show yourself how much you love yourself every day. No matter how you look, no matter what llamas are going on around you. You care. You matter. Your alignment matters.

Once you know all of this - *truly* believe it - you can't go back. The slightest misalignment will niggle you until you adjust your vibrations to match your Higher Self. After seeing yourself the way she sees you, nothing else will do. And, although it takes self-reflection and time, this takes no effort. Once you drop the expectations of others this becomes your base line. You are no longer reliant on the external validation from other people because you know in your bones your worth just is. There's no validation needed for who you are, how you look or how you feel.

So why are you still feeling self-conscious about looking less than perfect?

Your Body needs to play catch up.

She still holds on to the beliefs that are going to keep you safe. She still feels the need to protect you like a loving mother.

Most of us are brought up with the belief that seeing yourself as beautiful is the equivalent of being vain. Being modest and humble is put on a pedestal whereas being confident in our looks or unabashed about compliments is seen as being egotistical and conceited. From a very early age we internally focus on our imperfections while living in a world that tells us that perfection and attractiveness equals worth and admiration. So, we are taught to rely on other people's opinions of how we look and the validation by others about how attractive we are.

Trouble is even if you have a social media following of thousands of people, all telling you how gorgeous you are, if you are still focusing on your imperfections, you won't believe a single one of them, no matter how many compliments you are fobbing off. You will always be striving to be "more perfect", and you'll still be mortified if even one person points out one of those imperfections that you have been worried about or hiding.

Why does it feel so bad to believe the negative comment and yet so easy to brush off the thousands of positive ones?

You might not give a single shit about what that person thinks of you, but you do give a shit that it confirms a belief that deep down you really don't want to believe about the way you look or are perceived.

Logically you consciously may or may not know that the belief goes against your Higher Self's belief...either way you can definitely feel that it does.

That uncomfortable feeling of misalignment.

So, is this just all about not wanting to face up to reality?

My saggy podgy belly is real.
My zits are real.
My cold sore is real.
The bits about my body (and life) that I used to want to hide from the world are real.

It's all there in the mirror to see.

It's real.

What's not real is the belief that any of those things about my body, or those seemingly imperfect things about your body, have

ANY...
ANY ...
ANY ...

...sway on your attractiveness or worthiness.

Your looks are not a measurement of your worth.

They do not distract from the utterly perfect beauty of who you are both on the inside and out.

That is the belief that kills your alignment.

Big U knows how perfect you are and the belief that any of that is lost because you have a perception of yourself that is less than your own standards of beauty is fucking wack.

So, any attempt to hide any part of you is because YOU don't want to see it. It's the protection you give yourself from this fucked up belief that you are holding on to.

This was the point where tears started flowing freely and I puked on my boat. The grief of this belief dying in front of me overtook my entire body. I laid on the bed sobbing knowing that life would forever be changed but not knowing how. It felt like I wasn't sure if I'd ever be able to stop crying again. It felt like the nuke bomb of hearing someone had died because I'd carried this belief my whole life but could never consciously put my finger on what the belief was or why it held so much power.

This belief was a loving protection from my Body but in the most messed up way. She protected me from seeing my own perceived imperfections because she knew what the true belief was and knew how misaligned it was to my Higher Self's view on just how perfect I am.

In that instant I KNEW the truth.
And that belief had no choice but to die.

This relates to EVERYTHING.

Why you care about how other people see you is never about
them or about how *they* see you. It's about your own alignment.
It's about how YOU see YOU. It's about the scary thought of how
your Higher Self sees you.

Dancing like no one is watching.
Being in photo's no matter what type of day you are having.
Swimming...
Sunbathing on a beach...
Wearing whatever the fuck you want.
Making videos...
Singing in public...
Being SEEN.
It all *all* matters so much.

Because when you have that belief that the way you are seen or
seeing yourself makes any difference to how worthy you are, you
are so scared that something is going to prove to you that that
bogus belief is true, you avoid doing things, wearing things and
going places.

You live scared.
Unseen.
Try to blend in.

It filters into everything you do. Even after you've let go of that
need for external validation, if that belief is still there it festers
and eats away at your alignment. It can literally kill the joy in
your life, in your truly living, and the ways you express how you
feel and who you are.

You miss out on living.
You need to unlock that belief.
Kill it dead.
Grieve while your Body catches up to this new knowledge.

How you are seen.
Viewed.
Thought of.
It's all bullshit.
None of it matters.
Your Higher Self *sees* you.
Your Higher Self loves you.
Your Higher Self knows the truest truth.
The whole entire truth.
You are seen every single day.

Seen by others...
Seen by yourself...
Seen by the eternal consciousness...

The eternal truth.

YOU ARE HERE.

Fucking beautiful.
Fucking worthy beyond measure.

Seen by the never ending, never beginning breath of life itself.

Held in her eternal loving gaze.

She is seeing your fucking amazing self.
She not only loves all of your humanness and all of your
imperfections, but she revels in all your gorgeousness and in all
that you are.

You are fucking magic.

Pure magic...
Pure power...
Pure fun...
Pure youness.
BEING SEEN.
BEING LOVED.
BEING WORTHY.
BEING THE TRUE YOU.

The death of this belief changes everything and seemingly nothing at all. How this death impacts your life will be up to you alone. But now you know, and you can never unknow this. You can use this knowledge with zero judgement on yourself because if you hold this belief or not, if you let this belief rule your life or not, if you let this belief die or not, you will still always be seen as beautiful, worthy, as you. Just as you are.

Go fucking live.
Go dance in the sea.
Go sing as loud as you can.
Go wear whatever the fuck you wanna!
Go be seen as the beautiful badass fucking goddess that you are.
And see yourself through the eyes of your Higher Self.

Love how you are seen.
Love how you look.

Chapter Nine - Using Fear to Chase Your Dreams

I held onto my fear
Like a warm thick heavy coat
On a bitterly cold,
Windy day

I snuggled in
It felt uncomfortable
And truly comfortable
All in the same moment

I held onto my fear
Safely afraid
Safely trapped

I held onto my fear
She caressed me gently
Wrapped her fingers around me

Held me back

Feeling small
Feeling Unseen
Feeling Unwanted

Is this what no expectation feels like?

No, it's all expectation
Fuelling the fear

Still, I held on tightly

White knuckles
Struggling against the movement
I didn't want any movement at all

Dug my heels in

I can't grow if I can't move
I can't feel if I can't move
I can't fail if I can't move
I can't succeed if I can't move

I know her so well

There's no fear
In fear
Except
All the fear

No Unknown
No possibilities
Just a comfy pimped out cage
Door seemingly locked impossibly tight

The fear embraces me
Not enough to move

It feels so bad
I know it's not true

It feels so good
I know that's not truth

Each tiny step forward
Feels like a leap

Leaping alone
Body holds me back

You are never alone
Unless you choose
Not to go

Better the devil you know
Than the devil you don't

Shitty little cage is mine

What could be out there for me?

Only everything I am becoming
Only everything I want
Only everything I can be
Only everything

Only freedom

Is it time to take off the coat?

Am I ready?

She is ready
She is free

Infinite freedom
Infinite possibilities
Infinite power
Infinite strength
All at my fingertips
All just beyond my fear

All if I just trust
All if I just believe

Can I believe?
Will I be safe?
Is it safe to be free?

Sweet courage stirs from her slumber
A glimpse of my true power gently slaps me on the arse

Pure grace for my humanness
Pure gratitude for my Body's sweet protection

I can do this
There's no such thing as failure

I've had enough of the devil I know
He's killing my soul with boredom

I'm ready for the Angel inside
I'm ready to see my true being
I'm getting ready to step forward

No leaps needed
No fear needed
Excitement awaits

Trust
Trust
Surrender
Melt into the unknown
I flow and ooze around
The bars of my cage

There is no lock
There is no devil
There is no knowledge
There is no safe

Only me
And my Body playing catch up
And then comes the knowing

Always supported
Always surrounded by goodness
Always on the right path
Always free

Choice is my freedom
I am it all

Devil and Angel
Dark and light

Cage and freedom
The lock and the key
The fear and the courage

Hand in hand

Like a thick coat on a sunny day
Take it off or keep it on

I'll still be worthy
I'll still be free
I'll still be loved
I am it ALL.

What Dreams Do You Actually Want To Chase?

Before you jump balls deep into how to use fear to chase your dreams, it might be a good idea to establish what your dreams actually are, if they're actually yours, and also if the ones you've given up on need to be revisited.

Oh so often we will think about a dream or desire, get really excited and then shoot ourselves down with logic or reality to make that dream seem impossible before we even give it a chance to marinate.

It's like we are so afraid of being wrong or wanting something that we feel like we can't have, so we poohpooh the dream before it can even get started. What's a sad fact is that most of us are so wrapped up with what's in our reality right now that we don't allow ourselves to open up to the possibility that our reality can change. That actually *anything* is possible. So, we squish down our dreams, live our lives as practical, logical boring adults and miss out on a whole lotta fun and a whole lotta magic.

Why do we automatically shut down these dreams and desires even when just thinking about them can cause us to feel excited and hopeful for the future?

Fear.
Fear of everything.
Failure
Success

Looking like a dreamer
Looking like a knob[36]

Losing what we already have, even if it makes us desperately
unhappy

Not living up to other people's expectations or our own

Fear of change.
Fear of everything.

Our Higher Self, however, knows how powerful, supported and
resilient we are, so when we get an idea that excites us, she's in
the background shouting yes, yes, yes!

She knows you can't get it wrong and whatever comes out of the
idea, that you are on the right path, and it will set off some
beautiful expansion. She also knows that you have unlimited
possibilities ahead of you and that you are worthy of anything
you desire.

Your Higher Self has zero fear.

It's your Body that wants to protect you from change; good or
bad!

As we learnt before in order for your Body and Higher Self to be
in alignment you need to live true to yourself and that means
that your goals and dreams need to be in alignment with your
true beliefs and your core self.

To dream and desire is to be human.

---

[36] Knob: A very silly person

To move towards those dreams and desires, regardless of fear, is to be truly satisfied and truly happy.

To expand through those dreams and desires, to allow the Body to catch up with all that you have already become, to trust your Higher Self's guidance and nudges, to cause the expansion of others and impact the entire Universe through the ripples of your own expansion...now that is the purpose of life.

That might just sound like some hippy dippy bullshit but believe me, as soon as you step into alignment **that's** when the magic starts happening...but you already know that don't you?

Once we know what makes us happy, we can start looking at where we've been settling or even punishing ourselves in our own lives due to not feeling worthy enough or feeling like we don't deserve to be happy.

Most of the time, if you feel yourself immediately pushing away desires or hopes for your future, or if you realise you have dismissed your dreams of the past, it's a sign that you have created yourself a little cage.

A cage is a time of your life or a situation that you are in that feels impossible to get out from. It's a hopeless place and you feel trapped. Even if you are mostly happy, certain areas in your life can still feel like cages.

Everything in this Universe is constantly expanding. Eternal expansion. To expand does not mean to change what you are but to grow into more.

Everything is energy.
Always in motion.
Always with the potential of movement.
Ready to move, grow and expand.

The idea that we as humans have been thrown into these magnificent bodies just to be here to struggle or prove our worth is beyond absurd. Our worthiness comes without a cost. It's in our nature to want a rich, satisfying experience that causes our spirits to soar. Oh, of course there will always be struggle, but we were never made to wallow in it. We were never made to settle for the struggle. Life is supposed to be fun, exhilarating and exciting. We are made to move. We are made to take the struggle and mould something beautiful out of it. We are made to know our worth as a given and expect a life that reflects that. We are made to move forward, expand and enjoy our life.

We know this in our very bones but yet, after a lifetime of being spoon-fed the idea that we have to struggle, overcome shit to prove our worth for just the smallest good to come to us, we forget. We get knocked down. We are afraid to move. We are afraid to hope. We put up with other people's shit. We put up with our own shit. We create cages. We sit in them and stagnate.

It's almost like we settle in our little cages, and we put up with shit every day just because that shit is more comfortable than the uncertainty of what lies ahead if we try to make things better.

"Better the devil you know than the devil you don't."

So, although we may be miserable, feel trapped or hate waking up every day...at least we know how to cope with it, we know how to live with it, we know that we will survive it. Take away the cage and then what's next? Who can you blame if you don't then go after your dreams? Who can you blame for feeling miserable? How do you know that you will cope...even with the good?

As much as this truth bomb hurts, even if you are stuck in a cage (of anyone's making) the responsibility still comes down onto you. I know how easy it is to blame someone else when you feel like they are holding you back.

But your cage has a door, and you hold the key.

Thing is you can make anything into a cage. As soon as you decide to do or not do something you hold yourself hostage to that belief. If there's no flexibility to it or it's not aligned with your core beliefs **that serve you** then you are taking away your freedom to express yourself in whatever way you've chosen.

If it doesn't feel "right" then you won't feel free and then that's just another cage to break free from. If you are feeling trapped right now, it's good to always test your beliefs, to test why something feels so hard and to test your alignment.

If we are actively staying stuck there's always a reason. Sometimes the reason is because we are unsure of ourselves. Like if things got really good, we don't trust ourselves to not fuck it up or we don't know if we would be able to sustain the good, so the struggle becomes addictive.

Like, seriously, most people are just as afraid of success as they are of failure.

Think about that for a moment, think about why that could be? Why have you felt stuck for so long, why do you continue in a job that you hate, stick with a relationship with zero love or fun?

Why keep doing something that makes you unhappy every single day?

Because your Body knows it's safe. It may not even be a safe situation (think about people who stay in domestic abuse relationships) but at least it's not change, change is unstable, change means you are unsure about the future and so for your Body, any change - good or bad - is unsafe for you. Success *or* failure equals change.

So lovingly, to protect you from the unknown, your Body will tell you that you are not good enough to try that or you are not clever enough to pull it off, or that you are not lucky enough for it to succeed. She will also give you every reason to fear the success too if you did succeed. She tells you that you are not enough to chase your dreams because she wants to keep you stuck.

To be stuck is to be safe.

Now we've found yet another way your Body is trying to protect you. Now we know why, how do we use this to become unstuck?

What Your Fear Really Means

Ultimately, fear means you care about something so much that you are scared of the outcome, but your Higher Self isn't. Fear is *excitement* when you are aligned.

Fear is a great measuring tool for where your true self really wants to go. If there's something you feel you want or should do and it doesn't fill you with fear or excitement, that means you don't really care too much about the outcome. If you don't care about the outcome, it's not really deep in your heart but you're feeling like it should be for some other reason.

Now while doing this is fine, if you are doing things that don't feel scary (i.e., you feel safe all of the time) this may mean you are following someone else's path or that the goal or thing you are doing isn't really what you are passionate about.

When you "follow" the fear and take notice of those things that start your blood pumping and make you feel jittery just by thinking about it, that's when you know you've hit on something you really want to do. That's the path of true passion. If it feels like fear and not excitement, it doesn't really matter *what* the fear is. It could be success, failure, what people will think of you or if you are really good enough, if it's just a pipe dream or if you'll end up looking stupid. No matter what the fear, you are feeling it because it means so much to you. Fear is your Body's way to protect you and also to make you stuck where you are right now.

I.e. It's your Body not wanting to catch up to your Higher Self.

But take a few moments to explore the "what ifs"?
Explore that fear.
What if I do? What if I did it anyway? What's the worst that can happen? What's the best thing that could happen? What if I was enough right now? What if I didn't give myself the choice at all?

Why am I feeling this fear? What does doing this mean to me? What would it mean if I did it? What would it mean if I accepted that I want this to be my goal? What if I realise that this is my first step? How will this change me? What would need to change? Would I feel freer than I do right now?

What is the biggest thing stopping me?

Listen to your Body's fear and turn your whole attention towards it.

That's the way you need to go to get back to you, and to your heart's true goals and desires.

The fear is like a map, use it to guide you through. Normally the more something terrifies you, the more it would excite you.

Did you know that fear and excitement are actually the same emotion? They cause the same chemical reaction in our body and exactly the same physical responses. The heightened heartbeat, the shortness of breath, sweaty palms and butterflies in your tummy... The body actually doesn't know the difference between fear and excitement. So, she checks in with our brain to see which one we are choosing to feel. We are literally making a subconscious decision on whether we see this reaction as a positive or negative thing. But fear can be positive. It can be enjoyable, if we allow it to be. If we choose not to fear the fear itself.

Without fear there's no such thing as bravery. You can't be brave or courageous if you're not scared in the first place.

"Feel the fear and do it anyway" is a fucking epic book by Susan Jeffers, that if you've not read you seriously need to. It lives up to the hype. I put off reading that book for years and decided to pick it up about a month after losing my brother. The way she describes fear and brings every fear back down to its core message which is: "Will I be able to cope?"

Blew my fucking mind. That book touched me when I was in a place of full fear and grief, because what's your biggest fear when someone dies? That you won't cope with your new reality. Death is the biggest uncontrollable change there is.

But you do cope. You do have days when you fear you won't, but you do. During grief the most courageous thing you can do is to keep living.

With goals, dreams and cages it's a little easier...but not much.

Revisit your old desires. Think about what made you give up on them. What fears did you have? Do those fears still ring true? Think about the desires you have right now. Focus on just one. Daydream about it without any fear. Try to see it unfolding through your Higher Self's eyes. If you had the belief that life is unfolding magically for you, that you have unlimited power and resources, that you can cope with anything that is thrown at you...would you step towards that desire? When you drop the fear does that desire make you feel good?

True Courage is Feeling the Fear and Doing It Regardless

Now we know why we feel fear, you may be one step closer to knowing what your true dream really is.

What do you do with that?

You see your dream, the one that scares you the most and you start writing the small steps that you need to take to get you there. You feel excited, this could really happen!

"My dream is possible..."

You plan each step to the tiniest detail, and you can see yourself in the future, living how you truly want to. But now each tiny step scares the shit out of you. Everything you have to do, no matter how small, feels like a mountain. Even if you've been feeling the love for yourself and you're feeling Already Enough.

Now this starts to rock your core. It's scary, isn't it? You decide to do the easiest step... for example, just register a domain name. You umm and ahh because you feel that you are not allowed to get this wrong. It's vital that it's easy to remember and spell...the future of your whole dream, nay the future of your whole life depends on this tiny step, fuck what will people think of the name? What if...what if...what if?

Suddenly this tiny step has become huge. It's become really scary. You think, *"I'll tell you what I'll sleep on it."* Days go by. *"It doesn't matter, it's really important so I'm going to take my time, I don't want to get it wrong, I can't get it wrong..."*
Oh shit, there you are...stuck in fear. Just like that, a tiny step on your fantastic plan has become a huge stumbling block.

Fear gets you by the nads[37] once again but here's the kicker, you can feel the fear and still move forward.

Being brave doesn't mean that you have no fear, it means that you do it regardless. You face the fear and do it anyway because any fucker can do anything that doesn't scare them.

True courage is being shit scared and still going for it.

Forgetting the outcome, knowing that you're strong enough to deal with any outcome, trusting in perfect timings, doing what needs to be done and always from a place of alignment.

That doesn't mean that it's not hard to do. Each tiny step may be the hardest thing you feel you've ever had to do! Sending one email may feel like you need a 2-hour pep talk just to get you to the point that you feel brave enough to hit send. You may find you waste days or even weeks preparing yourself to be brave enough to just do the shit that you know you want to do.

It's OK, breathe, dude, breathe...

---

[37] Nads: I.e., Ballbags; genitals

As long as you feel satisfied as often as possible, it's never a waste.

Even getting shizzle done imperfectly, as long as you feel brave on the way, trust that you are being directed and as long as you preserve your self-love while you are gathering your courage, it's really OK.

Without that self-love and self-belief, following your true dreams that are deep in your heart will be useless. If you are beating yourself up for feeling fear or not feeling strong enough, there's not a chance in hell you will get to where you want to be. The vehicle to completing your dreams is fuelled by love not shame. The journey of getting there needs to be as satisfying as the end goal and is meant to be enjoyed.

You see, you will never really fully "get there". As an ever expanding being you are always going to have new desires and evolving dreams. What feels scary and exhilarating to you today, might be normal and boring to you after you've done it numerous times. The soul wants the thrill, wants the exhilaration and so will give you plenty of opportunities to feel stretched. The journey of stepping outside of your comfort zone is what makes life exciting and gives us that feeling of satisfaction, so really time is irrelevant.

Your time is not running out.
There's nothing you can do to do it wrong.
The journey enriches your life experience.
We are here to feel it all.

Fear is normal.

Never be ashamed of being scared.
Never be ashamed when fear stops you in your tracks, because it will, and that's when your love is more important than ever. That's when you need to be full of self-love and have the kindest inner voice you can.

Fuelling yourself with love and acting through alignment will get you closer to your dreams than ever. Fear tells you that you are going the right way and love gives you the courage to feel the fear and do it regardless because you know you deserve your dreams, and that however it works out, your love means you are safe enough to cope with anything that happens.

Shame and guilt have no place here, there is no space for them. As soon as you start to feel either, stop what you are doing and turn your focus onto loving yourself harder. Bravery will come when you are in your self-love flow, when you can be gracious enough to give yourself empathy and room to fail, if it comes to it. Ultimately there is no such thing as failure anyway. You are being guided to expand. You deserve all of your desires, and life wants to give them to you. What others perceive as a failure is really just an unfolding. Having grace for yourself and a knowing of how loved and supported you are will remind you that you can never really fail.

Remember each tiny step brings you closer to your goal but each tiny step is not a one chance deal. You can always try again. Some things you try will fail and we need to not be so harsh on ourselves. Each tiny step is not a life-or-death situation. We are imperfect. Seeing it as a failure is shitty and makes it super scary to try again but remember we can take as long as we need to make something work.

One tiny step failing isn't the end of the world or your dreams. But, never trying to do it again might well be.

Like I said before, sometimes the fear of success is just as great as the fear of failure.

It is brave to remember that even if something succeeds beyond your wildest dreams, you will be able to cope with it. You have whatever strength, power and courage you need, already inside of you as an unlimited source that you can tap into at any time.

The moment you decide you are strong enough; you will be strong enough.

You will be given exactly what you need rather than what you want. That is a given. Embrace all your dark and light so that the big U can know you are ready to get unstuck. Ready to move forwards.

You can cope with whatever the future brings.

Believing Anything Is Possible And Forgetting Limits

We all have limiting beliefs in some areas of our lives and these beliefs never serve us well.

Some of us learn not to dream too big in school, some of us are told to be realistic by our parents, sometimes friends will "tell us as it is" as a way of bringing us down to earth, siblings make fun of us if we believe in the impossible and work colleagues feel threatened if we aim too high.

When we start to dream close to our hearts, we are dreaming big. Dreaming big means being brave, it means change and breaking the norm. This normally means we start acting and thinking differently to the people around us. This can threaten the people close to us because by choosing a different path, it can feel to them that we are actually questioning *their* choices and, ultimately, as we do braver things and we challenge our own limiting beliefs, we are challenging theirs by proxy.

We know our fear of change comes from a place of love. Usually (unless they're complete arse hats) their fear, expressed as disbelief in our new way of thinking, comes from the same place.

They don't want you to change because 1) they love you and want you to be safe and 2) they don't want to believe your dreams are possible because that means that theirs is too. They want to stay safe and stuck without being challenged.

This can even be true not only for finding your dreams but also when you start to love yourself.

Frank and honest discussions and, if you need to, agreeing to disagree is normally all it takes to get family and friends on board. Sometimes just knowing why they are acting this way can help you empathise but not knock you back to your old way of thinking.

We'll dig deeper into this later but ultimately, if someone truly loves you, they will want to see you soaring high in your full power, loving life and genuinely being happy. That will outweigh any self-reflections they have to make. If you keep aligned and take the responsibility to care about how you feel as your main vibration, then anyone who doesn't match it will fade away.

But is anything possible and if so, how can you believe it's true for you?

-Cut-
-Hold up, heyyyy-

Disclaimer time:
When you are super brave and decide to break out of the fear and do the "new thing" you will have a vision in your head about how you want it to turn out. It will be perfect (or close to) in your head. And now I feel like I need to include this warning, there's a highly likely chance that at first it will be crap. We are talking shitcakes here people. Changing anything normally means you are going to have to waddle through some shit before you get to the promised land. A story as old as time itself.

The *Hero's Journey*.

I'm talking about a new business, new skill, new home, new singleness, new relationship...any new situation in your life is going to drudge up the shit you've been sitting on because you are now moving and that shit has been sat undisturbed for years while you've been safe, small and still. Now it will rise to the surface, and you will need way more compassion and empathy for yourself than ever before.

As you learn and progress you may find yourself feeling frustrated because the vision in your brain gets clearer, but your skills are not matching up to it. You feel like you are producing crap, and it's at this point where the fear overcomes most people. When the shit hits the fan and is splattered across your face, the negative voice becomes louder and most people will give up and run back to their shitty, but at least it's shit they feel safe with, their boring cage.

If you can allow yourself the grace to be imperfect and remember how long you need to keep going to catch up to the vision...that's when greatness happens. That's when magic happens.

This is the moment your self-love will propel you forward and allow you to sit in that crap for a while.

You can push through it.

You can reach your vision and achieve so much more than you've ever believed.

You are allowed to not be amazing the first few times you try something new, or even the first few hundred times!

Every time you want to beat yourself up for not living up to your own standards, remember to love yourself harder and just keep swimming. If you can't swim then just float for a while, just keep your head above water. Whatever happens, you are closer to your greatness when you are soaring the sky or bobbing in shit than you are when you're tucked up safely in your cage.

Your brain believes whatever you tell it.

A brain not only believes what you tell it, but it will also look for evidence to support that what you are saying is true. If you have failed at a goal in the past and still believe in your own limits, it may be that your brain is actively looking for evidence constantly to confirm your limits and prove that they exist and they must be true. Once you set your brain to believe that you have no limits, your brain will then switch tracks to look for evidence that you have no limits and can achieve the goal that you want to. It will actually try and prove what you really want to believe.

Infinite Possibilities

The moment I tried to write this section the big U decided to have some fun with me.

"You want to write about infinite possibilities, my beautiful Mirrie? Then I will give you a fish slap right across your cheeks with your own impossible situation and see how you handle that one."

Yep, I got a message that made me feel like I'd been fucked in the feels from behind ... aggressively.

A misunderstanding.
A friendship never to be repaired.
I'd hurt someone I really loved.
The impossible situation.

I felt sick. Anxiety rose in my throat, and I couldn't even articulate the sadness in my own brain. Body stepped in and poured me a glass of wine. She took over, allowing me to feel just enough hurt to put me off writing but not enough to draw me into the pits of hell.

So, I thought I'd sleep it off. But I woke up and the sadness was still there. I tried to switch my mindset. I tried to talk to the person involved. I couldn't even talk about it, let alone write about it.

My anxiety took me to the future, all the way into my old age and this situation was still the same and I was still sad. I felt like I was going to be sad forever. I knew these were my own internal Llamas. I knew I was taking myself into the future for no reason apart from to convince myself of the impossibility of the situation.

I was in a spin.

This was never going to be able to be forgotten.

How can you explain your beliefs of infinite possibilities and allowing yourself to feel your limitless potential when your brain is in the place of the impossible?

Then this happened...

I'm on voice message with my friend Rachel, just sending normal "how are you" messages and Indie is just bugging me,

"*Mummy, Mummy, Mummy.*" He wants more food - "*I'm hungry Mummy.*"

He's already had a croissant that he didn't eat, a cupcake that he just ate the sweet off the top and he also had a banana which he discarded after just one bite. Yet he's still like,

"*I'm huuuuuuungry!!!*"

and I'm like, "*Oh for God's sake what the hell am I going to do with this boy?!*".

He grabs an apple and then he just literally eats, like, four bites. You know what a kid does when they just eat around the edge of the apple once and then they're saying "*I'm all done now, I want something different.*"

While still recording the voice message I said "*Indie, there's more apple on that apple...go eat some more apple!*"

I start laughing and then my friend Rachel messages me back and she says:

"*There's more apple on that apple...Mirrie, there's more apple on your apple...there's always more apple...that's so deep and profound you need to put that in your book!*"

Well, that gets me thinking, that's got nothing to do with infinite possibilities really, has it?

But then I'm reflecting on it and I'm thinking, yeah there is always more apple on the apple but then there's going to be a point when you've eaten all the apple.

Then it hit me: FUCK ME, THEN YOU GET TO THE SEEDS!

You eat the apple and then all that's left of the core is that really gross stringy bit and then the seeds.

Each tiny seed contains a possibility of a new tree.

The possibility of a tree contains the possibility of more and more and more apples.

And that's the possibility of more and more seeds.

That's the possibility of an orchard of apple trees...with even more apples and seeds and trees.
And the infinite possibility doesn't stop there. One apple can feed you, but lots of apples? Now we're talking cider, we're talking apple juice, we're talking apple-bloody-strudel...the possibilities are limitless! You can take that apple and get the benefits in hundreds of different ways.

Then, if you actually take the effort and the energy to go and plant the seeds, they grow into mighty trees and then those trees can provide shelter, they can provide wood, they can provide heat, they can provide life-giving oxygen, energy and more apples and then each of those apples has got the same infinite possibilities within them as the one that you've just eaten. My mind was blown.

Even just the simple act of eating an apple can lead you to the fact that everything in this life has infinite possibilities inside...if you're willing to eat all of the apple and then actually go plant the seeds.

And the stringy gross bit that gets stuck in your teeth before you get to the seeds...I guess that represents your own limits. The limits you put on yourself to get stuck in the impossible. To keep yourself small. To stop yourself from planting any seeds. To keep you safely in your cage.

There's more apple on your apple.

I thought about my own seemingly impossible situation. My friend who was feeling hurt. There was definitely more apple on that friendship. Although I wasn't able to see how it was going to be resolved in that moment, although it brought up lots of emotion, guilt and sadness, it didn't mean that it was impossible to find a solution. In fact, through talking and expressing our feelings to each other, that impossible situation actually strengthened our friendship, deepened our bond and took our relationship to a completely different, expanded level.

There's always more apple on your apple. This is true in all situations in life.

A dream may feel impossible but it's only your perception that makes it so.

To Indie that apple was eaten, and he was still hungry. To me the apple wasn't eaten. It took reflection and an epiphany for me to see that not only wasn't it eaten but that it held the potential to feed us all for the rest of our life. For others they could see an apple business, an orchard, a change in their whole way of life.

The half-eaten apple remains the same. Slightly browning on the kitchen table, the reality of the apple hasn't changed. Only the expanding limits of our perception of the possibilities of that apple have changed...which changes everything.

This really is a stretching of your brain to be able to see past your current reality and past what you believe right now to be true. Everything in life starts off as a passing thought. The biggest ideas in the world could have easily been dismissed as crazy or impossible, and probably were by multiple people. It just takes one person to have a different perception of what's possible and it can impact the entire world.

Maybe your dreams don't involve changing the world but would be a huge change in your life. That dream is just as important. Every time we decide to go forwards towards our true self or desires, we do change the world. Our world, our family, the people we meet...the ripples of you being happy and satisfied will gently rock other people's perceptions of what can be possible for them. So, with every dream you decide to be brave enough to go for, you are changing the world around you.

The impossible is really very self-indulgent. The randomness and energy of this universe means that your life can change dramatically at any given moment. That's without your own responsibility of reflecting on your fears and using them as a guide as to where you go even when faced with an impossible situation that scares the shit out of you.

Remember, there is no impossible and your potential is limitless. That's what makes life so magical *and* so terrifying. There's energy and possibilities buzzing around us all day. It's only when we decide to notice and tap into that, and push our imperfect, loving, protective limits aside, make a tiny courageous step and open ourselves up to the fact that anything can happen and we deserve all the good, that we are able to see that magic.

The thing is, sometimes to dream of, say, creating your own business, may feel as impossible as being the first person to accompany a moose to the moon...but fuck it, if you want to hang with a moose in space even that is possible! Wait, I mean, fuck it, if you want to run your own business, open a shop or make your grandma's secret sausage recipe famous - of course it's possible. It's all possible.

All it takes is unearthing your belief on why you feel it's impossible, focusing on the solutions rather than the problems, allowing your brain to look for evidence of your new belief that serves you, trusting your Higher Self to give you inspired action, being brave, believing you are worthy enough and then having fun along the way.

The only limits you have are what you give yourself and sometimes we don't even notice that we've given them to ourselves.

See your potential as that apple. You can leave it to go mouldy, shrivelled up and half eaten OR you can say "There's more apple on that apple" and go fucking chase your dreams.

Ever expanding
Circles of Time
Sparkling
Twinkling

Ever Knowing

Trust
Trust
Surrender

Trust
Trust
Surrender

Each spark a connection

Dots connecting
Without effort

One path
A million possibilities

Just a little
Trust
Trust
Surrender

The perfect moment
Directing your moment
A million moments

Trust
Trust
Surrender

Ageless
Endless
Limitless
Infinite

Trust
Trust
Surrender
Co-create
Feel the power
Flowing around you

It's Her
It's Me
It's You
It's We

Trust
Trust
Surrender

Ever expanding
Possibilities multiplying

Feel into the fear
Take the uncomfortable action
Be Brave (Little One)
It's all unfolding perfectly

Trust
Trust
Surrender.

Chapter Ten – Family Matters

Homies
Famalam
Bros
Crew
Blood
Tribe
Village
Family

Whatever you call it...we all need one. We all have that human need to feel like we belong. Knowing there are peeps[38] who are out there who have our backs no matter what. It feels good to belong. It feels good to be supported. It feels good to be loved.

It is very human to want to be a part of something bigger than us. We are lovers to our core so it's natural to want to love and be loved. Whether it's building a tight family unit, a gorgeous collection of friends or a beautiful community, it's a lovely thing to share parts of our lives with others.

It's human to want a family but it's a flawed belief that we need any validation from that family (whether blood or chosen) or that we need to be understood by them.

You have no responsibility to explain yourself to anyone, not even the people who love you.

You have zero responsibility to have to be understood or have your actions or emotions be validated by anyone else.

You have no responsibility to make anyone feel happy, comfortable or secure.

---

[38] Peeps: Cuddly term for people you dig

Are You a People Pleaser?

When you love another, of course you want them to be happy, whether it be your partner, children, family or friends. The more you love someone, the more it can seem that the stakes are higher, the thought that if you have boundaries or please yourself, you may upset them or change the way they view you.

Surely if self-love is an inside job, this shit shouldn't really matter so much? If loving yourself is all about you, does having a network of support and love around you really matter that much? Does family matter?

Family matters.
The family you choose matters.
The people you surround yourself with matter.
How you love yourself and therefore feel about your family matters.

External validation from any source doesn't.

As your self-love grows, the pure love from all around you grows too. As you expand, the people around you expand too...or they don't. The people who love you will want to see you soar but change often brings with it an unsettling of dust so will often shakes thangs up. Family can be a tricky subject at best. No family is perfect, but add in your self-love awakening and things might get a little messy.

Don't Be a Doormat

There comes a time in your self-love awakening that something will trigger the fucking rage storm in you.

Someone may do something, call you something, ask something of you or assume something about you.

You will feel the heat of a thousand dragons rising up and shouting "*Fuck NO!*" into your throat. It may be such a little thing but to you it will be so powerful that it will stop you in your tracks and surprise the hell out of you.

You see, chances are you've been putting everyone else first for such a long time that it's become second nature to you. When people have slightly put you down or asked too much or assumed too much of you, it's not been that big of a deal because you've agreed with them, not had the strength to stand up for yourself or just gotten so used to it that their words are normal now.

Before now you've not had the self-esteem to believe you deserve better or the drive to believe you can have boundaries that people treat with respect and that's because you've never treated yourself with respect.

Slowly but surely as you work through this book and make the decision to love yourself every single day - imperfections and all - you will also see your undeniable worth.

Your worth, that is there day in day out.

Your worth, that is within you regardless of your mistakes or shortcomings.
Your worth, that is as immovable as the sun.

Your worth, that is based on just the fact that you are you.

And so, you deserve respect...just as much as everyone else.

Your wishes, dreams and plans are just as important as the people who you love.

Your dignity, your time, your health, your peace, your future and your freedom are worth standing up for.

There will be a moment where you will realise you have moved the bar on what's acceptable anymore and guess what, bitches? It's higher than ever.

Remember all these changes have been happening inside you, slowly inside, you are loving and respecting yourself a little bit more each day but the people around you may have not noticed that yet.

This life-changing realisation that you are already enough has not yet filtered to the people around you, who are used to treating you in a certain way (sometimes like crap). They don't know that you have new boundaries and expectations. It may even come as a shock to you!

Why do people put up with shit?

They want people to love them.
They have no personal boundaries.
They expect others to take control.
They don't like making decisions.
They are worried about how people see them.
They think that's how you are a kind person.
They don't respect themselves.
They don't know their own wants or needs.
They've put themselves last for so long it's become normal.

So, someone will innocently (or not so innocently) say something, and it will be like:

BAM!
HELL NO!
FUCK NO!

I can guarantee that when it happens, it will be hard to breathe, like you won't know what to do with it because it is SO powerful and SO scary.

Why is it so scary? Because this will be your moment and you will know that the next thing you say or do will represent a massive change. A huge decision.

The knee jerk BAM moment happens and then you choose:

Shrink or grow
Speak up or shut up
Stand up or fade
Keep taking the same ol'[39] shit or demand some damn respect
Will this be the point you decide to love yourself enough to make
that hard choice, no matter what the outcome, no matter what
the cost? Deep down you'll just know what you need to do.

Is this the point where the way **you allow** the people in your life
to treat you changes?

Is this where a part of your cage falls down?

Now depending on the situation, the other person will probably
be dumbfounded because it will be something so tiny to them,
but they need to know you have new firm boundaries.

I'm not saying everyone who lives with not loving themselves is
some weak shy wallflower. It's totally possible to be assertive (or
opinionated as fuck) and have high self-esteem but still not
actually love yourself. I'm also not saying that once you love
yourself you are going to start being a demanding diva all of a
sudden who only wants her own way.

This is different. This is your life, and we are talking about the
people who mean the most to you in it.

This is like a fundamental new love you have for yourself, so now
you realise you matter as much as everyone else (not more or
less) so now you need to stick up for yourself and make sure that
you are heard too.

People who genuinely love you don't want to take your love, time
and resources for granted. People who love you do not want to
hurt you on purpose. People who truly love you want to see you
succeed, love yourself and have high self-respect. Of course they

---

[39] Ol': Ye olde way of saying old.

do, it's just that most people don't even realise when they are overstepping your boundaries.

When we are being a doormat, we don't want to say no or rock the boat because we are scared. We're scared to change someone's view of us or love for us. We don't set boundaries because we feel people should respect us just because they love us. That pesky fear again about being lovable seeps into so many areas of our lives...

Here's the thing: *most people* just don't even realise they're taking the piss and if they do realise and keep doing it...do they really love you? Do you really need people like that in your life?

Now I'm going to tell you this amazing analogy about gardens and boundaries. I'm pretty sure I didn't make it up, but I've just spent an hour googling it and I can't find out who to give the credit to. Whoever came up with it, I love it and it's been stuck in my head ever since. I've also expanded on it because I'm poetic and fancy innit[40].

Imagine your life is like a garden. You've spent years taking care of your big trees (your time, self-respect and inner peace). Every year you plant flowers of hope, trust and respect. There are happy little bees that look like kindness flying around. Little money trees are popping up all over the place. Blades of empathy and goodness making your garden a lush green colour.

But there's no fence. Any ol' person can come in. So come in, they do. You hope they will care about your garden but most of them are selfish fuckers and they're dropping their beer cans all over the place, taking whatever they want and ripping up the flowers.

You believe these people are your friends (even family) so surely they don't realise that your garden is becoming a mess, so you put up signs, suggested paths even, but you don't want to offend

---

[40] Ol': Ye olde way of saying old.

anyone or make them leave so you make them as tiny as possible, just hoping people will see them.

But people are quite self-absorbed and so the signs go unnoticed.

When people start letting their llamas (dramas) in and they are trampling your flower beds, poking at your trees and you are exhausted with trying to tidy up the mess, you decide to put up fences. Your boundaries. They are feeble at first because you are worried that you'll be seen as offensive (see what I did there?). You don't even bother putting up a gate just in case it will put people off.

Of course, the same things happen again, and again, and again. So now you have a choice...

1. You either take down the half-arsed[41] fences and put up with a shitty garden (I.e. Appease people out of fear that they will leave or prove to you that you are unlovable)
2. You build a MOFO huge wall which keeps EVERY fucker out (I.e. Lose all trust in people and close yourself off to connection).

Or...

3. You take responsibility for your own garden. You build firm fences and a fat ol' heavy gate. You decide who comes in. You decide where your boundaries are and the ones who love you will enjoy your garden, respect it and help you to grow it.

Your boundaries are your responsibility.

You deserve a beautiful garden, and YOU get to choose who enjoys it with you.

---

[41] Halfarsed: Not jumping in with both feet; Only doing something with half of your heart in it, barely trying at all.

Your "BAM" moment is really just you standing in your garden, fully loving every part of it and having the knowledge that you deserve people in there who fully support and love you no matter what.

It's the knowing that the people you invite into your life are there to enrich it, not validate it. You have no need for their validation when you have your own. When we are all taking care of our own gardens while respecting other peoples and all growing together, this world becomes a beautiful place to live in. But it starts with a BAM.

It starts with you deciding you are worthy.

Supporters vs. Doubters

Which leads us nicely into this section.

Maybe you've been a doormat.
Maybe you've allowed some people to take advantage of you.
Maybe you've been appeasing.
Maybe you've been playing small.

Maybe self-love is just stupidly radical compared to how the people closest to you live.

The framework of people closest to you will notice the differences in you the most. You might be rattling many feathers without even knowing.

They may be questioning what this is all about.

The change sparks the fear in them too.

Remember, most fears are your Body's way to sabotage you into keeping small. To keep the same is safe. Your Body works in any way that she knows will protect you. This works for the people around you too.

Change is scary even for the people not going through it. Seeing you change, seeing your opinion of yourself grow, is going to trigger the fear for them too.

When you hate yourself, you strive to change yourself in order to feel worthy.

When you love yourself, you will grow, flow and the change is organic. It happens easily because you know that you are worthy regardless.

So certain things will change as you start to love yourself more. People will see you and even judge you and this will cause them to start questioning themselves.

This is the point that they will choose to support you or doubt you.

Support means: they are in a good enough place to not fear your change or make it question themselves, rather they can reflect on their own self-worth in a healthy way.

Doubt means: they are coming from a place of fear. It maybe that love for you is showing up as doubts and questions, or the fear of losing you, or fear that this will change their relationship with you. This makes them want to cause doubts in you.

Sabotage/Pull down means: they are projecting their own feelings of self-loathing or lack of self-worth onto you. They want to bring you down so that they don't have to face the truth about themselves. THIS IS NOT ABOUT YOU.

Remember, self-sabotage may project your own emotions onto other people's reactions. Always remember to use "This moment's truth".

Bring yourself to the present moment, only allow facts, don't project your own truth onto other people's actions and talk to find out what people are really thinking. They might be saying one thing but actually meaning another. Have the courage to have those awkward, honest conversations before you decide you know where they are coming from.

So normally, people in your close circle include (if you have them) your partner, kids, parents, siblings and a couple of close friends.

Partner: This might be where you have the biggest issues, especially if your relationship isn't very solid. Your partner will know you so well that they will notice any changes quickly. They might be afraid to lose you, or they might be cheering on your success. Make sure you communicate and really open up to each other.

Kids: Children and even older kids are learning from you all the time so it's really important to be brave and talk to your kids about everything.

Parents/Siblings: Usually the most judgy, but at the same time the most supportive. Your actions will most likely trigger your family and get them questioning their own actions. If you have toxic members of your family remember you are allowed to love them from a distance, but allow forgiveness and grace to guide you (but also take no shit!).

Use the BAM knee jerk reaction we spoke about to gauge how respectful people are being to you. Encourage people to talk to you about what they're seeing changing or what scares them. Lead with kindness and understanding.

Apart from your kids, you still have a choice who you let into your life.

Being with you is a blessing, you may find even your kids rebel but once they realise your love for them is unconditional, they will come around, you are teaching them how they will treat themselves and others when they grow up. Chances are, if they are already grown up, you may have some things to apologise for or explain. As adults, your kids have the choice of how they respond to you.

What teachings did your parents try to give you? What beliefs did they have about themselves? What did the way they treated you or themselves teach you about self-worth? What were their core beliefs and how did they act on them?

Reflecting on how they both acted and talked about self-love might give you some insight as to why you feel the way you do or how you acted in the past and give you the power to change the cycle, especially when it comes to your family and own kids.

Breaking that cycle can be scary and you may face opposition because you're not doing things the way your family has normally done it in the past. Of course, you might not, you may find everyone close to you is supportive and even embraces some of the changes you are going through for themselves, but it's the fear that they might not be supportive that actively stops so many people reaching the point you are at right now.

Changing your core beliefs about self-love and accepting your flaws might mean going against the grain when it comes to your family, and the thought of possible conflict or judgement from parents, siblings or your partner is fucking scary.

But ultimately, if they love you and want the best for you, they'll come around when they see the amazing way self-love has touched your life once you accept yourself and start to love yourself.

And if they don't?
Fuck 'em!

Jokes!

Kinda...

That's ultimately up to you. There should be zero reason out there that anyone could not be happy about you feeling enough and falling in love with yourself, but no one can tell you what to feel or think about your family if they turn out to be long-term doubters.

At the end of the day, you can only be in charge of your own feelings and actions. It may be that you yourself need to forgive, confront or distance yourself from certain people. But ask your Body, trust your gut, acknowledge your emotions around it and do what's best for you and your emotional health.

The main thing I've heard from my doubters is that self-love is selfish.

If you hear this, you need to stand your ground. In order for you to be an amazing parent, partner, family member or friend, especially when you are always giving or serving others, you need to be the most rested, healed, happy, contented, fulfilled, loved up person that you can be. You need to be OK with yourself; then you can be your best for others.

You deserve love from people who respect you and want you to be happy. And if someone is constantly sabotaging you or bringing you down?
LIFE IS TOO SHORT.

You deserve supporters.

Teaching your Children to Love Themselves

Family can be a tricky thing; it should be the first place we learn about unconditional love but for some people that's unfortunately not the case.

Our family instils our deepest-rooted beliefs about who we are and how deserving we are of love, but it seems Self-Love isn't really up there on the menu.

Take this moment to think about your core beliefs regarding self-love and how much worth you give yourself.

What would you want your child's answer to be?

This will be the greatest gift you could ever give your child. As I've said before, when you love yourself everything in life is easier, having more confidence is effortless, making friends (because the fear of someone not liking you is less when you feel comfortable in yourself), going for your big dreams and goals regardless of fear becomes more normal, loving and connecting with your Body is second nature. Self-love touches everything, there isn't one area in your life that isn't improved and brightened by self-love.

Isn't that exactly what you want for your child? That unconditional love you feel for them, for them to have it for themselves? For them to be so sure of who they are that anything feels possible to them?

Of course we want this for our children, but the question is how? I'm afraid the answer isn't a fucking easy one.

We all know our kids copy us.

We also all know the value of telling our kids how much we love them. There's scientific evidence that a child's brain grows with the more love, affection and physical contact they have. You've probably heard about the research that was done in Romanian orphanages that found nurturing a baby actually changed the shape and wiring of their brain?

For most parents this comes naturally. Our love for our kids overflows. We constantly praise them up, tell them how proud we are of them, tell them how amazing they are and how loved they are. So why do we still end up with kids who are depressed, with little to no self-confidence or who feel unlovable?

You can tell a kid until you are blue in the face how much they mean to you but those are not the words that they internalise. Yes, the words that you say and the things that you do for them have a huge impact on their inner voice and core beliefs, but the most impact on a child's self-love is how **you** feel and talk about love and how you show love towards yourself.

That's what they are watching and that's how they learn.

When you are expressing your love for them, it teaches them how to express love for other people.

When you shower them with compliments or gifts, it teaches them how to give compliments and gifts to others.

When you tell them that they are amazing and show them that you love them unconditionally, it teaches them how to love unconditionally and to be an amazing parent or friend.

When you react with compassion and empathy, it teaches them how to react when they feel wronged or annoyed.

When you talk about yourself, your Body or your dreams, it teaches them how to talk about themselves, their Body, their dreams.

How you treat yourself will teach them how to treat themselves.

Teaching them about parenting, expressing love and having empathy is amazing and vital in them having a happy future.

Teaching them that it's OK to be imperfect, to accept themselves fully and to treat themselves with kindness is just the most beautiful gift you can give your kids.

The good news in all the carnage and smoke I left with that nuke bomb though? You don't have to be perfect in your self-love in order to help your children develop theirs. We all slip up. We have years of conditioning, other people's beliefs and shoulds to wade through. For a lot of us our first impulse is to go to that harsh inner voice inside where we pull ourselves down or doubt ourselves.

Don't beat yourself up for how you were before you knew what you know now. You can teach your children about fear, about the way their Body protects them and about how amazing their brains actually are.

When my son decided to sleep in his own room, he went through a period of feeling super scared of monsters coming into his new room and eating him. Yes, kids can have real scary fears...like actually being eaten alive (it actually makes our fears a bit crummy in comparison!).

I tried to explain that monsters aren't real, we tried to draw what the monster looks like, we checked under the beds, but nothing was working. Instead of focusing on the monster I focused on the fear. I asked him if he knew why he felt so afraid, even when I showed him that there was nothing there or told him a million times that monsters didn't exist. He said he didn't know but that his brain told his heart to be scared. I spoke about why his brain was telling him that. I helped him understand that his brain and Body loved him so much they wanted to protect him and keep him safe. So, the fear he felt was a loving protection, even if the fear wasn't about something real.

Together we came up with this mantra: "*Thank you brain for trying to protect me but I'm already safe, everyone I love is safe and it's safe for me to sleep.*"

That was over 7 years ago, and we still say this every night before bed.

Little things you learn about yourself, your own beliefs and your own self-love, have a huge impact on your kids.

As long as you make the commitment to give yourself time to reflect, empathise or be compassionate to yourself, your kids will see that.

And that is real life. True self-love takes commitment, and your children will internalise each time you come back to your own self-acceptance or love and know that it's OK to be imperfect themselves.

Remember, it's not your responsibility to make your children happy or even to make them love themselves. But it is your responsibility to show them what you now know is true and to teach them about aligning with their Higher Self so they can find ways to make themselves happy and satisfied, not only now but for the rest of their lives.

Finding Your Village

Up until I had kids, I never really felt like I needed a "village". As a very self-assured teenager I was definitely one of the lads and although I had a couple of very close girlfriends who I loved dearly, did lots together with and I knew they had my back, it seemed like I didn't really fit in. To be honest I never really felt like I fit in anywhere.

After the birth of my first son something inside changed. I was sure of most of my parenting decisions, but I started to feel lonely. I was different to the other mums and making new friends at the baby groups felt like I was back on the fucking dating scene or something.

When was the right time to ask for someone's number or to talk about meeting outside of the group? Would they think I fancied them if I asked them to meet me down the park? Am I coming on too strong, should I be playing hard to get?

Because my first son's birth had been epically traumatic, I had a devastated body, grieving for the perfect birth I never got and now I was left with this tiny human, with tongue-tie and I was struggling to feed him. Because I had been so out of control during his birth, I became passionate about breastfeeding and I wanted to help other women feel safe at a time when I had felt most powerless, vulnerable and alone.

After doing some research I found out about doulas, and I decided I would really love to become one. The course was about 6 days long over two weekends, Eli was 9 months old and permanently attached to my boob, so it seemed a bit like a pipe dream. But somehow, I managed to secure funding, arrange for my mum to come to help look after him while I was in the class and before I knew it, we were on our way to Cambridge with the car loaded up with toys! I remember walking into the first class. I was the last to arrive and everyone was already sitting in a big circle of beanbags, and we went around the room telling each other why we were there.

On that first day we laughed, cried, hugged and held each other's space while we opened up talking about things we'd never told another living soul. Some women had grown up children, some had lost family members, some were going through menopause, some still had little babies. But no matter the age, background or even beliefs, the one thing that had pulled this little group of women together was the shared passion to empower other women while giving birth.

Just in that first day I realised what I had been missing all along. A group of women who were powerful, vulnerable and completely supportive. I realised my whole life I had been avoiding female companionship like the plague. Instead of feminism - which I thought I had been showing - I had been completely sexist!

I had favoured hanging out with the guys because I thought it was "less drama" and I had been proud of the fact that I was considered "just like a bloke but still sexy". I had been acting masculine my whole life and seen feminine traits as weak. I had been thinking "I am a woman, but I can still do" rather than "as a woman I can do".

In short, I'd dismissed the absolute power that comes from being a woman, I'd tried to be as close to being a man as I could be.

I always remember getting invited to a stag do and when my boyfriend at the time said "hey it's supposed to be boys only", his mates laughed and said "yeah but it's Mirrie, she's pretty much one of us anyway".

Thus began my lifelong mission to try and prove to the world that not only was I as strong as a man, but I was also super desirable to them and also that I could have as many guy friends as I wanted that I could keep "just as friends". I was sick of being told that guys were only my friend because they had a different goal in sight.

After I got married my husband made it very clear that I would upset him if I had male friends, so that left me with 15 years of barely having any friends at all.

But with this new knowledge under my belt, I could let go of that need for other people to see me a certain way or that belief that I could only get on well with men. Women had amazing unique strengths and could make an amazing village, so I set out to find my own little village and I wanted it to be full of powerful women.

How do you find your village though?

As my social media demon of choice was Facebook (at the time) I used my message of self-love to attract a small but amazingly supportive group of women and imparted the fucking impactful wisdom of self-love in there for years. The only problem was I wasn't being completely true to myself.

Because this message of self-love was so important to me, I wanted the message to reach as many people as possible, so I kept up an image on social media. I couldn't risk repelling people because if I put them off, they might miss out on this life changing knowledge. The knowledge that they were already worthy was far more important than how they saw me, so I needed to be likeable, or so I thought.

Fuck, I was also keeping up a (rather shitty) image in my personal life as well. As my partner at the time wasn't fond of me having any friends, let alone male ones, I kept all people at an arm's length, especially male ones.

In my group I allowed myself to be conditionally vulnerable and pushed my limits as to what I shared, but I was always aware of having a non-confrontational approach and rather bland voice because this message was just too important to risk offending anyone. Also, as many of my friends and family were still in the rather strict religion I grew up in, I didn't want them to judge me either. This led to a rather wishy-washy vanilla message that wasn't connecting with hardly anyone.

It wasn't until that fateful day in Jan 2020 that I was on LinkedIn and I thought *"Fuck it, I don't know anyone on here, I'm just going to be my sweary, horny self and use this platform to just have fun"* that I started getting really vulnerable and actually my connections blew up. I was making a real impact and having real fun.

LinkedIn is very male dominated too. That meant the connections, banter and fun was with both men and women. I'd forgotten how easy it was for me to connect with both and when I saw the impact of my *authentic* self-love message had started to impact the guys, in just the same way as the women, I realised I'd been given all of this knowledge about self-love for a reason and that it needed my unique voice to attract the right people to me. That made me free to just have fun and make myself laugh. I didn't dilute my dark humour or sarcasm, so I did put some people off, but the people I attracted were really ready to hear what I knew to be true...

They were enough.
Life gets messy but even in all the mess we're all still enough.

I didn't need to water down this message or water down myself. Speaking freely was liberating and started to filter into all other areas of my life. I could feel my cage start to break and I really started to connect with people.

I felt stronger.

Then, lockdown hit.

Within days of lockdown being announced I felt more caged than ever. So, I did what I always did when I felt unable to help myself... I thought how can I help others?

Mindset meets. The answer was scary. Daily mindset meets. I knew this would cause huge issues with my partner, so I sold it to him by saying it was to promote my coaching, but that wasn't my intent. I knew I had the power to help but the thought of doing these daily zooms made me full of fear. I knew this meant more than just some marketing, I felt like I was being pulled to do this by the Universe.

1 hr a day I thought, to give people just 1 hour of my day, for just one week, to help in a way I knew I could, with no money intentions behind it, surely that would be doable.

After sitting with the idea for a few days and feeling like it would kill me through nerves alone, I followed my fear and set it up. I had no idea of how it would go, how it would affect my already rocky marriage or what people would think of me.

The amount of times I wanted to give up and cancel the calls in that first week was every fucking call. My partner was calling me selfish, and we were arguing before each one, sometimes with me sobbing minutes before I was meant to go on. But go on I did, and I decided that a week wasn't enough. We were having new people coming on every day and we could have all talked for hours.

There was a core group now coming on regularly and I knew they had my back supporting the newbies when things got rough at home. I'd invited my "bestie in real life" to join and she fit in amazingly and told me how much of an impact the group was having on her daily life.

Lockdown V.1 was hard on everyone, but we had a little group we could rely on. To pick up our spirits, to give genuine support and to dish out love bombs at the perfect times.

Weeks went by and this little group became family. Without this family I wouldn't be here writing this book, nah fuck it, FINISHING this book right now. We no longer do the daily zooms, but we are there for each other exactly when we need it (which has been multiple times a day for me with birthing this book!) and we accept each other unconditionally.

Through the past couple of years, we've helped each other through homelessness, marriage breakdowns, losing jobs, not being able to find jobs, family dying, pets dying, lockdowns galore, the whole world going to shit, illnesses, depression and that's not even it! We've celebrated the great together too... the highs and the lows... A complete village. Men and women being a powerful force together, that all started with a question on Linky[42]... *How's your mindset?*

Imagine if I had stayed vanilla and never been brave enough to use my true voice?
Imagine if I had appeased my partner and not followed this soul niggle?
Imagine if I had let my fear of what other people thought of me stop me from helping how I knew would make a difference?

The Rona Love Story for this bunch of fucking amazing peeps around the world wouldn't have happened.

Everyone has their own unique qualities, strengths, opinions, perceptions and beauty to bring into one another's lives. Your family and friends are anyone who you choose to allow to touch yours. With all relationships there's opportunity for conflict, love, support or contrast but the extent that you allow it to move and grow your life is completely up to you. You are attracting your current relationships with your beliefs and how aligned you're allowing yourself to be.

This is why family matters so much to self-love. Once you realise that the happiness and satisfaction in your life is solely your own responsibility and that you are not responsible for anyone else's, it allows you to see that the relationship with yourself is totally the most important relationship you can ever nurture. Once you've got that down and you actually care about yourself, like yourself, feel comfortable with who you are and feel safe to be authentically you.... that's when you will attract the most beautiful relationships into your life.

It's OK to feel like you want to belong, it's OK to want to know you have people who love and support you, but you won't need to base your happiness or worth on other people's opinions of you. Others will be there to enrich your already rich life and you

---

[42] Linky: Cute, affectionate term for LinkedIn

are there to do the same for them. It's so freeing because as soon as you let go of that need for love or acceptance you will get it tenfold.

I guess what I'm trying to say is you can find your village anywhere you want. As long as you are brave, authentic and allow yourself to be vulnerable, **then** take inspired action - even when it's hard - the people who you need and who need you will be drawn to you...and the results will be nothing short of magic.

You deserve all that beautiful shizzle.

Chapter Eleven - When Life Gets Messy

Trust...
Trust...
Surrender.

I'm sitting here in tears. This is the chapter I've been fearing the most. This is the chapter I've been running from for all these years. This chapter is the main reason why this book has taken so fucking long to get written.

It starts off simple, but my Body knows what's coming. Grief. My Body is scared shitless. Sobbing. I want to eat. I want booze. I want distraction. I want anything. I would take anything rather than facing up to the bag of trauma and emotion that I've been carrying around with me every fucking day since it happened. The heavy weight of trauma my Body has lovingly carried for me because I'm afraid I'm not strong enough to cope...or if I let a little out will I ever be able to stop? Or if I let it all out what's next? Am I really ready to heal? I don't feel ready. I feel weak and vulnerable and just so so so fucking scared.

Leaning into your fear when it's work, family or goals is hard enough. But when it's grief, when it feels like your soul is ripping in half, when it's an actual possibility that you will end up battered, broken and never the same again...this is when you need to tap into something deeper. It's too much for your Body, because we are not designed to feel pain like this. This is when your Higher Self needs to scoop you up, wrap her arms around you and tell you that you are going to be OK. Life gets messy, but you will survive. Battered and bruised, but never broken.

Trust
Trust
Surrender

It's going to be OK.

It's easy to be upbeat and positive when things are going well, it's even easier to show the world your best side when it's all going to shit.

When things go wrong and life gets tough, that's when loving yourself can get messy.

These are the times when we need to love ourselves more than ever. These are the times we need to love ourselves harder.

Just how do we do that?

When Life Seems Against You

Things are going relatively good, you have a roof above your head, people you love and food in your belly.

You're feeling creative.
You're feeling happy.
You're feeling hope.

Then *bang* something breaks in your car; do you have enough money to fix it? You get caught in the rain, you miss the bus, you start to walk...that voice inside your head starts to murmur: *"Why do things like this always happen to me?"*

You get home, wet to the bone and there's a letter on your doormat. It's an overdue bill - they are taking you to court because you forgot to pay...the voice returns, louder this time: *"Great I'm useless and now I owe £100 extra, why the fuck didn't I pay the damn thing?"*

You go to make dinner, there's nothing in the cupboards except tins of beans, the voice now screams: *"Oh My literal Lordy, I haven't even been shopping yet!? Beans on toast it is, I guess. No dinner for you, knob cheese[43]."*

---

[43] Knob Cheese: Do you really want to know?

You burn the toast... Now there's a barrage of insults you start calling yourself.

You catch a glimpse of yourself in the mirror... "*What a mess, no one will ever love me. I look disgusting*" you say sobbing into your cold beans straight outta the tin.

Can you hear your Inner Bitch piping up? Oh, she's happy to come out to play. She's been bored (and quiet) while you've been happy.

Things like this can happen during the day, sometimes it lasts a week or for some people they feel like their whole life has been like this and life is just always working against them.

Are you singing the *Friends* theme song too?

Can you still love yourself when life looks like this?
The short answer is yes, of course you can. You need to more than ever. The trouble is, how do you love yourself despite the crap and the insults you hurl at yourself? Why is it so important to?

Ah, that beautiful Inner Bitch that we spoke about in Chapter 3. Almost everyone has her lurking in the shadows during good times, then she springs out with the "*I told you so's*" and throws "*you're so crap*" at you even when the smallest things go wrong.

Let me give you a hypothetical. If your laptop breaks down and your thought process is:

It's the end of the world as we know it
Shit like this always happens to me
I may as well give up
What a fucking idiot, I'm so useless

It means you are reinforcing this situation and using it as proof to back up what you already believe...i.e., *I'm a fuckup*

Remember your brain believes whatever you tell her.

With a little bit of compassion and self-love you can turn this thought process around.

Wow I'm so glad I did a backup
So grateful I can get it fixed
I really appreciate my laptop now

It's a mindset shift that uncovers a deeper belief inside. That things going wrong doesn't reflect on you, your entire life or your worth.

Sometimes when the Body doesn't believe you are ready or can cope, she will decide to take over and use fear to lovingly protect you from the situation. Just by telling her that you can cope and that you ARE safe, it means she can relax and not feel like the whole of the weight of the situation falls just on her.

I'd like to take this moment to point out that sometimes your brain and body come together to make the decision that you are not strong enough to cope with some situation, circumstance or event and they are right on some rare occasions. But mostly, they won't be.

In extreme circumstances such as trauma, grief or child abuse though, your Body will take over for good reason.

Your Body will trickle your memories, emotions and you may subconsciously block stuff out until you or your Body decides that you are strong enough.

If this event is recent or you are feeling weak, you need to feel completely grateful to your Body for doing this. It's a survival mechanism for when the pain is just too much, or the feelings are just too overwhelming. The period when grief or trauma hits you in waves is your Body's way of giving you Grace.

Grace:
1. Smoothness and elegance of movement
2. Courteous goodwill

Writing this book has been a lesson in grace for me. I'm someone who loves instant gratification. In terms of life getting tough and money getting tougher, sometimes I need it. As you also may have realised, I'm a perfectionist in recovery. I need things done, like, yesterday and they need to be perfect which is the exact opposite of the messy, fucking long process of writing a book. So sticking with the writing process has taken years because of my Body taking over, I've had to have pure love for my Body for giving me so much protection and pure grace to myself for taking so long.

Perfect timings.

Debt

It's hard to put your trust in doing something so long term as this when everyday life and pressures are knocking (loudly) at your door. I've always felt the pressure of needing to make money. One area that I've always hidden or avoided talking about (mainly because I used to be really ashamed about it) is my financial situation. I really couldn't afford to write a book, let alone the time to write a really long-arsed[44] book without any expectation of a financial return. Although there have been times when I've been flying high with making money, the shame and immense pressure of debt has made it a real effort for me to not live with a lack mindset. Fuck knows, once you go down that rabbit hole life starts looking really shitty.

People do love a rag to riches story but I'm here to give you the lowdown while I'm still in my rags. My glorious, glamorous Boat Folk[45] freedom rags.

This is the shit the 50K coaches like to paint their pretty Canva flowers all over...let's get it all out in the open.

Most people have debt.
Most people live hand to mouth.

_____

[44] Long-arsed: Really fucking long.
[45] Boat Folk: Hardy badass crew of peeps who live on boats

Most people feel shitty about their financial situation.
Most people feel shame, guilt, stress and lack when it comes to money.

Not having money makes life fucking hard.

No one talks about this shit because

It's depressing
It hurts the ego and soul
It doesn't sell

If someone is trying to sell you something, they want you to have the problem so that you either pay them to fix it or are inspired by how they fixed it for themselves. Showing the whole fucking world your own messed up situation, especially when it comes to money (whether you are a coach or not) brings up so much shame and guilt especially when you have kids. Debt or money struggles suck the hope out of you and who wants to hear about that?

No one (supposedly). Especially when you are a "professional" or run your own business. So, you just decide to hide away, struggling on your own, trying to put on a brave face that everything is great...it's no wonder people print such an unrealistic "highlight" reel on social media and are afraid to show their true self.

Guess what? You don't have to do that!

You can be messy and still professional, struggling and still capable, real and still fucking beautiful. Almost everyone will go through ebbs and flows with money, especially if you work for yourself. As we saw in chapter 7, money has nothing to do with your worth as a person.

I've been in a place where money has been flowing, getting 3k clients and I've been in a place where I've been working three jobs just to make ends meet. I had a fire and lost everything...didn't even own a pair of shoes and then I've been sunning myself in 5* hotels in America.

I've been at a place where dropping £300 on shopping was just an expense and where £10 was the difference between me eating or not. I've felt shame about debt, and I've felt grateful for what my debt has allowed me to do.

Thing is, whether I'm flying high or struggling in the depths counting my pennies, I'm still the same Mirrie. Yes, life gets easier, life feels lighter, and you have more opportunities to actually LIVE when you have money but the person you are, and your worth, does not change.

Money has no emotion other than what you give it.
Money has no emotion other than what you give it.

So as soon as you can view money for what it is, just a blank canvas and realise it's our brain that colours it and makes it:

Good or Evil
Hard or Easy
Desperate or Flowing
Shameful or Exciting

Then you can see that self-love can change your beliefs and mindset around struggling with money too.

If you've ever had a bailiff come to your door, then you'll know first-hand the disgusting taste of shame that hits you. Seeing someone waiting there with a fucking clipboard and a judgy look on their scary mug fills you with fear. Even when you know all your rights (i.e., don't let the fucker set foot in the door) the guilt, shame and fear that's trudged up in that split second makes you want to vomit.

Let's break down where the feelings are coming from.

Fear -

What will they do to me
What if this happens
What happens when I tell them I can't afford to pay them

Shame -

What will the neighbours think
Why am I so useless with money
Why me

Guilt -

How did I let it come to this
What's this teaching my kids
When will this ever end

That's a whole lot of questions and a whole lot of emotions to work through before you've even answered the fucking door. The whole experience just leaves you hopeless. As much as I'm sure there are some nice bailiffs out there, just doing their jobs, most that I'd met have been condescending bullies.

But what if the bailiff standing there had no reflection on you as a person, your current situation or your worth as a person? If their opinion of you, the neighbour's opinion of you or society's opinion of you didn't reflect or affect *your* opinion of you, then how would you feel?

Remember money is blank. It has no emotion. It is just numbers to the value of stuff. Most bailiffs have no authority to do anything anyway and they know that, so they use shame and fear in order to control you in that moment. They know the panic you'll feel as you open the door. Their job is to get blood out of a stone. They know you are in financial trouble before you've even opened your mouth so of course that's what they will try to use.

Imagine you are opening the door, you feel the fear, the judgements and the shame but you KNOW that it's a belief that doesn't serve you. So you fling the door open with a smile on your face and exclaim "Hi!" like the fucker is your best friend!

"I'm SO glad you are here! I've let that bill get on top of me, and I've been afraid to sort it out... I'm sorry you had to make a trip out here! but grateful you have come to help me sort it out! Fancy a cuppa tea?"

IMAGINE THE LOOK ON THEIR FACE!

Think about how powerful you would feel in that moment. How much more in control you would feel. We hide away from this shit not just because it feels crappy to see our true situation down on paper but also because it reflects how we see who we are as a person, our core beliefs about ourselves and to what extent we are fucking up our lives.

With the simple mindset shift of looking at your problems with self-love, you see past mistakes with money as just that ...past mistakes.

Just as YOU are allowed to be imperfect, YOUR LIFE is allowed to be imperfect. Life is unpredictable, sometimes messy, sometimes beautiful, but it will be all of these things regardless of who you are. There are going to be some things in your life that you can't control but you can always control how you react to them. Be kind to yourself. Be kind to Tomorrow's You. Drop the shame around your current situation and look forward. Forgive yourself for what you didn't know before. Now you've got self-love and infinite possibilities on your side, *anything can happen.*

Sometimes though life gets so particularly shit you will feel like your entire world is crumbling down around you. Death is just about the messiest life can get.

How do you love yourself when you've lost everything?

Grief

When I first started writing this book the whole reason was because, through having my missed miscarriage, I learned how to love myself. It was during the hardest time of my life, and I did it by holding onto hope, the feeling of compassion for my Body for the very first time, the realisation that all my Body wanted to do was protect my baby and all she'd ever been trying to do was protect me. My whole life, no matter how badly I treated her, abused her, saw her or even hated her, she still wanted to protect me and the people I love, including my little spark of a baby bean.

When my Body finally let go of my baby, I was as close to death as I've ever been and drifted in and out of consciousness in front of my children and my husband.

In the hospital my husband lost count of the times he thought he'd lost me. My Body fought hard, and I survived, and it was only after a month of being so ill I could barely stand without fainting, that my Body was strong enough to allow me the honour of doulaing my friend as she gave birth to her beautiful baby. Although it took a lot longer to fully recover, I learnt to be gentle with my Body, actually look after her and allowed myself to actually "be ill".

It was after doing that, that my self-love hit me. It was in one instant of realising why she had been protecting me, and my whole world changed.

Self-love and knowing that I deserve to look after myself and not constantly hate on myself was nothing short of life-changing. Like I've said; that's what inspired this book.

"When times are tough" has become the phrase for when you get messy.

As you may have gathered, I was dreading writing this chapter. So, I started writing it one paragraph at a time. For a month it dragged on, but I was preoccupied. At the time my dad just had an operation, my husband was having a cancer scare, I had just had a baby and my big brother was in hospital.

I kept thinking, when everyone is at home and on the mend, I'll push through this chapter in no time. I'll find the strength to describe the depression I'd felt after my miscarriage. I'd find the strength to let people in and describe just how much of a beautiful fucked up mess I was and how I learned to love myself regardless. Because that's the most important time to love yourself.

I was waiting, for a time I'd feel less vulnerable, not knowing that I would look back on this time marvelling at just how strong I'd been and how life was going to show me just how messy it could get.

It was an innocent, perfectly normal Thursday afternoon when I got a phone call that would change my life forever.

The day before I had been on a mission, my brother had been in hospital for a month but every time I'd visited, he was his normal cheeky self and they kept telling us that he would be home anytime soon. They kept taking him to critical care because he needed more oxygen, but we got told that this was normal procedure and that when he didn't need it, then they could get him back on the normal ward again. We were told this was pretty standard and nothing to worry about. My mum and dad had gone to see him but because my baby had a cold, I thought I'd wait until he was back on the normal ward to visit so I didn't make anything worse. Mum and Dad said he was laughing and joking so I wasn't too worried and knew he was in the safest place he could be for what he was going through right now.

So anyway, it was a Wednesday and my brother's 20th Wedding Anniversary but with the month we'd all had I hadn't even got them anything. They were supposed to be on holiday but kept having to rearrange the dates and I knew my brother Sam would be gutted to still be in hospital, so I wanted to do something nice for them both. Sam and his wife were just couple goals. They had a crazy relationship but honestly, I don't think I've ever met two people who loved each other more. His wife had been juggling their three kids and still going to the hospital every single day and I'd never been so grateful that my brother had such a bloody amazing family.

Mum had mentioned about maybe getting them a cake, so I spent the day arranging a photo cake to be made. I felt an urgency but the cake place said it would be a day and I tried to tell myself that this was just my OCD playing up, so to relax because a day won't make too much of a difference, especially as

Sam was only eating jelly so he'd have to wait a few days for his slice anyway.

On Thursday I took the cake to my mums and told her I wanted to go and give Sam a cuddle even just for a few minutes, so he knew I was thinking of him. While I was at mum's, they got a text saying he'd taken a turn for the worse and so they told me to stay at home but promised they would keep me up to date. He was still joking about with the nurses so there was no need to worry.

I was getting mixed messages all afternoon but had an uneasy feeling and at about 5pm my mum called me to tell me the doctor had pulled dad aside and said there was nothing more that they could do, Sam probably only had a couple of weeks to live.

To say I was in shock was the understatement of my fucking life, but I got my baby in his car seat and drove the half an hour to the hospital in our rickety old car praying it wouldn't break down on the way. Praying the doctor was wrong. Praying my mum had got it wrong. Praying that this was just a mistake.

My brain did awful things to me on the way there. I've not spoken to anyone about that journey. Thankfully my baby slept. I remember keeping my breath calm and repeating "Hope, Hope there's always hope" and during the eternity to get there with my brain going wild to calm to wild again, I kept saying to myself out loud:

"Brain, thank you for trying to protect me but it's time for you to rest now. Body it's your turn, please take over, please look after us."

I got safely to the carpark and my Body was on autopilot as I got a ticket and quietly wrapped my sweet sleeping baby to my chest. Indie was only 3 months old, and I felt a wave of calm sweep over me as I smelled his tiny head.

When I saw my dad in the family waiting room he broke down. At that point it was only the 2nd time I'd ever seen him cry. I've lost count of how many times I've seen him cry since that day.

The doctor was now saying my big brother had days left, maybe a week. I knew doctors had been wrong before and I knew I had to cling on to any hope we had. I cuddled my brother, we spoke, he sat up and I had hope. Miracles happen every day, right?

We got dad sorted to stay the night and I went home with Indie and mum. My Body took over and I was strong when I couldn't sleep and my brain was trying to run away with me. I did yoga and meditated. I slept. I cried. I hugged my mum. I told her she must have hope.

But at 3am we got the phone call that he was already losing the fight, so we needed to come and say goodbye.

When I got there, he was still talking, and he was scared. I couldn't allow myself to believe that this was it. I told him to stay strong but deep down he knew. I believe he knew. His kids came to the hospital very shortly afterwards and he had the chance to cuddle them and spend some time with them. I still had indie strapped to me and took on the role of mother hen. Trying to keep his boys as happy and comfortable as they could be, even making them laugh and playing with them because I knew that's what Sam would have done for me.

It was hours of me trying to look after everyone who came. Popping in to see my brother and leaving again to cry silent tears, trying to keep it all together. Changing nappies and making hot chocolates while dealing with the most powerful trauma I'd ever been through.

It felt like a bad dream, but my Body took over. She gave me such grace.

I remember a nurse telling me to take a minute on my own and holding Indie for me. I fell to the floor uncontrollably sobbing but the moment Indie started crying for me my Body just snapped into this strong mode again, instantly stopped crying and scooped him up to give him some boob. Once again, my Body carried my emotions for me.

I lost my brother at about 10:30am. He really, really fought but we kept telling him that it was OK, to do whatever he needed to do. That we'd keep his family safe. He died surrounded in love.

Over to YesterMirrie as she was writing this chapter...

"I never, ever imagined I'd be writing this chapter a week after my own brother's funeral.

I never ever imagined I'd be dealing not only with depression, but with my OCD the worst it's ever been, my eating out of control and with this fucking painful raw grief.

I never ever thought I'd have to learn all over how to love myself through grief and loss.

And yet here I am. Loving yourself is hard when all you are feeling is regret."

You talk to someone who hasn't experienced this type of loss and honestly there's no way for them to know how it feels.

There's only one way that you truly "get" what grief does to you and your family and that's when you are in the thick of it. It rips a hole through your entire existence, not only is your future never going to be the same again, but all of your memories are now also bittersweet. Your past feels different. It's all-consuming. There's so much to sort out afterwards too. I remember being in the supermarket, just hours after going to the funeral parlour and the whole family sitting with my brother, telling each other stories and crying while laughing at the same time. One moment you are sitting with your dead brother and the next you're buying bananas in Asda. Life just becomes surreal.

After the funeral life doesn't change for you, but for everyone else, life just carries on. It's like you are walking around on the edge of life and death's door but it's your little secret as you watch people get stressed about tiny things. Honestly you just can't get it unless you've experienced it.

Thank fuck, eh? If you knew what was to come, life would be unbearable right?

Except even afterwards, it isn't unbearable - well, not all of the time.

The seven stages of grief are shock, denial, guilt, bargaining, anger, depression and acceptance.

But we all feel like the stages will happen in a certain order or over a certain number of days, weeks or months and once we have got through one, that will be it, it will be over and then we will "get through " the next stage.

But in grief there is no timeline, and they are not stages but rather moments. They are mixed up and no one knows how they'll feel, when they'll feel or even why they are feeling what they are.

Writing and editing this nearly five years later and I still couldn't tell you what stage I'm at. It took so much for me to even tell my story, to get to the point where I felt "strong enough" (I didn't by the way, I just knew in my gut it was the right time) to visit this again feels like I've just gone through this epic journey.

I accept that Sam is gone, kinda. It still feels very unreal. I'm proud of myself and I know that he would be proud of me too. Sat here on my little boat, surviving a snowstorm and keeping my boys happy and warm. Facing my fears and emotions and loving myself regardless. He would be proud that I followed my heart and followed my freedom. Fuck, I believe that his spirit is out there fucking proud and happy as he watches his boys grow up and his family thrive even with all this sadness and trauma.

Now back to YesterMirrie, just a week after the funeral being a beautiful, brave badass without even knowing it...

"I thought because I loved myself and that me and my inner bitch are besties (my inner voice is super kind and understanding) that I would not feel guilty- I mean I was done with ever feeling guilty because I've accepted myself as the imperfect human I am and I

*know guilt serves no purpose unless it's to motivate you to put
something right...*

Grief did not get that memo
Guilt did not get that memo

*I'm wracked with guilt. In my life I've only had a couple of regrets –
things I'd genuinely change if I could. But they are also to do with
death and with death there is no going back.*

*Now, right at this moment, I'm completely swimming in regret.
And I'm so unsure of myself, who I am, everything I've done, of how
I feel.*

*Some lovely random person on the internet just told me that I'm
allowed to heal, and I breathed a sigh of relief. It didn't last long.
But I keep reminding myself of what I tell other people: there's no
wrong way to feel, you are allowed to feel whatever you are feeling
right now. It's so easy to say that to someone else, I need to give
myself that grace too."*

If there was ever a time to be allowed to be unsure of yourself,
it's after a huge loss. Whether you are grieving a family member,
unborn baby or just a different future to what you've believed
was possible, there's no wrong way to feel. Guilt is working to
help and protect you, but that still should not be an excuse for
your inner bitch to awaken and start shouting at you.
Compassion is key here and it's vital that you keep that
compassion and empathy for yourself because you **need** self-
care now more than ever. You need to be extra kind to yourself.
Give yourself as much time as you need.

That lost feeling is normal and is yet another way your Body
protects you, and actually, when you're in the fog of deep grief,
it's OK not to be found for a while.

The other day my friend wrote on Facebook about losing her
mother. She said I can't just grieve for one, I grieve for all. That
hit me like a ton of bricks. We say things like "Time heals" but
really do we ever heal from grief? I lost my best friend nearly 16
years ago. Sometimes I'm still hit by grief like a punch to the gut

and get transported back to that moment when I was woken up with the phone call to tell me she'd had an accident and died. The pain is still overwhelming and very very real, and when I grieve for her, or my spark or my brother or my grandparents...I'm grieving for all of them. The pain and loss never changes.

But you change.
You grow.
You continue to somehow live.

Although the pain never gets smaller, your life, your Body and your emotions are expanding. You grow around the pain like a strong tree with roots around a big rock. The rock remains the same size but as the tree gets taller, as the roots get longer and the tree gets stronger...the rock is easier to manage, easier to cope with, easier to grow around.

If you are going through the trauma of grief right now, I'm so glad you found this book. Read these words as a big fat soul hug surrounding you with love and compassion. Connecting to your Higher Self is connecting to the collective consciousness and whatever you believe has happened to the person you are grieving, know that their pure love energy can never die. They love you and want you to have that kind inner voice. They don't want you to live with regrets, guilt or pain.

Everything you did or didn't do is actually OK. Make peace with yourself, my darling. You are so loved, so supported and surrounded by the love of all before you. You deserve to feel that peace. You deserve to feel that love. Death is not the end, just another form of expansion. Grief is probably the most messy you will ever get. It's human, it's raw and it's a beautiful expression of all the love you have for that other being. Your Higher Self knows this and will gather you up and love you so hard, it's time for you to allow yourself to feel, heal and let it in.

Negative Feelings

Being a positive person doesn't mean being all buttercups and sunshine every day. Real life just isn't really like that. There's going to be days when you are feeling negative, and the negativity may hit you like a passing cloud, or it may stay with you all day like a thunderous storm.

At the end of this chapter there's the Messy "Un-tools" that will help your mindset but sometimes nothing will work - and it's hard to feel gratitude in these moments, it's hard to feel joy, sometimes it's hard to feel anything except anger!

Why is it when one moment gets us feeling negative it can start a spiral into suddenly our whole life is shit? Like, it can't just be about the one person that pushed past us in a queue, all of a sudden it's now how shit our morning was, and how so many people take us for granted, we spin about that boy who rejected us in high school and how our house is so cluttered so that means we must be a shit mother and we've been trying to lose weight but we ate a donut and so now we are a failure at everything we've ever tried to do...

And breathe...

This negative spiral is yet another way our Body is trying to protect us.

It starts with a mood or a feeling and it's shitty; it's not nice.

It doesn't feel pleasant to sit with and suddenly alarm bells pop up in your Body because she senses you are about to face emotional pain.

So, your Body lets you sit with this negative feeling, empathises with why you are feeling this way and lets you see it's only one aspect of your day/life and it doesn't reflect on your worth or who you are as a person...right?

Nah that would be far too easy! Your Body goes into full blown protection mode. Like a mama bear when she thinks someone is going to hurt her cub, your Body will shut down all emotions, she's like: "*Numb the bitch quick! She can't handle any of this!*"

With all emotions in shutdown mode, you still won't be able to stop thinking about the "thing" that set you off so now your Body gives you two options:

Go into victim mode
Go into angry mode

The only feelings your Body can't seem to block is you feeling sorry for yourself and getting angry (I.e. finding someone to blame)

This sends you into survival mode, your Body knows you can cope with this and lap this energy up. Whichever one you choose to switch to the outcome is always the same.

You spiral downwards in a tornado shitstorm - sucking in every part of your life and spitting them out as the worst things in the world. Everything gets sucked in and everything sucks and it's not fucking fair, so it's time to blame, get angry or just feel fucking hopeless.

Suddenly, instead of coping with just one thing that's upset you, you are now facing a lifetime of regrets, anger or unattainableness. A lifetime's worth of every problem or shortcoming you view yourself to have.

And now it just all feels too much. Ultimately if you go into the eye of the storm, there's a reason that deep down you blame yourself for everything. Remember how we've already talked about blame? Whether we are blaming someone else or ourselves, we go into victim mode, where everything is "poor me"

We do this because it's overwhelming dealing with a lifetime of stress all in one sitting and victim mode takes away all of our power which conveniently takes away all of our responsibility (this happens even when we are blaming ourselves). It takes away our energy to change anything about our situation so that means we are allowed to stay in this angry childlike state for as long as we want. With no hope or power, it feels like:

We can't change the situation.
We can't change our life.
We can't change our feelings.
We can't change our mindset.

We say things like:

This always happens to me!
What's the point?
Nobody cares!
I may as well give up.

What does this achieve for the Body who wants to protect you from emotional pain? Because it will feel like you are swimming in pain at that moment.

It allows your Body to keep you stuck. She now has no fear of change as long as she can keep you in this state (angry or victim). She knows you will feel like a helpless child and so...

You won't be brave...
You won't take any chances...
You won't make yourself vulnerable...
You won't be self-confident enough to make any changes...
You won't feel strong enough to address or deal with any *real* feelings or confrontation.

You won't reach out to other people...
You won't trust other people...
You won't trust yourself...
You won't even risk being nice.

You will feel miserable,
You will feel "Not Enough".

But you will be safe.

Safe from "possible pain"

Safe and stuck.

And some people stay like this for years.

Living but not really living.
Feeling but not really feeling.

It's not quite survival mode, not quite depression but it still sucks hairy balls.

Maybe your Body doesn't want to feel either, like she is scared of your being able to cope with it, not being able to cope with it, changing in some way and opening yourself up to the opportunity of being hurt again or even maybe it's hard for your Body to let go of these emotions so she's avoiding it as much for her as she is for you?

But here's the kicker: everyone has days like this. Everyone has feelings like this. Not everyone spirals out of control in the shitstorm though.

So, what's their secret? Why can some people just feel crappy but not allow it to affect their whole day or even let it seep into weeks or years?

The answer is already in the question…*they feel.*

If you find negative feelings affecting your day or making you feel shitty even when you know you are going down a spiral, please don't beat yourself up over it. We are not only imperfect beings, most of us also have not been taught this simple fact:

Feelings need to be acknowledged, validated and expressed before they can be healed and released.

That's it.

The secret formula…

The Feeling Process.

Maybe this process hurts our bodies as much as it hurts our spirits and that's why almost every person on this glorious planet blocks their feels out to some extent, in some way or another but this is what every feeling needs in order to heal.

Every feeling inside your Body is needed.

Not one person will come earthside and go through their entire life without feeling jealousy, anger, joy, love, hate, hurt, excitement, fear and every feeling in between.

Every emotion you can name has a reason behind it and teaches us about the world and about ourselves. Our feelings are like a map for our entire life, and we are killing ourselves with all these unhealthy blocking mechanisms just because we don't want to feel them!

Why? Because as children we are taught that some feelings are "good", and some are "bad". Some are "acceptable" to show, and some are not. Some kids have even been taught that some feelings are unacceptable to even have.

Over years of being told, shouted at or even punished for this, we not only believe it and push our feelings down, but we also become scared of what it may mean about ourselves when we feel them.

We say "*push our feelings down*" because it is impossible to just not have undesirable feelings even if you see a feeling as bad, you'll still have that feeling there.

Say you've been taught that feeling jealousy, for example, is bad. It means when you feel it, you'll subconsciously believe that you are bad, which is nuts because everyone feels everything at some point.

A feeling tells us a truth about ourselves or our situation, it doesn't define who we are, unless we act wrongfully on it or live in it.

Let's stick with jealousy because it's a feeling that doesn't feel nice, there aren't many people who actually enjoy being jealous, are there?

When you are triggered by jealousy you won't stop feeling it until you go through it. It's needing you to explore it.

Acknowledge:
"I feel jealous of Lucy because she is going on holiday *again* and she always has really nice clothes."

Fuck I sound petty. Lucy is my friend. But she always looks so fucking perfect and has such a perfect life...it's not fair...

This is the point where you choose where to go:

Angry Mode
Victim Mode
OR Feeling Process mode

Validate:
"I have been struggling with money for a while and I feel less than worthy because I can't afford a normal life, let alone a holiday or new clothes right now. Lucy talking about her holiday has made me see how upset I am about my situation"

Express:
"Even though I feel jealous I still love, honour and accept myself. Even though I am feeling unworthy because of my money situation, I still love, honour and accept myself. Even though I can't afford a holiday I still love, honour and forgive myself."

And in this case, because the jealousy is not Lucy's fault, healing may look like this:

Heal:
"I love Lucy and it's not her fault I feel this way. I honour my feelings and forgive myself for feeling jealous, sad and even unworthy (even though I know I don't need forgiveness for this.) I have the power to change my money situation but even if I choose not to, I still love, honour and accept myself."

The goal is not to just "get rid" of the feeling as quickly as possible or even explain it away. Once we know that no feeling means that we are "good or bad" it means we don't fear exploring the "why" we are feeling it and then once they are felt and honoured, they are happy to be released until they are needed again.

Remember, no feeling is good or bad but some feelings make us feel awesome and some make us feel crappy. They don't reflect who we are, and they are all needed.

So even when you are in a funk and you can't seem to get out of it or don't feel strong enough to deal with it, you are still worthy of your love.

You don't need toxic, fake positivity or a mask to cover it.

Whether you feel great or shitty...
Positive or negative...
Hopeful or down in the dumps...
Grateful or jealous...

You can still love yourself,
Feel your feels.

All of your power is in the now.

Give yourself the courage and bravery, the time, the grace and the compassion to just "be" in the feelings. You don't need to live there, just acknowledge, validate, express and heal. Loving yourself at "every stage" no matter how long it takes.

You are allowed to feel.

Depression, Mental Health and Chronic Illness

In my twenties there was a time when I was practically housebound for a year, it was too painful to even sit in a car. I had to give up work, I was on so many tablets that I had to take tablets to combat the side effects of other tablets, sometimes I'd spend hours in the bath because codeine wouldn't work. I ate too much, drank too much, couldn't sleep and because I was so often bent over in pain I was severely depressed.

I always felt like my Body was betraying me, like how could she treat me this way? Especially when doctors couldn't find a reason for the pain after my first operation. I felt so much anger at my Body.

So useless.
So betrayed.

This wasn't my first time feeling like I was battling with my Body. Growing up I had multiple panic attacks a day to the point where I would just faint. There was no reasonable trigger and it impacted me so much I couldn't even sit my normal GCSE's.

After a lifetime of my Body serving me, me abusing her with partying every night, eating shit, going to the gym and biking miles every day, losing my best friend and never allowing my Body to grieve, pushing down every emotion...I still couldn't see why she would stop working. I didn't see her as mortal, I didn't see her as having any purpose apart from looking good and actually working.

I didn't have a shred of sympathy or empathy for her.

I was betraying her.

I had been betraying her my whole life and after the doctors couldn't explain it? I was still using too many drugs (legal but destructive), alcohol and food to push down pain, push down anger, push down grief, push down imperfection, push down limitations, push down everything I've ever known.

Where was it all supposed to go? Looking back now, I see my Body as abused, neglected and just so sad with no way of escape.

But I didn't care about her. I didn't see the fact that she needed to escape from the way I was treating her, all I cared about was that I could no longer use her to escape from me.

I then saw my Body's weaknesses as my own fault for not looking after her for all those years but it's totally possible of course that I'd have been this way even if I had looked after her.

To a certain extent, eating right, moving your body and looking after yourself helps your Body stay fit and healthy but there's still a chance you might suffer regardless of how you treat her.

Your Body is not perfect
Your Body is not indestructible
Your Body will not last forever

The goal out there always seems to be to fix.

Sometimes that can't be done.
Sometimes it can.

The goal is to love yourself even if it feels like your Body is broken.

Accepting your Body as a mortal being with weaknesses, imperfections and failures, but still being worthy of love means we can love ourselves broken, even if we don't understand the why.

Take depression, for example. There've been times I've been actively doing the stuff I know helps depression (fresh air, good food, exercise etc.), nothing is immediately wrong with my life, no major dramas going on. I wake up OK and by lunchtime I feel like there's no point in living anymore.

Now we all have negative thoughts from time to time, but have you ever felt so hopeless it feels like you are running a marathon in treacle, and your only goal was just to get dressed by 3pm or make yourself a fucking cup of tea?

If you have depression, you know where I'm coming from, maybe a little too much. It's no wonder our bodies want to find a way to block this out and lovingly protect us from these feelings, but how do we repay this kindness?

We beat ourselves up about it, not seeing it as an illness but as a weakness. Not just a weakness but a hateful, disgusting trait that we define ourselves with. No wonder we belittle and get angry with ourselves when we get like this, especially when there's no obvious reason to feel this way. Depression is one thing, but deep depression is a whole other level. It feels like there's no way out, nowhere to hide from yourself and it's a dark and hateful place to be.

Surely you can't love yourself while you are depressed? Surely that needs fixing first?

Two weeks ago, I was soaring high, writing was going well, home ed was amazing, I was down the allotment every day, beach a couple of times a day, created my new website, feeling so happy and so hopeful...then *BAM*...deep depression.

Depression for me feels like I'm walking and living deep in treacle. Everything is slow and so much effort. I can almost touch the happy go lucky me, but she feels unreal, just out of my reach at all times. Like a floppy fish gasping for water but I can't quite move my Body to get there.

I have so much I want to do but moving from the bed or sofa is hard work. It's too much bother. It's like I can feel my brain is actually ill. All sensations are heightened and overwhelming. So fucking tired, bored of life, paralysed by both the day ending or beginning.

When you are in this place your brain is actually ill. Unlike some people, I don't feel like this is a mindset issue, a lack of gratitude for life or an excuse to be lazy. This is a situation where your Body and brain need to recover, rest and heal just like any other illness.

The trouble is the way society sees mental health as a whole, that it's avoidable or just in your head (no shit, Sherlock), so it's often like the person suffering is actually at fault.

Depression makes it easy for us to feel useless and like it's all our fault and yet we fall into a sucky victim mode too. It's easy to hate yourself, blame yourself and go into an even worse place.

There are ways to help your Body when you go to that dark place but remember our goal is to heal not fix. When it comes to any long-term illness or condition the goal is never to fix yourself, the goal is always to love yourself regardless, even when you feel broken.

The Messy UNTool Box

I keep this list on my phone and have set up reminders to pop up randomly throughout the day for when I need an extra "Self-Love Boost".

I keep to the 4-minute rule that no matter what is going on during my day, or what I need to do, I can always spare *at least* 4 minutes to take care of myself.

Looking down this list some actions will take longer than 4 minutes, others you can fit in 2, 3 or even 4 actions into them! It's just about doing what feels good within the time period that you can carve out for yourself. It may be that doing any of these just feels too much. That's OK too. Be kind to yourself. Make yourself a priority. Remember they are designed to heal, not fix.

- Drink Water
- Meditation
- Affirmations
- EFT
- Visualisation
- Yoga
- Walking outside
- Dancing to loud music
- Reading
- Writing
- Creating
- Hugging
- Playing

- Journaling
- Learn something new
- Eating real food
- Bath
- Nap

And with that the messiest chapter of the book is done. Shit can get really messy. You can feel really messy. Life can feel so incredibly messed up it feels like it will never be the same again.

No matter how messy it gets there will always be sparks of joy. No matter how messy you feel you will always deserve self-love. No matter how shitty, negative or ill you feel, there will always be moments of wellbeing, positivity, gratitude and love just waiting for you to let them in. It's all part of this messy, raw and beautiful human experience and ALL the emotions you feel makes you the gorgeous human that you are. Light and Dark, you are ALL loveable. Trying or surviving, you are ALL loveable. Messy and imperfect, you are ALL loveable.

Loveable by others...
Loveable by source...
Loveable by yourself...
Give yourself permission to love yourself messy.

Chapter Twelve - Fuck Like You Love Yourself

Pssssst
Shhhhhhhhh
Ayeeeeee Upp
How you doing?

I couldn't possibly write a book without including a little wee (not that type of wee you perv) chapter on sex, could I? A sprinkling of spicy Italian self-love...

Mum avert your eyes, I'm going in... That's what she said!

As I've been rewriting this whole book, I've been doing it in order, until I got to this one. I'm sat here writing this from scratch and it's the last chapter I need to send in. The only one I waited to do. I know deep down there is a fear of being judged, and the chapter title itself is enough to scare off even the most liberal of us, but here I am writing it anyway. I think I left it until last because I was viewing it as "just for fun" so if I didn't have time to write it, it wasn't important to the book anyway so I could leave it out. But I made time for this chapter. The thought of leaving it out was not actually an option because this chapter is important to me. Sex, masturbation and orgasms are fucking important.

There are so many people out there who are missing out on the fun, the creativity and the feelings of love that cum from these three things (oh the puns could be never fucking ending, but I promise I'll stop).

There's so many people using sex to hurt themselves or to hurt others.

There are so many people out there putting up with shit sex and not having the big O that they deserve.

There are so many people out there that have feelings of shame, self-disgust and unworthiness after the deed is done.

An orgasm is a beautiful thing and can feel amazing both before and after. This is what you deserve and I'm finding it the perfect chapter to finish off on (I must resist the pun) because both the subject and the act are messy as fuck.

Sex fills a need.

Which Need Are You Trying to Fill?

The subject of sex is still a bit taboo with some people and so will often just get avoided. This leads people to clam up about it and put up with all kinds of messed up shit like:

- Being with a partner they don't even like anymore
- Doing uncomfortable things to please someone else
- Not allowing themselves to let go
- Having sex when they don't want to
- Having shit sex and pretending they enjoyed it
- Keep going back to shit sex just for the feeling of being loved even if they know it's a lie

...to name just a few.

Because it's hard to talk about, people will just put up with it. If you think about it, it's like you'd rather ram a dildo up your arse than have an uncomfortable conversation about not wanting to ram a dildo up your arse because you risk being rejected. Just don't forget the coconut oil.

Here we can see our self-respect and boundaries come into play. But also, what is behind your decision-making surrounding sex is your intent for having it. It's the need you are wanting to fulfil by having sex.

We've been taught that anything other than two people making love is wrong or dirty. But the truth is, when sex is used for fulfilling any healthy need and the fact that you want to help to fulfil somebody else's healthy need, sex is pretty fucking awesome, right?

Sex is a basic adult human need.

We are all craving some sort of connection.

It is a type of expression, and it confirms what you already believe about yourself.

It's when your intention is unhealthy that this becomes dangerous.

Having sex, making love or yep just fucking like you love yourself, means finding someone (or more peeps if that's your thang, we ain't judging) who you trust to explore and embrace you.

Someone who you feel free to be your freaky or not so freaky self with.

Someone who actually sees you.
Whether it's with someone else or by yourself, it's about having the courage and self-respect to have clear boundaries.

It's about having the confidence to be yourself, show yourself, and be wild and free.

If you are using sex to fill a void in your life, to feel powerful, to validate yourself or to fill a desperate need to be loved...it isn't going to be fun.

First you need to step into your power. Take care of loving yourself first.

75% of all women can't orgasm through intercourse alone. Have Google read out this stat and have a giggle hearing her say "without the extra help of sex toys, hands or tongue."

43% of women and 31% of men report some degree of sexual dysfunction and have trouble orgasming. There's around 10% of women who report having never orgasmed in their life.

Sometimes it might be a physical reason, sometimes it could be a mental block, other times it can be down to your situation, worries or mood. Sometimes it's to do with the intent, the need you are trying to fill, other times it can be judging yourself or being distracted.

Whether you haven't been able to come for a while or you've never even experienced an orgasm …well it's a bit shit innit?

There's a beautiful release and creative energy that comes from coming when self-love is involved. I've noticed this is different when you're just beating one off to porn. That can feel empty and unsatisfying.

But orgasming with the intent to express love to yourself, connect with another human on a whole other level or to enjoy and appreciate the human body is fucking mind blowing.

We all deserve this.

I guess it starts off with who we are with. Whether that person has the same level of love for us as we do of ourselves. But what about when you are on your own? Can it still be an act of love?

Wanking…Yeah, I Said It...

A self-love wank just sounds dirty doesn't it! But the act of pleasuring yourself can be just as fucking epic as when there are more people in the party.

It can be an act of love.
It can be a gift of bliss.
It can be a gift of time, attention and love for your Body.

I actually can't believe I'm about to do this but I'm going to describe how you can turn a quick wank into a gift for your Body. Buckle yourself in, my notepad is about to get wet…from the bath.

You can do this wherever of course but baths are kinda my thang, so I'm sticking with it. Also, whatever sex you identify with, you can still do this, but it would feel weird to write about touching my cock when I haven't got one, so I'll stick with what I know...adapt as necessary people.

OK so first I give myself the time and energy. I check my intent and make sure it's to show my Body gratitude. I'm doing this for her, not to her.

I step into the bath and feel the hot water soothe my feet and legs. I start gently rubbing my legs and massaging them telling my Body why I'm so grateful for my strong legs and weird ass toes. I submerge the rest of my Body and feel the hot water against my skin.

My shoulders relax. My belly is the last thing to feel the water and my first thought is it's because it's so big, but I bring myself back into gratitude and rub my belly while I say thank you to my belly for growing my children, digesting my food and being a soft pillow to snuggle into. Next, I go all the way under the water, sinking in. The outside world sounds muffled and distant and I'm feeling bliss just being alone there. This is my time now I tell myself.

I start to massage my head and the back of my neck, releasing any tension or stress that's built up. I thank my Body for carrying it for me and for letting go of it now.

Here's where I have a quick cuddle. I wrap my arms around myself, rubbing my arms, thanking my Body for allowing this time and expressing this love.

Of course, my boobs have perked up now and are feeling cold, so I warm them up while I thank my boobs for feeding my babies, giving me so much excitement and past fun.

I experience a flurry of energy flowing around my Body.

I remind my Body:

You are safe...
You are loved...

My hands go back to my belly and tightly hold my hips. I allow my arms to heavily rest against my pelvis, the source of all my daily pain but I tell my Body I appreciate and love her regardless.

I've got cold knees, so I sit up and I'm massaging my thighs, thanking them for being thick and strong. I'm back under the water as my fingers find my clit. My powerful pussy. The vulva and vagina being a portal to another world. Literally so much to be grateful for, birthing my children, giving me pleasure. My Body feels a yearning, she's ready.

I tell my Body to relax, to enjoy the sensations. She deserves this. As I experience the sweet relief and the buzzing flowing around my entire Body, I tell my Body how beautiful she is. How appreciated she is. How loved she is.

I ask my Body what she wants next. What would feel good to her? Now my Body is in control of my fingers, and I make no judgements. I try to turn my brain off and allow her to control the flow, the movements, the speed. I listen to what feels good.

I feel myself start to hover around outside of my head, so I bring myself back inside my Body. Back to this moment. I'm feeling pleasure, warmth and a whole lot of love. I'm creating this for her.

I don't allow myself to drift my thoughts to memory fruits, past experiences or imagining someone else there. I want to feel exactly what she is feeling. What I am doing for her.

No time limits...
No judgements...
No expectations...

Allow her to orgasm in any way she wants.

If the brain starts to wander off, I keep saying

You are so beautiful...
You are so loved...
You are so appreciated...

Until it's time to allow the bliss. The release of energy. The explosion of pure, real love.

Bring myself down slowly,

Hand on heart

Safe...
Safe...
Safe...

Breathing slows down.

I come back earthside.
Feel the love.

Revolutionary act of self-love or a just really hippy way to wank? Try it out first, then decide for yourself.

Hey mum, you can start reading again now...

Unconditional Orgasms

However and whoever you decide to share your Body with, make sure you keep her safe, appreciate her and use it to enrich your life.

Your Body deserves to feel unconditional love from both yourself and others. The commitment to love yourself daily extends to the commitment of making sure you fuck yourself and others for the pleasure. You are worthy of an expansive, healthy sex life. When you make time for yourself and set boundaries around how to use your Body in a loving way, you will shine and appreciate your Body more.

There's zero reason why you shouldn't be enjoying yourself in this way. There's zero reason why it should not be as important to you as the other areas in your life.

If you think about it, an orgasm is a beautiful connection with your Higher Self. It's the ultimate alignment. Sex with yourself or cocreating that moment with another person is tapping into pure love energy. A sacred act but not a dirty or forbidden one. Shame or expectations shouldn't need to come into the equation. Open yourself up to the possibility of unconditional pleasure. Unconditional Orgasms. Unconditional Sexual Alignment.
Open honest communication is an act of self-love in itself. Knowing that you are worthy of all the pleasure and more can inspire you to be brave and care about how you express that love.

Sex matters.
Orgasms matter.
You matter.

So go fucking enjoy yourself and make yourself cum hard.

Whoops, sorry mum!

Chapter Thirteen - Fuck Me in The Feels

I want to feel
I want to feel
The pain
The anger
The goddamn
Fucking lot
I want the black
The darkness
I deserve the flies
The stench

The Ocean
Covers the broken
Shells
Death
Beauty in suffering

I give away my power
On a platter
My energy
My mask
Slipping
Vulnerable
But no movement
No silence

Empty broken shell
Held together by
Responsibilities
Expectations
Hope, I said it.
Trust my Body
She holds it altogether

She is my power
But she grows weak
Unable to stand

Forever

The flies land
They love my bullshit

The stench
Of giving
Giving
Giving
Hypocrite
LIAR
SELFISH

Dark shadows
I see in mute

What did I expect
The mask is slipping
Falling
Into boredom
Impatient energy
Shaking with anger

Hot sun burns my
Neck
Water touches
My feet

It's coming
I'm running out of
Time
About to get trapped
Again
Who truly deserves freedom?

This night was the night I sat down to write but instead I started
sobbing. It was the first time I'd cried in weeks. Not just tears,
but ugly thoughts and hopelessness filled my heart.

"Who the fuck do I think I am to write a book on self-love?"

My life was indeed a fucking mess. My heart was battered like a grey, lifeless sausage. Life had been relentless, wearing me down night after night, one moment to the next, not knowing what llama was waiting in the side-lines poised and ready to kick me in the throat while I was already down.

2020, what a fucking joke.

2019 was the year I put my health first. I was determined to heal myself, I owed it to my brother. I was alive so I was determined to live the best life that I could.

Basically, for about 13yrs I've had this chronic pelvic pain. I'd tried everything the NHS offered me, but nothing worked. Before I got pregnant with Eli, I was on a downward spiral. A huge cocktail of drugs every day, mixed with getting drunk, smoking, junk food and anything else that gave me a moment's relief. I always say that Eli was my miracle baby because not only had I been told I couldn't have children, but I was also on medication that could have killed him in just one dose, and also for the fact that it feels like he saved my life.

The very day that I found out I was pregnant (in an Asda toilet by the way, but that's another story!) I went cold turkey. Stopped it all in an instant. The thought of even causing him the slightest bit of harm was enough for me to just deal with my pain. What I wasn't prepared for was the huge physical withdrawal symptoms mainly from the codeine. Good Lordy, for two weeks I was a mess.

Anyhow, 3 babies later and I coped with the pain in my own ways, put on a shit ton of weight, found myself miserable and was waking up every day at 4am, having to cry myself back to sleep in pain. So, in 2019 I thought enough was enough and I set out to heal my body. In true Mirrie fashion I became obsessed with research and embarked on a 100-day juice feast. I lost over 50lbs, lost Self-Love, found Self-Love, healed nearly all my physical pain but I was still having long bouts of depression and what I called "The Rage".

I recently found a video from that time in Oct 2019 when after three days in bed refusing to get up, I'd had an "aha" moment. I didn't want to heal. I was waiting for someone else to give me permission.

Permission to feel better.
Permission to not be OK.
Permission to be angry.

I realised in that moment, on that fucking video, that other people's permission meant shit. Other people's permission was good to hear, it made me feel better for a moment, but it was just empty. I needed permission from myself. It was the first video I'd ever said "fuck it" in. My true self had been hidden for so long, caged up like a wild animal. Controlled by my marriage and other people's expectations. I could see the flick switch in my own eyes.

Roll on a couple of months and there we were in 2020. This was my year of saying "Fuck This Shit." I decided to be me. Regardless of the consequences. No more vanilla Mirrie. No more people pleasing Mirrie. I would talk how I wanted to, and BE who I truly was. I felt ready to break free of my cage and set a mother fucking burning flame across the sky as I soared free.

The first few months were amazing. I gained a following on LinkedIn and made real friendships with people who believed in me and were willing to support me. I attacked the year like there was no tomorrow, constantly in "Beast Mode" creating content, self-love spilling out of me as I left puddles on the floor. It felt like my wings were unfolding, creaking as they spread out, strong and determined. It affected my marriage though. After so many years of appeasing my husband, under the weight of my newfound strength, the cracks began to show and we were having blazing arguments daily. I knew I had to leave so I tried to go but after three days of what can only be described as a barrage of emotional tomfuckery[46] I agreed to stay and give it one last go for two weeks.

Just 3 days after that, lockdown was announced, and the "try again" bubble popped. At each other's throats and this time there were no options, nowhere to run. The toxicity was inescapable. It felt like the universe was saying:

"Hey bitch, you thought you were trapped before? I'll show you what trapped really is."

I tried; I really did. But for weeks I knew the truth. Our expectations were just set too high. The only way to live up to his was to appease and squish down my true inner self. And this year I'd promised not to do that. But I did do that.

So. Many. Times.

I started concentrating on just having a good day for the kids, doing whatever I had to do in order to make that happen. It wasn't pretty. Most mornings I'd dance in the kitchen for three hours straight just to dull down the rage. I started smoking again and then came the day drinking. I was chasing fun as an escape and I didn't, actually no, I COULDN'T give a shit what it was doing to my Body because I was in pure survival mode. Doing whatever it took to not feel like a wild animal being prodded in a cage, forced to play a sweet perfect mother role because the kids needed me to. To stay quiet. To stay small. To stay obedient.

I couldn't feel. I couldn't heal. I couldn't eat. I couldn't even cry. Every day was just a battle. A push against those bars. One step forward, three steps back. It felt impossible to escape.

Eyes
Someone else's
Words

---

[46] Tomfuckery: Cluster fuck of drama llamas

Someone else's

I still can't cry
I want to feel it

Tiny Pebble
People
Eyes
Risk
The edge

I've worn my mask too long
It slips but
Never falls

It slips
But never falls

Tangled hair
Twisted humour

I share my dark with you
My ugly skin

Mash up legs
Scared, bleeding
No pain
As the sharp edges
Twist in

Ego Untamed
Fucks not given

Eyes
Eyes
Seeing
Sleep beckoning

I feel no pain

I deserve the flies
I deserve the anger
I deserve the knife

No such luck
No such grace

Time still ticks
Sand in my knots

I feel nothing
I see the darkness coming
To swallow me up

Eyes
Eyes
Gone

So, I was drinking too much, smoking too much. I started playing with my darkness, toying around with it. Becoming much braver to look my ugliness in the eyes. I stopped appeasing my partner, half the time only giving a fuck about arguments if the kids were there. Nights became a battle ground again. But still I felt trapped. Nowhere to flee to. I tried again with him, like really fucking tried. I remember one day I bit my tongue all day. I was dressed up how he liked and whatever he suggested I said yes to. I made sure I tidied the house, didn't spend time on my phone, and didn't talk to anyone else. At the end of an argument-free day, he said: "See, we can be so happy."

Inside my head I was like "Yeah, if I fall in line, if I am mute without any opinions with one goal to just fucking please you, yeah look how happy we could be!"

It was at that point I knew it wouldn't work. If I wanted to be me, I had to be free.

But I was scared. 15 years is a long time to be dependent on someone. He obviously had his bad points, as did I, but he was amazing at making me feel beautiful no matter what I looked like.

He supported me in his own way with all my crazy obsessions. He had bought me my first camera, we had gone through 15 years of loss, joy, babies, kids, exes...everything. Hardly spent anytime apart. I didn't want it to not be what I wanted. I thought we would be together forever.

The good times were so good and that's why I stayed..
In a way, I must have liked someone else making all the decisions. I didn't want the responsibility on my shoulders. What started as me feeling safe to let someone take over turned into me diluting myself and constantly appeasing to make other people happy. That was on me though, for so long I saw my cage as safe and being alone terrified me.

Alone.

Would I be able to cope? Could I manage money? What about on the days the darkness hit? Who would I turn to?

Then the end date for lockdown was announced and I fucking crapped myself. All of a sudden, the possibility to leave felt real. Not just talk. Excitement quickly turned to fear as I remembered the last time I had tried to leave. I went over to my mums when the rules loosened and told my parents my marriage was over. They said they'd support me in whatever I chose and although officially the lockdown wasn't done, if I needed to go there, to just do it.

I can't remember how long that was before the infamous Cunt-Gate[47] night, but I remember using the lockdown as an excuse not to leave...I mean I can only go to my mums in an emergency right? So, I'd struggle in my little cage in order to not cause anyone inconvenience.

And so, with the cage feeling tighter and tighter, the date for possible freedom looming (which scared me more than being

---

[47] Cunt-Gate: A suffix to refer to scandal

trapped) my rage was prowling around me like a hungry lion ready to feast.

I started losing days to the beast. Feeling snappier and snappier. Unable to bite my tongue or keep the peace. I was having zero time to myself. I felt wild and reckless, and poetry was pouring out of me, my only outlet outside of my head.

At my most desperate, for some form of release I arranged a mini girl's night at my friend's house. I suggested this to my husband and told him how important it was to me, just to have something to look forward to, to hold on to. He said sure if I could get the boys to sleep first and I couldn't be long in case Indie needed me. I wanted to flip him off, but I thought "just keep the peace you fucking need this".

Friday night rolled around, which meant zoom party night and I was on my extra good behaviour because I still wanted this girl's night to happen the next day. But here was the kicker. Our group had just gone through its first family fight. People were hurting and I was hurting so I wanted to make sure I was there to support and get my point of the story across. Of course I had potato net, so my connection kept dropping. I was super pissed off because the members of the group who caused the fight in the first place were all shit stirring in the background but wouldn't pick up the phone to actually talk to me, and my friend had some other serious llamas going on at the same time. I remember thinking I JUST NEED TO HAVE SOME FUN.

Life had been so heavy for days, I needed to just not worry about everyone else for a night. Surprisingly my husband was being really supportive but when I got stressed again at about 10pm and told him I'd rather stay on the zoom because I was trying to sort things out, he got super pissed. He used to get so jealous but that night there were only three women on, and it definitely wasn't a party. We were talking deep shit.

It ended up being very late and he started shouting at me. I was embarrassed because one of the women, although family, was also a client. So, I moved from room to room with him following me shouting and calling me names. Of course Indie woke up so now I had a little one crying to deal with too. I took Indie to bed and waited for everything to settle down.

I knew it was late, but everyone was asleep, so I thought I'd pop back on zoom to see if anyone was still there. My cheeks were still burning that they had all seen first-hand the side of my marriage I'd tried to hide away. I hadn't turned off the light when I got indie to sleep and he was sound, so I left it on. The ladies were still on asking me if I was OK...before I'd even said a word my husband came bursting in screaming the selfish cunt bomb at me. There was certainly no hiding it anymore. There was my shame, that I put up with this ranting and raving at me, live on camera for everyone to see. I felt sick and Indie woke up again. That was my fault too, apparently.

You'd think that would be my breaking point.
You'd think that would be my knee jerk reaction like I described in chapter 10.

You'd think that would be the moment my self-respect would have made me strong enough to say no more.

But no. I appeased.

I went to bed shaking.
I cried.
I felt so ashamed.

In the morning I made him a cup of tea and pretended everything was normal. Afterwards I phoned my friend:

"I'll never have the strength to leave. I'm going to be here forever. What more could he do that I couldn't forgive him for? I just gave him a fucking morning cuddle and he's not even apologised for Cunt-Gate. What would it take for me to leave? I'm stuck here forever, I'm so weak, I'm not ever going to be strong enough to leave."

Little did I know that the knee jerk reaction that I described four years ago would be happening to me, pretty much word for word (that gave me goosebumps!), just a few short hours later.

My sister-in-law phoned, she was coming to the beach and wanted to meet up for the first time since lockdown started. I said to my husband for him to come but he had loads of excuses and said he wanted us back for dinner time. I told him I wanted no time restrictions because we'd not seen Sam's boys for so long and I just wanted to have fun without having to worry about time. My sister-in-law said it was like talking to the old Mirrie again, I was so free and just being myself. She said she couldn't remember a time when I sounded so happy. I told her things had gotten so bad over lockdown I was going to have to leave my marriage, but I had no idea when or how.

We all spent a silly afternoon together and I was getting so excited for my girl's night, especially after the shitstorm of last night. We didn't make it back home in time for dinner and I knew that had irked him, but I didn't care. If I was to stay in this cage indefinitely, I had to at least rattle it to see my family, I wasn't going to miss out on that ever again.

I reminded him about the girl's night, and he was a bit pissed but not too bad. Then my neighbour phoned to say she wasn't well enough to meet. My whole heart sunk, I'd been holding on to this, it was the only thing keeping my thick, dark bubbling rage at bay. I didn't check with my other friend, but I thought if I took Indie with me, I could at least stay on the boat and have a little knees up there to expel some of this energy out of my Body.

I said I'd do this instead of going to my neighbours and said I'd still wait until the other kids were asleep but that I really needed to go. He got angry and said what about just having an evening with him. Considering we spent every fucking waking moment together, I was fucked off, but I said OK what if I spend the evening with you but go to the boat later on and still take indie with me. We argued for a while and the kids started getting upset.

Right in the middle of shouting at me for being fucking selfish or a liar again he says:

"Case closed, I made up my mind, you are not going so that's the case closed."

I got transported into a dialogue with myself that felt like it lasted an hour but was over in a millisecond. The voice inside bellowed out loud and clear:

"If you allow this now, you allow this forever."

Fuck no. I did not allow this now. Fuck no. I would not allow this forever.

From what felt like nowhere, the collective strength of the entire Universe was felt in my veins.

THIS was my knee jerk reaction, Fuck no.

My decision was made. I decided I was strong enough, so of course I was. I decided it was time to save myself, to save our children, to save my future.

The moment I made that decision it was set in stone. I knew that this time it was right. This time I meant it. This time was the last time.

I didn't go to the boat. What followed was days of him going off saying that he'd only return if I said I'd give him another try. When he returned the emotional barrage would too, so on the Sunday I went to my mum's but went back home afterwards because I was scared of what he would do. That Sunday night things got so toxic that I knew I had to take my kids out of that situation.

It was the Monday morning, and he was sleeping in so I could have gotten my shit together and left, but for some reason I waited until he was awake, I probably felt like I deserved the punishment. That entire morning though, I relied on my own strength, I didn't phone anyone, ask anyone's opinions or wait for someone to come save me. As much as it felt like I was trying to swim through cement, I got our basic shit and got out of there. The drive to my mums felt robotic, like I wasn't in my body, but when I parked outside her house, I felt my entire body drop. I could barely lift my arm to reach my phone. Undoing my seatbelt felt impossible, I called mum and said you better come out here, get the kids.

By this time, I was sobbing and shaking uncontrollably. Mum got the kids out of the car but left Indie. He climbed over to me and instantly my Body switched off my emotions and switched-on mum mode. That gave me the strength to get out of the car and walk into my mum's cuddle.

Knowing I had done all that on my own was everything to me. But the fact that it took so long? It taunted me. As soon as I was on the outside of that situation it all seemed so clear, but when I was in the thick of it, I felt so weak, so powerless, so hopeless. I had kept everyone at an arm's length because I knew I couldn't be fully authentic while I was living in a cage, existing with that dark rage inside of me, and what killed me was that rage still wasn't enough to stand up for myself...

Until it was.

I can't explain why or how I got to what felt like the point of no return so many fucking times, and somehow returned to learn the same old fucking lessons again and again. I'm not sure why I'm even writing all this apart from the showing you that everyone has their demons, what they see as weaknesses or something in their life that scares them shitless. If you don't stand up for yourself this time it doesn't mean you never will. All these things happen with perfect timing. You get what you need, not what you want.

It's never a test.
It's never a lesson.
But fuck does it feel like one.

Remember you are Big U. You are the Universe. You are source energy. You attract the lesson you believe you need, and you (probably unconsciously) will attract the perfect people again and again to make sure the lesson is really learnt, not just skimmed over. My lesson has been learnt; I'll never shrink myself in order to make someone else feel better ever again. I will never compromise my personality to appease another person. I'll never settle. I'll never set foot into another cage again.

Freedom has no price too high.

But yet that leaves me with the same question:

Who Am I To Teach You About Self-Love?

I like my old jeans
Tattered and torn
hangs tight to my skin
I like my old hoodie
Dirty and comfy
Like my old personality
I like the smoke
Feeling the filthy poison
Hitting my lungs
Struggling to breathe

I like the struggle
It feels familiar
Like family
I like the self-deprecation
The swamp thang
The uncontrollable
Lust
Need
I like the empty feeling in my tummy
The grace of numbness

I like the not being enough for you
It confirms my darkest fears

My darkest fears are comfortable
My inner pain is safe
The fears that are known
Are welcomed

I like the misery
I need the guilt

Unhealthy
Bad mother
Imposter
Dirty bitch

It's nice
The flames are toasty

I'm enough
Yet not enough
I love myself
Yet can't be loving
I'm safe
Yet living in fear
I'm laughing
Yet my heart has the jabbies[48]

I like the mess
I like the overwhelm
I like the uselessness

If I don't have all this
What would be left?

I'm just a normal person, seriously. not even that! The fact that
this book has been drilling a space into my brain for years,
hurting my ego, never letting up, never letting go is beyond me.

---

[48] Jabbies: Feeling pain like a knife to the heart

The message contained in this book always felt bigger than me but now I know it IS me. To dilute myself is to dilute the message.

You deserve to love yourself messy even when you feel beyond messy. Even when you've created the mess. Even when you feel too weak to clear up the mess. Even when you're stinking, drowning in the mess.

There's no need to save yourself because you are always safe. There's nothing to fix, there's nothing to clean, there's not even a mess.

A single mum. self-employed. Living on a tiny boat that only just got hot water. Honestly to the world, to society, I'm the lowest of the low, right? Little education, legally homeless, in debt, messy break up, messy head, messy mental health, don't even have a toilet I can flush! I mean, I know I'm hot, but this peachy arse can only take you so far innit! When it comes to actually writing a book, I'm probably the least qualified person out there (to quote Emmet[49]!)

To be talking so deeply on self-love is kind of fucked up too. I've spent most of my life in self-loathing and abused my Body in so many ways.

When I think about it, just the plain fact that my vision and message has been so clear and so forceful for so long speaks volumes. This shit has been a lived experience, but this knowledge comes from somewhere else. There was something bigger out there that needed this message into the world and, like Moana, I was chosen...so I had to learn how to sail before I could even begin this epic journey (what can I say except *"you're welcome"*?)

But the more I think about it, of course I've been the one to carry this message. Being so close to my dark, but still loving myself regardless. Looking my ugly in the eye but still seeing my beauty.

---

[49] Emmet: Inspirational character from the Lego Movie

Knowing the fucking hardship of making this daily commitment when self-love isn't my first instinct.

Of course it's me who had to write this book. I had to show you all my mess so that you can see it's OK to show yours. If Mirrie can love herself messy, you can too. It's so easy to talk to other people when you are full of self-worth and life is going great...here I am reaching up from the depths of hell showing you FUCK YES, IT'S STILL POSSIBLE.

This might be your version of hell, but it is my creation of heaven. My freedom. Me being able to be fully me. I may need to time my poos so I can flush with the tide but it's just the beginning of the life I am creating. I'm starting back with nothing and I'm grateful AS FUCK for everything that blesses me along the way.

This reminds me of a Linky post I made last New Year's:

At the beginning of 2020 I refused to make any resolutions, but I did make one promise...

"This year I will be me, no matter what"

Seems easy and simple right?

Fuck no.

Some moments it was exhilarating, others heart-breaking.
I had to make rough decisions, have difficult conversations, face change, face fears, face both my beautiful & ugly self.

I had to accept flaws
Create boundaries
Love without a safety net
Share my soul

I had to risk everything I'd ever had.

Be happy to lose it all
Just for the freedom of being me.

I saw alignment
I saw magic
I saw carnage

I saw the world fall apart
And I saw the power of those willing to rebuild it.

I've fallen apart many times
I've had the most amazing people around me who were willing not
to bounce and hug me back together until I'm ready to heal myself.

I've felt a lot of rage
I've felt a lot of hope

But singing "Happy New Year" doesn't stop the world from turning
or life from spinning.

Each day brings new llamas to herd, new risks & healing.

But it brings the chance to renew that promise. Recommit every
day...

To love yourself regardless
To lean into the fear
To make yourself vulnerable
To feel your own power...

"This year I will be me, no matter what"

Fuck me, I'm ready to do it all again, are you?

And so here I am, ready to do it all again but this time slightly
differently.

Zero expectations, but ultimate trust.
Ready to **do** and letting go of the perfection.
No failures, only expansion.
More grace...
More time...
More determination.

If I can finish this book, you can do anything.
If I can love myself, you can too.
If I can inspire someone, you can too.

No matter how messy...
No matter how dark...

Your light shines through...
My light shines through...
We can be ready together.

No One is Coming to Save You

I was watching a random inspirational video at about 1am last night and it ended on the words:

"Life doesn't give us what we want, it gives us who we are"

Not sure who said these words, but I call bullshit. There's plenty of really good, kind people who are being royally shafted right now. There's also a lot of people with evil intent who are winning right now.

I do believe that good always wins.
The light always outshines the dark.
One way or other things will work out for you at the perfect time.
Life (I.e. The Big U) does give you what you want, and she also gives you what you need.

Soul deep lessons
Strength
Courage
Resilience
Love
Pain
Pockets of Joy

We need all these things in order to grow, to expand and to live more fully.

Trust that you CAN cope with whatever shit the fan is splattering over you.

Trust that whatever is happening right now WILL become apparent in hindsight that it was perfect timings for you.

Trust that good will always win.

Trust that you are safe enough to feel your feels.

Trust that you are Already Enough just as you are and what's happening in your life doesn't define you as a person.

Having that trust is fucking hard. Especially when you're dancing in the darkness. But there are little signs everywhere.

I feel like this thing of having to do everything on your own and in your own power is actually really toxic, because if you think about it, if we're all part of the collective, all part of the same consciousness, then obviously we're going to need each other, obviously we're going to need the different connections and a different styles of support from other people in order to keep us going. It's actually these deep connections that makes life worth living.

We need the support.
We need the help.
We need to lean on each other and that's actually OK.

It's OK to admit! We obviously need to find all these things in ourselves as well and take on the responsibility, but we also need it from other people because they are part of ourselves.

From here it gets a little bleak. We won't always have another person there to fulfil these needs.

Although most people won't mean to be, when shit goes down, most of the fuckers out there will be self-absorbed, and rightly so. They might be having a drama llama in their own self-pity while totally forgetting the shitstorm you are actually in. There are exceptions to this rule always and it won't be every time but a lot of the time, if you are in a long-term fucked up situation you may find yourself alone. Having to rely on only yourself to pull you through.

These are called the sink or swim nights. You may have little ones relying on you, business clients who are super understanding but still need the job done. You may have health problems, be mentally weak or even feel unstable.

When you find yourself in that position and you're feeling abandoned, you have two choices - sink into that shit-infested rabbit hole and leave someone else to pick up the pieces, or swim, swim head down through the rough, through the dark, through the salty. Barely giving the night a second glance, swearing about the tossers you put up with as you do. Loving yourself, giving yourself grace, allowing the progress to be messy and imperfect.

Your love story needs to be with yourself.

Other people are going to fuck up on the daily, as will you.

You need to be someone you can rely on. It's not about inner strength, it's about inner kindness. It's about that unconditional love.

It's so romantic and alluring to think that there's someone out there just ready to come save you... most of the time in relationships, we are looking for someone to come and save us from ourselves. This often means getting involved with the most fucked up people because until you are ready to accept yourself as you are, you're using them to fill something inside yourself that you think is missing.

It's all very well to surround yourself with a village of the most supportive people. It's fucking amazing to find your soul connections, the people who accept you no matter what, for you just as you are. But only you can do the work.

There's going to be a time when you have to face yourself

Your ugliness...
Your mess...
Your demons...
Your seemingly impossible situations.

You have to face up to all of that. No one is coming to save you.
No one is going to be able to love your unworthiness, your fears,
your un-lovableness away.

That responsibility is yours alone. Only you can do it. Your Body
doesn't need anyone else's love; only yours alone.

And now is the time.
It's time to stop waiting for your knight in shining armour.

You are nearly at the end of this book. You know you are worthy.
I know you can do it. I have complete trust in you. I see your
power because it mirrors my own. You pull the strength to align
and love hard from somewhere deep inside your gut.

When there's no dings from notifications.
When there's no distractions.
When there's no one else awake.

You have to jump in.

You have to find your own peace, your own strength, your own
willingness to survive.

This isn't just a mindset. This is being human. Allowing yourself
the grace to be imperfect, to feel your feels. To allow them to
fuck you gently and still pick yourself up and carry on. Making
that commitment to love and care about yourself regardless.

You have the entire collective consciousness of the Universe
surrounding you, supporting you, loving you. The very power
that creates worlds that YOU are a part of.

You need *you* to be your own knight, slaying dragons, swooping
in and protecting your Body, having those uncomfortable

conversations, making those uncomfortable decisions and taking the uncomfortable actions.

Sometimes you've got to fuck yourself in the feels, dust yourself off and be the warrior that you've become. You got this, it's time to save yourself.

But wait...

You do not need to be saved.

Even by yourself.

When you are there, wishing there was someone to save you, what would they be saving you from? The shitty situation? Your life? You?

You alone are an unstoppable force.
You are backed by the entire Universe.
There is no situation, emotion, life event or even inner crisis that you need saving from.
Even when it feels like you are sinking, really you are flying.
Coping. Surviving. Thriving.

Getting fucked in the feels is always an expansive momentum. Seeing your ugly and still loving yourself through it always exposes your true inner strength and makes it grow beyond anything you ever felt possible.

The life beyond the cage is such sweet freedom...but it wouldn't taste so sweet unless you knew what trapped felt like.

In this moment you now know you are capable of any fucking thing you want. With others or without. You have all the support and love you'll ever need. Being you no matter what and flying free has never felt so fucking satisfying.

Chapter Fourteen- The Gift of Anger

Hold up, did a bitch say Gift?

Yep, this bitch did.

Getting dumped
Getting cheated on
Getting rejected
Getting swindled
Being unappreciated
Being abused

When we have been wronged, normally we go to two places.

Sad and victimised, or angry and indignant.

We know feeling like a victim (even when we are) means it takes away our power, but it also takes away our energy, our hope.

After a lifetime of being told that anger is wrong, or a "bad" emotion...if you go to that hot place of pure rage, you can feel out of control or even like a bad person.

But here I am saying anger can be a gift. Sounds weird really, when anger nearly always leads to harmful or dangerous behaviour.

But I think that's because we've never been taught how to deal with that anger. We've never been taught how to channel it. We've never been taught that anger is actually another way our Body protects us.
Being sad or going into victim mode is soul sucking. We have no motivation to change things because it doesn't feel like it's in our control to do so. So often, if we're feeling like this, we'll avoid confrontation and hide away, trying to make ourselves as safe as possible.

Being super angry and not knowing what to do with it normally means we'll lash out, make rash decisions or seek revenge. Especially when we feel wronged. It will feel like a rush of unfairness and all the energy and focus goes on our version of making it right. We'll often have high expectations for the person who has wronged us and it's likely that, even if they do apologise, they will do it in a way that's unacceptable to us.

Revenge Is Never Sweet

The next step after anger is often revenge, and if we act on it, it fucking never turns out good. It often makes us more upset, causes more llamas and ends up hurting us more than the other person anyway.

Hurting someone else (in any way) is never serving us or anyone else. It's just a sick game with no winners.

So, I want to let you into my 15-year-old mind for a minute and take us back to the only time (apart from one other time that's way too messed up to mention, even in this book) I decided to take matters into my own hands and plot revenge.

I was 15 and in love. He was 23 and not.

My first love was also my first rejection. He was my best friend; we spent every day together and it took me nearly a year to 'fess up to the feelings I had for him. It was actually a very grown-up version of love. I had deep respect for him and loved spending time in his company. Yes, his dark lashes helped the matter along, and in hindsight, at his age he did the right thing, but I told him that I would wait for him (which became a running theme in my life). No matter how long it took, I would wait, as long as I knew there was a glimmer of hope. After being told there was no hope, I went into full blown teenage drama llama mode and played the "Phantom of an Opera" album while crying into my underaged wine way too many times than I should admit. I felt a mess.

I wasn't enough for him.
Which meant I felt like I was not enough at all.

I got really really sad.

The day for vengeance didn't come until one day, months later.
We were all sitting around drinking coffee talking about our
futures. My mates were joking around saying who we'd all end up
marrying or which of us would have kids and this guy, the
fucking so called love of my life, who had already rejected me,
pipes up saying...

"Mirrie, who would marry her?!"

Fuck me, if he sacrificed my hamster, it would have been kinder
than the soccer punch of those words. I felt like he'd ripped my
heart out and fed it to the dogs. I looked at him in shock, in
disbelief. My eyes darted to my friends who were all looking
shifty because they knew how heartbroken I already was. My
cheeks burned as I mumbled something about never wanting to
have to put up with a man anyway. I walked quickly to the toilets,
tears springing up to the corners of my eyes, but I wasn't sad
anymore, Teenage Mirrie was pissed off.
I'd like to say in that fit of anger I extracted some sort of revenge
but in truth I pre-planned the whole thing. I wanted him to pay. I
wanted him to feel humiliated. To feel the pain he'd just caused
me so the next part I'm not proud of.

I knew we'd be back at the cafe the next day, so I got one of my
parents' constipation pills and pre-ground that bad boy up. I
offered to order everyone's coffee and before I took his back,
hands shaking I took out the diarrhoea inducing powder and got
a split second of conscience pop up. Should I really do this? Did
he really deserve it? Would it really make me feel any better?

I felt my friend's hand on the back of mine, tapping the powder
in. She had this straight, knowing smile, like she was pissed too,
and I thought *"fuck it"* as I stirred the blobby powder in.

When I gave it to him, I felt sick, evil and incredibly satisfied all at the same time at the thought of what might happen.

To be honest not much did happen. There were a couple of times he went to the toilet quickly and me and my friend fell into fits of giggles. There were a few times we thought someone had farted and we knowingly looked at each other thinking it was the funniest thing in the world. Anytime he put his hand near his stomach I felt like I may actually puke because deep down I was seriously sick to my stomach with worry that I'd done the wrong thing.

Was it funny? Erm...yes.
Did it make me feel better? Honestly yeah, a little, but I did instantly regret it.

Was it clever? Not really but...it was funny.
OK, that might not be the best example. Thing is, if he had had super powerful diarrhoea, I'm not sure it would have been funny, and I didn't feel proud about my actions. It still makes me chuckle because I was young and dumb but that's mainly because I got away with it and because I very much doubt he'll ever read this sweary naughty book, so he is none the wiser. If anything more serious had happened? Even if he was only ill for a day or so, I would have seriously been upset with myself.

Why did I do it? I guess I wanted him to feel as humiliated as I did. Getting rejected fucking sucks, but when someone is a dick about it? Well it feels unjust and cruel.

Rejection hurts. What have we been saying all long about your Body? She loves you so much she will do anything to protect you from being hurt. She will use whatever she knows that has worked in the past to ensure you never risk being hurt again.

In order to avoid rejection, you have to avoid vulnerability. 15-year-old Mirrie fell in love, showed her underbelly and got her arse rejected quite spectacularly. My Body wanted to teach me a lesson about love. That it's not worth the risk. She wanted me to build some walls. Toughen up. She gave me anger and revenge as a motivating force. The anger felt better than the hopeless depression. The force itself is the gift. What you do with it is then your choice.

You can use it to hurt or heal. Only you have the power of that choice.

Some people choose to stay in that anger. They choose to keep those walls. They choose to harden their heart, never be vulnerable again, play games, control other people and seek revenge. This is totally fear based. They are staying in this protective mode because they are so scared of being hurt again. This sends a message to the Body that they are afraid they are not strong enough to handle rejection ever again and so their Bodies make them feel sadder, angrier and victimised their whole life, just in an attempt to keep them safe from the possible hurt that comes with actually loving someone fully.

The sad thing is that this energy will spill not only into all other areas of their life, but also when it comes to having another relationship, they'll often act the same way towards the person who is actually loving them. They'll try to control them, act out in spite and basically treat the other person like shite, just because they are afraid of being rejected. And so in most cases will end up being rejected and thus fulfil the circle and give them "proof" that love really just isn't worth the risk. Even when they've caused the rejection themselves by acting like a total knobber.

So, the key to anger is how you use the energy and how you reflect on the situation that caused you to be angry in the first place. To know how to use the energy of anger as an actual gift, first we need to take the taboo out of the emotion itself and learn about what anger actually is.

What Is Anger?

Anger is energy. Everything is energy. It's an emotion that serves a purpose just like all the other human emotions we feel daily.

We need to learn how to use it. We need to learn how anger can be a gift and take back our power when we are in that place, in a healthy way.

Really anger is the opposite of guilt.
Guilt is not the same as shame, remember. Guilt is an emotion that gives us motivation to change things when we feel like we've done wrong. It's the energy that makes us want to right a wrong that we have caused.

Anger is an emotion that gives us motivation to change things when we feel like we've been wronged. It's the energy that makes us feel compelled to right a wrong that has happened to us. When we feel we've (or someone we love has) been wronged or treated unfairly.

The same energy but for opposite reasons.

Anger is just energy.
Motivation.
It's up to us what to do with it.

Because it's seen as a negative emotion, it makes us uncomfortable. Because we've not been taught how to deal with it, or even that there is a right way to deal with it, we often take this energy and run with it in a way that hurts everyone involved.

But, when felt and processed correctly, anger can be a gift. It can motivate us to have stronger boundaries, to stand up for ourselves, to fight for what we believe in. Revenge barely ever has positive outcomes, but facing a problem head on? Yeah, that feels fucking good. Especially if you've been in the victim mode for a long time. Sick of the same old shit but feeling powerless...anger kicks in and all of a sudden, the energy is high, you feel strong enough to say that's enough. You feel the huge buzz to get off your arse and actually DO something about it. To change your situation, to react to that knee jerk reaction and say:

"Fuck no, no more."

Anger is a gift. It gifts us the vision to see our own power and, if we want to, to use it to better ours or other people's lives. Anger helps us get out of the hopeless despair mode and lifts us up to fucking MOVE. While angry it's almost impossible to feel fear because our focus is on action. While it's helpful to know you don't want to be in anger forever, knowing it's a motivating force that can shift our arses into someplace better can help us see this unappreciated emotion as a gift.

Getting Dumped

If yo' got your arse dumped, you got yo' arse rejected.

Ahh Shiiiiit.

Getting rejected, dumped or cheated on really isn't fun.

How can I feel like I'm enough when I'm being told I'm not enough by the person I love most in the world?

When you love someone, it can feel really scary to go 100% in. It can be all consuming. When you decide to be brave and actually get a soul connection it's very rare, so if a soul connection sees all of you, loves all of you but then doesn't decide to take that risk, it can feel like even all of you is still not enough, so where do you go from there?

When you're not enough
For someone else
It fucking hurts
No fucking getting around it

There will be a time in
Your life when you
Give it your all

Totally make yourself vulnerable
Show your ugly

Show your light
And still that won't be enough

So when that person

The person you thought was
Your everything

Basically confirms your darkest fears
That you are not enough
What then?
What's next?

Fuck that shit
No one gets to tell you that
Legit fuck that shit

You become
Enough
For yourself
Because your worth is already
There

Just because they don't see it
It doesn't mean you can't.

Seems easy to say but when you're living through it, it feels like
pure hell. It fucking hurts. You feel embarrassed, shook to the
core, unsure of yourself, angry, or sometimes even desperate.
The thought of moving on hurts, you feel like maybe you are
unlovable anyway. You have to grieve the future you thought you
were going to have.

Everything feels uncertain and scary again.

Your very worth can feel wobbly.

How do you love yourself, heal and move on? Where do you even
begin?

It's a sad fact that most people never do. They may move on, but to actually process the emotions and beliefs feels too hard, so they'll decide to go into a victim mode or get angry and stay angry and repeat the same behavioural patterns they had in the first place; just with a new partner.

Many people just look for sex. They believe that sex is connection. That all men or women are the same as the person that wronged them, so what's the point of risking their heart again? So they settle. They settle for mediocre sex, mediocre connections, a mediocre life. Safe, but oh so unsatisfying.

Fucking exes, fuckboys (and fuckgirls), friends with benefits, hoe bros (I made that term up, ain't it just great?), booty calls, game playing on dating sites...this behaviour has all become normal because there are so many hurt arsed meat bags walking around, still angry, unhealed, hurt inner children with emotional baggage, in full blown protection mode, saying they want true connection but who are too afraid to actually *feel* fucking anything.

While true love is limitless, once the Body gets involved...ego, stories, expectations, hopes and past experiences can make love become just another cage to keep us small and afraid.

You can live in fear of loss or heartbreak. You cannot feel enough unless you are being validated by the other person, feel extreme jealousy and compare yourself harshly to other people, see everyone else as a threat or be consumed by jealousy. All these things are natural because love is scary, but these emotions are not to be confused with real soul connection love.

These are all fear-based emotions that come from your Body to protect you when she feels you are being stripped bare, when it feels safer to her to keep you small.

Real love is immense. It's all encompassing, but with infinite ways to grow. True love is powerful and expansive. It actually represents true freedom because it's boundless.

That's fucking scary, isn't it? Now we can understand why our Body feels the need to protect us from it.

To be in love - to fully love another soul, to let go of ego and shame, to be totally vulnerable - is nothing short of acting like an actual fucking warrior.

Connection is scary. To open yourself up, to reflect on your own behaviours, heal old wounds and not project or fulfil your needs through somebody else means fully being in your own power.

To connect with someone on that soul level is almost like ripping your flesh open and laying your heart and soul bare. It's the most intense and vulnerable experience you can subject your human self to. For your Higher Self this is a breeze; fun even. For your Body... this is some serious next level shit.

For most people this is just too much. It's too risky, too scary. They've not yet dealt with their demons: they are still in some sort of cage. Not only is it just too terrifying to try and do this for themselves but it's triggering to see someone else who is brave enough to risk this - all *for them* - and so it sends them running in the opposite direction.

To open yourself up, you must either not be afraid of what you are going to find inside of you, or you need to be brave enough to face up to it.

To not be afraid of your mind, thoughts, actions, feelings and past.

That is true freedom.

Everything we see in others is a reflection of what we think about or fear about ourselves.

Imagine being so free that you can face everything about yourself with grace, bravery, honesty and love.

And then, like the warrior that you are, you then lay this bare, with no games, no ego and no limitations, to another person. Offering to face their true selves without judgement. Being a squishy, vulnerable meat bag with your heart and imperfections flapping about in the wind.

Then the other person says no.

You're too much...
Not enough...
Too imperfect...
Too messed up...

A train wreck waiting to happen.

You'll think that it's you.

That you showed your true self so it must be true.

That you are not enough.
That you are too much.

You'll take that rejection and make it about yourself, internalise their words.

But it's not about you.

It's a reflection of your strength, a reflection of your power. Your vulnerability, your bravery.

To break free and see someone else in their true power really is scary for someone who isn't in the same place. It shows them the possibilities in themselves. Reflects to them their own vulnerabilities, their fears and their own cages. Their cage that feels impossible to break free of.

If only they were as brave as you. If only they could feel enough. It's a rare thing to witness because this is true bravery. The connection is rare because in order for it to work you both need to be on the same page. The same journey. To show the same strength.

It's not impossible, but it is rare.

And beautiful...
And petrifying...

So, if you are facing rejection, please know this... You are enough. You are a mother fucking warrior. There is someone out there as brave as you. True love flourishes when she is free. True love flourishes when you are both feeling enough to be able to face the possibility of rejection. To face all the possibilities in the eye. Square in the feels. To be open and honest with one another. To not judge. To not make stories. To not expect yourself from the other person.

Cages are oh so safe, they keep us small, and they come in varying forms. Living your life in a way that is unapologetic, expanding and not allowing the imperfections of yourself to rule your head or your heart takes true courage. When someone else cannot handle that, it's because they fear the fact that you are doing what they cannot.

It's like you've got this powerful beautiful strong eagle, hunched up in a tiny golden cage with his wings trying to stretch out through the bars...the door is open, but the eagle doesn't seem to see just how easy it would be for him to escape. The eagle doesn't know his power. It feels impossible to escape and besides, it looks scary out there, the cage is much safer. The cage isn't too bad anyway, right? Maybe he can't even fly if he tried? What if I fall?
What if I fly?

The thought of being free is sometimes as scary as the thought of being trapped. Failure and success both come with risk, it's much safer to stay stuck.

Breaking free from cages, be it unhappy relationships, drugs, shitty jobs or whatever, means your life can begin again. It's a place of stepping into your limitless power, trusting your Higher Self, it means the possibilities for your life are now endless because you are taking responsibility for it.

Full power.
Full responsibility.

100% Freedom means 100% Responsibility

There's no one to blame or to fall back on.

You have to reflect...
You have to feel...
You have to heal...
You have to grow...
You have to be ready to fall.

To break down.
To rebuild.
Face all of your dark...

Is it any wonder really then that people are too afraid and seem to rather stay in their little cages?

They pimp them out, making the cage more bearable. Distract themselves in any way possible, then sit in their gilded cages pretending that they are happy or just avoiding their emotions. They lose themselves in distractions. They buy every gadget under the sun and have a little flat screen TV hanging on the bars. Pretty it up, upgrade the cage occasionally, just enough so they don't suffocate but not enough to break free and fly.

Then you come along.

Show them what true happiness can look like. Prove to them that freedom is possible. Show them how love can be freeing, love can be imperfect, and love can give infinite possibilities.

And it's all too much, they can't cope with it. They can't face up to themselves with kindness. They believe they cannot leave their cage - even if the door is proving to be wide open. They want to be safe. They want games, security, a vision for their future that is easy, risk free... in other words, they want pretend-freedom.

So they reject your arse.

If it feels like it's about you it's because it both is, and it isn't. You've shown "all that could be". Everything negative you are telling yourself is just your Body's fear, she wants to protect you from ever getting hurt again. Your Higher Self already knows this, it's your Body that is going to need to play catch up.

Body will use this as proof that the risk is just not worth the pain and so will tell you loads of horrible things that this situation tells you about yourself.

Just so that you don't risk doing it again.

That heartache?
That's grief for unrealistic expectations.

That disgusting self-talk?
That's protection to not rush it again.

That self-sabotaging behaviour pattern?
That's how your Body has learned to protect you in the past, so will use it again.

That not-enoughness?

You are reflecting the thought patterns of the person who rejected you.

A few years ago, we were having fireworks in my parents' garden. Their garden is small, so I had the kids near the house with me. I was recording my dad lighting the fireworks with one of those long sticks and as he lit one and stood back, the firework fizzled but didn't set off. In the video, in a matter of seconds, you can hear me laughing and saying to dad: "*You never go back to a lit firework...you never go back!*"

Then, all of a sudden, the firework exploded while still on the ground. We gathered the screaming children and ran back in the house. In the video you just saw this flash of light and like a million balls of sparkles surrounding us while we screamed. Very, very, very luckily the kids were fine, just very shook up. The adults had a few burns but nothing serious. I was shaking for a good couple of hours and my dad said:

"*You've gotta laugh Mirrie, let's go out and do some more!*"

I was like: "*Hell no, I'm never doing fireworks ever again!*"

It took me ages to be able to watch that video back, replaying the trauma, but now I watch it and find it pretty cool...unfortunately, *You've Been Framed* didn't want to pay me £250 for it.

The phrase "*you never go back to a lit firework*" stayed with me.

For your Body, love is a firework waiting to explode. Up until now (if you are single) you may never have experienced healthy love before. Up until now you may have been burned by love, hurt time and time again. Imagine being scarred by a firework and then going straight out to light another one. Imagine if every firework you'd ever lit had exploded in your face. How likely would it be that you'd want to go straight back out and risk lighting another one again?

Hell no.

Your Body thinks you are legit crazy for ever wanting to risk getting hurt again. Your Body is expecting the fireworks to explode. Your Body is almost certain you'll get hurt again.

Your Body is protecting you.
Reflect on your actions, be honest about your feelings but don't listen to the negative voice inside saying that you were not

enough. A person who is truly free can never be with a person who is still caged up.

The two people are living in different realities, different levels, different worlds. One would always have to compromise. If they weren't ready to join you in your freedom, they would have expected you to join them in their cage.

Having this realisation actually puts you in a place of true power.

Yes, the other person ran from you, but now you know why, you can realise they would have just been another cage for you.

In order to feel justified in staying in their cage, maybe unknowingly or not, they would have tried to keep you small, trapped...just like them.

Even if they said they loved to see you free and in your full power, they would need to keep you small and keep your power at a bearable rate for them, because seeing your power would be a constant reminder to them of their own.

Keeping you at their level would mean that they have no need to step into their own power, grow, be free and be happy. They would have had to squish you down or you would need to pace yourself to stay in their world.

As much as you wanted and loved this person, you were not made to be small, you are too brave, too fucking powerful, too bright, too vulnerable and too full of limitless possibility to be squished into somebody else's tiny cage. You have fought for too long and too hard to be trampled back down.

You are allowed to feel.
You are allowed to grieve what may have been.
You are allowed to reflect on yourself.

But it has taken too many stars in the heavens moving themselves for you, for you to walk yourself back into another cage and willingly give another person the key.

Fuck no.

Fucking feel it but don't move in there, don't allow it to stop you living or to stop you loving. Use it to make you more free, use it to remember all that you've worked for, all you've given up, all you decided and risked your heart for.

You were not born to live in a cage.
You were born to live.
You were born to love.

You were born to love.

Healing

When you break up with someone why does it seem that every song you listen to now is a love song that reminds you of them?

You either avoid music all together or you curl up in a foetal position, with a tub of ice cream handy, pop on the songs that make you the saddest, like the masochist that you are, and sob into your raspberry ripple, feeling all you have lost and how no one will ever match up.

Once anger sets in, the songs change as you now shout-cry into your hairbrush, never losing eye contact with yourself in the mirror (or is that just me?).

The angry songs are normally self-derogatory or talk about how much you hate the other person, and yourself, and life. Your focus is still on the person who has rejected you, what they think about you, how you are not enough for them and how you can't live without them. The anger feels good but there's still so much pain inside you that YOU don't feel good.

Thing is, once you know what true love is, once you see love as two higher selves connecting, once you let go of the games and let go of using another person's love as a way of validating yourself, once you see that no one else on this planet has the responsibility of fulfilling your needs, your wants or your desires, once you know that no other person has the responsibility of making you happy, making you feel whole or giving you purpose…That's when you see these songs, almost all these songs, are actually talking about a toxic kind of love.

All the classic ballads that taught us about love as we were growing up, were talking about "needy" love. Possessive love. Conditional love. Love that's ruled by your human body rather than your higher consciousness. Rooted in how the person makes you feel.

The type of love where you can't live without someone else or where you hate yourself unless they are loving you IS NOT HEALTHY LOVE.

If you have experienced this type of love, which you probably have as that's normally the only type of love we are fed as real, you will know that once you lose it, it feels like you have lost everything. This is because you invest so much of yourself, your worth, your life into the other person and your feelings are governed by their actions.

So while things are going good, you are feeling loved and happy and fulfilled…but if they are actively hurting you, abusing you or cheating on you, your emotions, worth and purpose will have unwittingly been signed up for a rollercoaster ride. And then once they're gone, that's it - you are back at a place of *who am I* again.

When things turn sour, or you get rejected, it feels like you've got nothing to live for.

Really, love built on this rollercoaster ride is doomed to be rocky. Even if the other person isn't bringing their emotional baggage into the mix or their own toxic needs or expectations…the truth is this is just too much responsibility and pressure to put on someone else.

Your feelings...
Your happiness...
Your worth...
Your life.

That's your own shit. No one else can do this for you. It's too big of a job for anyone else. And it's too much of a job for you to take responsibility for someone else's shit too. When we talk about love being as close to freedom as we can get, does having responsibility for someone else's happiness sound like love? Does that sound freeing?

To be truly free you need to be your own anchor. Have your worth, your happiness, your emotions and your purpose anchored inside yourself.

In fact, you know what I've done? Got myself in front of the mirror and sung all those old love songs TO MYSELF. Yep, I pulled the old switcheroo on all the songs that made me feel like I couldn't live without someone else and looked myself in the eye and sang them to myself, about me.

"I can't live if living is without you"

"When you put your arms around me, you let me know there's nothing in this world I can't do"

"If you fall, I will catch you, I'll be waiting...time after time"

"And when you smile, the whole world stops and stares for a while, cause girl you're amazing just the way you are"

"I hope you don't mind that I put down in words how wonderful life is while you're in the world"

"How sweet it is to be loved by you"

You get the idea. I started it because instead of making me cry the songs made me laugh but do you know what... when sung from your Higher Self to your Body, these songs are far more powerful!

Often, if you've not been practising self-love and you are wrapped up in another person, it's euphoric, addictive and is like a bubble from your real life. The bubble is so seductive, especially if you've been in a place of self-hate for a long time. Finally, someone loves you for you (or a lighter projected version of you) and you finally feel loveable and worthy. The shift of seeing yourself through somebody else's eyes who seemingly adores you, is so new and novel it's easy to get lost in it. You want to experience the bubble at all times, it just seems all too perfect. And it is. Eventually the bubble will pop. Eventually the flaws start to emerge. We all have darkness and light, human flaws and especially if you are rooted in self-hate, toxic traits and needs will come bubbling to the surface. We may feel elevated while in the bubble but when we get slapped in the face with our real life again, distrust, jealousy or doubts can rule our days.

When we have taken the power back. When we anchor ourselves in the place of not needing anyone else's approval, when we feel loveable and worthy without any external forces, that's when we start to create the life that's better than any bubble. And truly that's real living. To have a life we don't need escaping from. To have thoughts and feelings governed by us that are fulfilling our own needs and feeling satisfied and accomplished without anyone else's input. To feel loveable because we can love ourselves.

To be your own anchor. To not need a bubble. To have love from another person in that state will be a bonus. It still feels euphoric, it still feels amazing, but it's on your own terms. It's a stable feeling because it comes from within yourself. Now you are sure of your worth, sure of your boundaries, sure of yourself so when someone amazing comes along, they are not validating you, they are just adding sparkle to your life.

Can you taste the difference? Can you imagine someone like this loving you? Loving you with no agenda rather than just to enjoy your company, to share the good and bad moments in life...but not relying on you to cope, not relying on you to be happy, not relying on you as a reason to live. Doesn't that sound freeing? Doesn't that sound beautiful? Doesn't that sound so much more satisfying than any bubble? Isn't that what you'd like to be able to offer to the person you love?

Basically, we are talking about the difference between love based from inside your Body and love based from inside your Higher Self.

Your Higher Self is fully powerful, she has infinite power, she knows she can cope with whatever life throws at her, she has boundaries and dreams and infinite possibilities. She knows who she is. She has unconditional self-love as her foundation. She knows her worth is unmovable, anchored and strong. Her worth just is, and nothing external can change that. She wants to create her best life, express herself freely and give herself grace for her imperfections.

Your Body is more human. She loves you so much that her only goal is to protect you from getting hurt. She's unsure of your power and so uses feelings of unworthiness, jealousy or neediness to protect you based on your experiences in love so far. She just wants you to be safe and so throws up all sorts of shit when falling in love with another person.

For a true soul connection, it does take bravery. To create a life that doesn't need a bubble? That feels almost superhuman. When you approach this anchored in your Higher Self's infinite strength it's more than possible though. It's undeniable, it's a given. As long as you can reassure your Body of your power and unconditional love every single day, do the inner work, face your fears and forgive yourself when you fuck up, you will create this anchor. You will create this foundation; you will create a life far more enjoyable than a fleeting bubble. But first, you need to heal.

So many people will jump straight into another relationship because the hurt and the belief that they need someone else to complete them is just too much to bear.

Hurt people hurt people.

If you have been hurt or you feel angry and loving yourself feels like too much of a leap right now, give yourself some grace. Start off with just the goal of feeling a little better. Tiny steps towards healing are better than no healing.

But then you ask yourself, am I ready to heal?

Fuck me, healing is scary.

Facing up to the reality that in order to heal it actually means you have to let go. Let go of the bubbles, let go of the anger, let go of the feelings of unworthiness and let go of the relationship that you may have thought was going to last forever.

You need to face up to the reality of your own humanness. The patterns and behaviours you have that may not be healthy for you. Face up to your ugly. Face up to your insecurities. It feels so much safer to jump into another bubble. To not rely on yourself for your happiness...to head towards another rollercoaster. But let me tell you, healing and loving yourself regardless of what anyone else thinks or feels about you is soooooo incredibly sweet. Feeling enough and satisfied with your own life is sooooo incredibly delicious. Fulfilling your desires, wants, needs and dreams and having that internal anchor is true freedom...and THAT changes everything.

That is worth being brave for, that is worth the inner reflection, which is worth facing your fears and pain for. That is worth letting go of anyone who doesn't align with your life for.

It's so much easier to let something go when you know in your heart that it isn't serving you. Once you know that your worth is rock steady and isn't dependent on anyone else's actions or feelings, that your happiness is 100% your responsibility, it feels like you need to protect it. That any person now entering your life does so because you've decided they add something special to your life. It's a privilege for you to share your time with them and that you are on equal footing with a mutual desire to support, love and cherish each other. Now you don't just give your heart (or fanny) to any old Tom, Dick or Harry because you see your value and appreciate the work it took to get you there. Being secure in yourself and the life that you are creating means anything you get from anyone else is a bonus.

This is so worth healing for, right?

Before you start it is helpful to put your hands on your heart and remind your Body that you are safe. That you can cope, that you are strong enough to heal and let go of all that doesn't serve you.

It doesn't have to be all or nothing. It's not logical to think that you can leap from self-hate and hurt into self-love and bliss. I mean, you could, but for most of us squishy humans it takes time, patience, grace and a whole lotta forgiveness. So instead of feeling like you "should " be feeling this or doing that, just set out to do something that makes you feel a tiny bit better. Do something for yourself that makes you feel a tiny bit cared for. Remember it's a process so it's OK to cry, it's OK to get angry and it's OK to feel scared...it's more than OK: it's human.

Most of us will never get to a point where we wake up one day and feel completely healed, completely in our power or completely in love with ourselves, or if we do, it won't be every day because we are human and just like self-love, healing is a daily commitment...it takes being extra kind and gentle with ourselves and actually processing our feelings like we've talked about all throughout this book.

Everyone's process, ways and needs to heal are different but to know you are on the right track you need:

- *Inner attachment*
  This means getting to know your true self and becoming actively interested in your own wellbeing and happiness. Becoming aligned with the beliefs that serve you and being committed to loving yourself to the best of your ability daily.

- *Self-care*
  Being invested in your self-love, healing, wellbeing and

happiness means you'll need to take care of yourself. Actually putting into practise the self-care suggestions you've learned about. Trying each day to make yourself feel a little better by finding out what brings you sparks of joy and makes you feel gratitude to yourself and your Body. Making fun and making your needs just as important as everyone else's. Carving out time for yourself and your passions. Enjoying yourself without guilt and basically just giving a shit about yourself.

- *Firm boundaries*
  Allowing yourself to love without expectations or fear doesn't mean you rush in blindly and let someone walk all over you. You still need firm boundaries with all relationships in your life. Having boundaries means you have respect for your time and energy. It means that whoever you invite into your life you won't resent or feel used by. Having firm boundaries means your garden is secure and anyone who is a part of it brings joy and support to the table. Remember you are allowed to give from your excess. You are allowed to fill your cup first. You are allowed to say No. Having boundaries also means you are more aware of people who want to push them or break them which can save you from a lot of heartbreak further down the line.

- *Build your own life*
  When you fall head over heels for someone it's natural to want to spend every waking minute with them...at first. But your life is YOUR life and theirs is theirs. You can't live for someone else. Even if you find love on a soul connection you are still going to have different interests, different energy levels or different social needs. **Build a life that's enhanced by another person, not reliant on them.** This goes for partners, family and friends. Enjoy being with other people but learn to embrace your own interests too and never miss out on something your soul is calling you to do because someone else doesn't want to do it...learn to enjoy doing things on your own. See your relationships as the cherry on the top - not the whole cake.

- *LET GO*

  Look at your current life with fresh eyes, feel brave enough and free enough to let go of whatever is no longer serving you. There's no wrong way to do this because if something or someone is truly meant to be in your life Big U will see to the fact that they will come back in. Let go of the emotions, hurt and anger that you've been carrying around for years, let go of your cages.... the shitty job, the crappy relationship, or the addictions. If it doesn't make you feel good, why hold on to it? Life is for living and you now know you deserve all the love, all the joy, all the support and all the bliss that life has to offer. There's really no time to waste - start TODAY.

Walk out of the door of your cage...see how easy it can be to step out and stretch your wings. Give yourself the care, time, space, grace and love to heal. Test out those wings, see how strong you really are. Prove to yourself that it's safe to fly. Pretty soon you'll be soaring high, burning up the fucking sky, with limitless possibilities, bliss and love stretching out in front of you.

.

Chapter Fifteen - Being Enough Today

In order for you to truly believe you are Already Enough, you have to prove to yourself that you are Enough **today.**

Today not tomorrow.
Just as you are right in this very moment.

You prove that by your actions, by the way you treat yourself, by how much time and effort you gift yourself, and by the grace you allow yourself.

Remember, whatever you believe is what will prove itself to you.

There's nothing to fix...
There's no "*I'll love myself when*"...

You need to be able to look at both your light and your dark and see each aspect of yourself as beautiful. Unique. Loveable.

There can't be light without the dark. There will always be shadows that will feel comfortable to hide in. Your light will scare you as much as your dark does. It's OK to feel that fear.

It's OK to not feel enough. It's OK to fuckup.

But you are the one that needs to decide that it's OK. You are the one who needs to give yourself permission and treat yourself kindly regardless. You are the only one who can commit to loving yourself messy. You get to choose.

Be Vulnerable to Be Strong

You walk into a room of happy faces – some you know really well; some you've never met before.

"*Hi, how are you doing?*"
"*I'm really good, how are you?*"

You meet up with a good friend for coffee.

"It's been too long, how are you?"
"So good, you?"

You see your mum.

"How are you doing?"
You burst into tears

Even when you're talking to a close friend, if you're the friend to lean on but you don't feel able to lean on anyone…maybe you're seeing vulnerability as a weakness? I know I did.

About 10 years ago, I *prided* myself on not needing anyone or anything. Being strong was so important to me. I had a couple of people who knew what pain I was hiding but my party trick was to be the life of the party. So much fun, everyone loves you, but no one gets too close. That was perfect for me. I was strong, independent, fun, loved, living life to the max.

Sounds good, right?

Well, it was until any time I was alone with myself. Being alone petrified me.

Waiting in a doctor's office, at the bus stop, quiet time at work…even going to the loo. I was a slave to my own thoughts, so scared of facing up *to me* that I'd do anything to avoid it.

So, it wasn't just not letting other people in – I had to block out myself too. That's the thing about being "strong". If you don't want or need help, strong means alone and alone is impossible when you are more scared of being alone than anything else.

So, what is it that you're scared of? *The unknown.* The emotions you've been avoiding. The "you" you really are. That it will all just be too much. That super-bitchy voice telling you that you're worthless and not enough.

Staying "strong" is seen as a strength. But strongness without vulnerability is really just hiding from your truth. It turns out "being strong" is quite a weak thing to do. It's weak because "being strong" means you don't feel strong enough to be vulnerable.

To me, being vulnerable is the ultimate, most powerful strength.

To be vulnerable, you have to be *brave*. Being vulnerable means being *you*; no matter where you are or who you're with. It's owning your emotions and *knowing* you can handle whatever comes up. It's *letting people in.* Showing people who you are and what you are feeling is *brave.*

You risk:

- Being rejected
- Being misunderstood
- Being laughed at
- Being told you're an imposter/drama queen/selfish/ [insert any scary term you don't want to be thought of as here]

You risk *losing control of how other people see you.* They may find out that you're *gasp*...*not perfect.*

That's some scary shit.

Letting people in means that they have to accept you for the real you. That you have opinions, hopes and dreams that matter...sometimes more to you than theirs do.

That you have problems too and aren't just a shoulder to cry on or someone to ask help from. Vulnerability means that *you* may need help too. You need other people to enrich your life. You risk people letting you down and *you* may let other people down.

Can you see why we prefer to stay "strong" and "independent"? Half the time these risks just don't feel worth it. Half the time we don't feel "strong enough" or "brave enough" to take these risks.

So, we shrink.
We stay quiet.
We stay hidden.
That is not being "strong". *Vulnerability* is true strength.

Writing this book feels like the ultimate act of vulnerability to
me. I feel like I'm laying my soul butt-naked to the world. Every
time I pick up my pen, I have to not only face the fact that
someone else will read this, but I have to face each emotion
myself too. I have to face each risk, each shortcoming, each
moment. It's fucking scary as hell. It's an act of bravery to pick up
this pen and write.

It's an act of bravery for tears to fall. It's an act of bravery to call
or text someone or look a person in the eyes and admit that
you're not coping well or need help. It's an act of bravery to leave
the house for the first time in weeks and smile at a stranger. It's
an act of bravery to ask for a hug. It's an act of bravery to admit
that you're not perfect, that you feel like you're screwing up, that
you want to cry, that you don't feel enough. It's an act of bravery
to meet a friend for coffee. It's an act of bravery to *let someone
in*. It's an act of bravery to be vulnerable.

Sometimes we spend so much time and effort hiding ourselves
from everyone else that we start hiding from *ourselves* too.
Sometimes, that hard outer layer designed to "keep us safe"
starts to grow into a hard outer crust. It starts to overtake any
softness and gradually becomes a hard inner layer too. The
longer it's left unchecked, the deeper it grows and the crustier it
becomes.

We start becoming numb to ourselves. Sometimes our
vulnerability isn't just opening up to others but opening up to
ourselves too. It happened to me. I hid from myself for years and
it's so easy for it to happen – you hardly even notice. But, all of a
sudden, your phone is stuck to your hand at all times and even a
moment's silence feels like a deadly threat.

Afraid and trapped is the opposite of loved and free. For self-love
to bloom and that feeling of power and freedom to burst, you
need to be vulnerable. You need to be brave. This means learning

who you are, what values you hold and the emotions you've been avoiding. It means opening yourself up to *risk*.

You may get hurt.
You may upset people.
You may find out things about yourself which you don't like or wish you hadn't done.

Today is a new day and the possibilities are endless. Face the unknown. Claim your truth, through your "real" eyes.

Speak your truth.

Let people in. You are allowed to be seen and heard, just as you are, every fucking day of your life.

Letting Go of Shoulds and Guilt...

Let's meet for a cosy cuppa and say a beautiful fucking farewell to our four friends:

Guilt
Shame
Shoulds
Perfection

First, we will talk about the partners in crime. Guilt and shame are two very similar emotions but very different in the results they produce. Guilt is something that pops its ugly head up when we feel that we've done something wrong. Something contrary to our morals or misaligned with our Higher Self or not aligned with the person we believe ourselves to be.

Guilt can move us to action, correcting the wrongs we feel have happened. It's something we feel when we need forgiveness, either from ourselves or others.

Shame has no real positive effect. It's something that overtakes us when we feel that we are a "bad person" because of our actions or non-action. Shame can be caused by our belief that someone is judging us for those actions. Shame fills us with negativity and self-loathing but doesn't normally inspire any action, other than to beat ourselves up harder.

So firstly, ask yourself this: am I feeling guilt or shame? Am I feeling in need of forgiveness or am I feeling unworthy of love? Am I feeling this way because of misalignment or other people's expectations?

Bringing in Shoulds and Perfection, which are normally the cause of our guilt and shame, is the situation MY truth or is it still someone else's?

We have been told from a young age what actions we "should" be doing or what qualities we "should" have. Next time you add the word "should" to your sentence, ask yourself if it's someone else telling you this so-called truth or if you really believe/know it for yourself.

Sometimes when we think of our failures or shortcomings, instead of seeing them as a small part of who we are or what we have done, we label ourselves a "Bad person".

We have been told actions are GOOD or BAD our whole lives. Pretty much every movie will have a goodie and a baddie. The baddie is to be hated, and the goodie celebrated.
We are told:

Good = Lovable

Bad = Unworthy of love

This is UNTRUE. We all have both good and bad inside us. The light can't exist without the dark, remember?

We all are neither good nor bad. We are ALL deserving of love.

Are you feeling in need of forgiveness or unworthy of love? If you feel like you need forgiveness from someone who won't give it to you, can you give it to yourself?

Are you asking for advice or permission?

Are your "shoulds" worth it? Is this worth denting your self-love over? Where do your "shoulds" come from and is it still YOUR belief or somebody else's?

Think about what a "should" is:
"Obligation, duty or correctness, typically when criticising someone's actions."

So basically, it's an expectation – either from you or someone else, based on your understanding of what people may think of you. Of course, there are expectations of you that are totally needed, like feeding your kids or keeping them safe and warm.

But then there are some expectations that are just ridiculous. Some expectations are just unrealistic or even soul destroying.

Because these expectations are fed to us (by society, parents, friends etc.) from such a young age, they get held onto by our subconscious mind and become beliefs without us even knowing. It can be uncomfortable that people don't think the same way as we do because we've never even thought of it as any other way, we believe that that's just the way life is. We forget that everyone has a different set of "shoulds", and these can actually rule your whole life or become a cage in their own right.

Add in bad mental health or the seriously unrealistic expectations that need you to be someone different to try to live up to and it can easily lead to you not ever feeling enough. Feeling like you're not measuring up, should-ing yourself throughout your entire life.

It can mean feeling unworthy, that your dreams don't matter, and that the person you are will never live up to who you feel like you need to be. You start feeling like you are always playing catch up, like the goal of feeling enough is never quite in your reach because you have all these unattainable expectations weighing heavily on you.

You might feel out of control because you are so used to people pleasing or appeasing that you believe you have the impossible responsibility to keep everyone else happy and no matter what you do you can never quite manage it.

It's like a spiral because once you feel this way, it can send you deeper and deeper into not feeling enough. Basing your "enough-ness" or worth on the "shoulds", and unrealistic expectations of yourself or your life is a dangerous game. It's *even more* dangerous when we aren't even conscious that we're doing it.

Imagine this: You're a kid and every morning your mum serves you porridge made with water and a sprinkle of salt. Your dad eats this breakfast, as do all of your siblings. *"Come and get your porridge"* your mum calls up to you every morning.

One morning, you ask your mum: *"Why do we have porridge every morning?"*. *"Everybody does,"* your mum replies. Your siblings and father don't even question it and every morning you wake up expecting porridge with a sprinkle of salt.

Then, you stay around a friend's house. Her mum serves you porridge, with a sprinkle of salt – of course she does – that's what your mum told you. Every person you know or you stay around gives you this every morning of your young life. After a while you wouldn't question it. That's what *everyone* has for breakfast. Your experiences have shown you that your mum's words were true. As the years pass and you have your own kids you serve them up porridge with a sprinkle of salt, and when they ask *"Why?"* you tell them: *"Everyone has this for breakfast".* Because, in your reality, everyone does.

Imagine now if after 30-odd years of having your porridge with a sprinkle of salt every morning without fail, your friend from out of town comes to visit. She sits down at your breakfast table and watches as each of your kids gets a sprinkle of salt on their porridge. *"You use salt?"* she says, shocked. *"Erm, doesn't everyone?"*, you laugh.

"No! I'll have sugar please, and maybe some fruit". You stop in your tracks. Fruit? Sugar? On *porridge*?

"Are you serious?" you ask her.

Your mind is blown. She has porridge sweet? You are allowed to have porridge sweet?

Then, you may start looking deeper. Pancakes. Full English. Omelette. Cereal. Toast. There are hundreds of options for breakfast! Your mum was wrong!

What would you make for breakfast the very next day after finding this out? Porridge with salt, most likely. Why? It feels "right" to your subconscious and feels wrong to have anything else. It feels like an effort to break your routine. It feels like you're admitting your mum was wrong. It feels like you're saying you know better than your mum. That *you* are better than your mum. It feels like you'd be going against the grain. All your friends would wonder why. You'd stand out as different. You don't have time to change. It feels safe to do what you know.

This all means that your conscious brain now knows this belief that *"Everyone has porridge with a sprinkle of salt for breakfast"* is not true. There's a whole world of possibility waiting for you and your taste buds out there, but your unconscious mind still holds this belief as *true*, so your actions will still match your original belief.

In a number of ways (even if you *think* you know the truth), if you haven't done the deeper work of accepting it on a subconscious level, the subconscious beliefs always win.

Why?

1. It gives you bad feelings about the new beliefs

- Feels unsafe
- Feels untrue
- Feels "wrong"
- Feels scary

- Feels too much like an effort

2. It gives you guilt and "shoulds"

- I should be doing this
- I should be feeling this
- This is not the way I should be behaving
  This is not the way I should be treating my mum's beliefs
- This is not the way I should be raising my children

3. It gives you a "storm"

- Hateful inner voice
- Things go wrong
- Life seems harder
- You feel worthless

What you learned = CORE BELIEFS
What you experienced = CONSCIOUS BELIEFS

Core beliefs often go unquestioned, so they work deep within us without us even noticing. This can be very dangerous if the people we've lived around have destructive core beliefs for themselves.

The scariest thing about core beliefs is that no matter what you say, if your actions match the belief, your kids will pick up on them and often adopt them as their own. Addressing, acknowledging and changing your core beliefs into loving, positive ones turns into an act of love, not just for yourself, but also for your children and their children. It's so damn important, especially if you're a mum, dad or grandparent. Actually, it's important for everyone.

Obviously, the porridge example isn't that big of a deal, but I've used it to show you that your "shoulds" go deeper than just a feeling of obligation or expectation. It's a firm belief of how you've experienced the world working. Injecting worth, self-belief and self-love into your core beliefs is lifesaving but if forced it can be like trying to use needles to make a hole in concrete – that shit is hard work!

Self-love can be effortless, and we are flexible, ever-changing, intricate beings. So, this process can be as hard or as easy as you make it. But either way, these beliefs run deep so there's deep work to be done to release and let go of guilt and "shoulds". That's because they may have started with other people's expectations of you, but now they're so much more.

Your shoulds are your core beliefs of what's expected of you in order to be a "good person" or a "worthy person". Now you know these simply aren't true.

Every time you get stuck by guilt or "shoulds", you need to look inside at your expectations and see if they're in alignment with your new self-love beliefs, and if they're serving you in living a happy, satisfying life. In other words, you need to question your "shoulds" *every day*.

What would my day look like without this "should"? What would I *feel* like without this should? Where/who did this "should" come from? Is this "should" true? Who would get hurt if this "should" doesn't get done? Why is this "should" so important to me? Does this "should" make me a better person or parent? Is this "should" positive or destructive?

Uncomfortable Action

Write down all of the shoulds and things that cause you guilt or shame. Write it quickly. Don't overthink it.

Look at each point and decide if it's something that you believe is true and that you can work on, if it's someone else's truth that you don't believe anymore that can be let go of, or if it's stuff you can't change and that you need to accept.

Then I want you to crunch up that piece of paper. Now, destroy it...even better, BURN IT!!

Today you will have a clean slate. Every "should" or guilt that comes into your heart from this day forth becomes a choice. YOUR CHOICE to keep it or LET IT GO.

Overthinking – This Moment's Truth

I have multiple anxiety disorders which means when I'm at my worst I'm always having catastrophic thoughts. I used to describe myself as having a battle with my depression and anxiety every moment of every day and it felt exhausting.

As I mentioned before, the moment I accepted certain parts of me as "just me" and stopped fighting against them, I was able to start loving myself regardless.

There are certain things I do, think and react to that aren't necessarily ideal, but it's just the way my brain works. Sometimes it's a bit messed up but it's not my personality, it doesn't show the type of person I am, but rather the way my brain has learned to deal with something. The way she's learned to protect me. She may be wired differently to another person's brain and that's fucking more than OK. It's what makes life so exciting and fresh. We are all different, yet we are all still one.

I am no longer battling against myself – there's times I'm frustrated by the way I am, for sure. But those times are when I need to love myself harder – more *fully*.

"You said unconditionally, right?"

Sometimes our brains run away with themselves like an unstoppable train heading off a cliff. We get so caught up in different scenarios that we forget it's *us* actually making it up!

Our brain doesn't know the difference between experiences in the real world and the ones just in our head.

Did you know there are people out there who have learned to play the piano without ever touching a piano? Just through visualisation, their bodies actually make muscle memory in their fingers just as if they were doing the physical act.

When you are down a rabbit hole of "what ifs" and imagining the worst-case scenario playing out in your head, your Body will create the emotions that go alongside it, and those feelings will stay in your Body even if it hasn't even happened in real life.

Our brains like doing this to prepare us for worst case scenarios, like a practice run of emotion, so it will imagine the same thing again if not consciously stopped. What another beautiful way our Body is protecting us...nah only playing, it's fucking torture! A torturous, beautiful way our bodies decide to protect us.

Whether it's a huge situation – Like you get called to hospital and you don't know what's happened.

Or a tiny situation – you send a text to your friend, and she doesn't text you back.

The brain isn't fussy, and your Body gets so entangled in your imagination. The emotions stay with you and then the story we've made up feels like the truth to us, even when we don't know the full situation.

So, how can you stop yourself from overthinking? I have this thing I like to do when I realise my thinking has become out of control. I call it:

"This Moment's Truth"

Firstly, I tell my brain – *"Thank you for trying to protect me, but I'm already safe"*. Then, I take a deep breath and list out *only* the bare truths of what I know for certain are facts.

Sent a text – no reply:

This moments truth:
I sent a text

Uncertainties:
I don't know if it's been read yet
I don't know if she's busy
I don't know if she's angry with me
I don't know if I've upset her
I don't know what she's doing
Because I don't know (a lot), I now choose to assume the best or nothing at all. Look only at this moment's truth. Don't allow that bitchy inner dialogue to chime in – you need to protect yourself emotionally and mentally. Even for serious situations.

You get a phone call – someone's been rushed to hospital:

This moment's truth:
They're in hospital
You need to go
They're alive

Uncertainties:
I don't know how bad it is
I don't know if they asked for me
I don't know what happened
I don't know if...

Assume the best or nothing at all.

What you're really afraid about (even though it sounds selfish) is whether *you* can cope with it. Of course, you don't want to have hurt anyone, or anyone to be hurt in the hospital, but, ultimately, the actual fear and overthinking comes from a place of being scared if you'll be able to cope with the situation. So, your brain gives you some practice (and stress).

Are you brave enough?
      Are you strong enough?
            Are you capable enough?

Notice what word keeps coming up? Are you "*enough*" to cope with this?

Overthinking with a traumatic event is totally normal – don't be hard on yourself. Overthinking day in, day out, about little things, though, is just you constantly asking yourself the question:

"Am I enough to cope with this?"

If your friend doesn't text you back because she's annoyed about something you've said, *are you enough to cope with that*? What does that say about you as a person? Will you beat yourself up about this situation? Yes? Then your brain may as well get your Body ready by giving you a dose of self-hate before you even know if your friend is upset!

If you are overthinking that usually means your Body is in a protective mode and self-love needs to be injected into your thoughts.

Breathe.

Allow the overwhelm but ground yourself in this Moments Truth.

As you get good at this you will find the overthinking will melt away quickly.

Trust And Joy

Let's go back to YesterMirrie and read how she was feeling on a random day for no apparent reason...

"It's only just 9am and I can tell I'm having a day where I'm craving external validation... This doesn't set me up for having a good day and I'll tell you why.

I feel needy – I'm looking for a miracle or "something good" to happen to drastically change my life.

If I stay in this mindset, it means I feel in a place of desperation rather than gratitude.

I feel like a fraud - I'm looking for someone else to validate my worth or my skills, searching for proof from *anyone* that I'm OK and enough.

If I stay in this place, I'll be in a "getting" mode rather than a place of serving or equal exchange. Plus, any complements or validation will be meaningless *because I won't believe it anyway*

I feel like I'm failing - again I'm looking for something or someone outside of me, to tell me or to happen, to prove I'm not failing.

If I stay in this place, I will feel unmotivated and powerless unless the "something" (which I don't even know what that is) happens AND if something does happen I'll dismiss it as a "fluke" or fake.

So why write this? Self-Love isn't a magic pill or one time realisation. It's an everyday decision AND sometimes it's facing the not so nice feelings we have in ourselves and finding out why. Why is me telling myself that I'm worthy and enough, not feeling enough right now?

When I realise my own beliefs are needing validation, I feel weak, lose hope and feel unmotivated to care for myself. My inner voice getting bitchy or needing more than ME is my sign that I'm not completely committed to self-love right now.

It's my sign that I need to choose love again, it's starting to grow weak. My human self needs attention, care and so much compassion.

So me getting vulnerable with you is to show you I'm totally crap at this sometimes too.

This is not a skill that we've been taught, no one is perfect at it. No matter what stage you are at or what mindset you are feeling today, Self-Love is something you can nurture & grow and it's totally possible for you."

You can't expect every day to go perfectly, and you can't expect massive miracles (outside of you) every single day, even when you feel enough. Life doesn't stop around you just because you decide that you are worthy. The good times are always splattered with moments of shit, sometimes it's the other way around. But just like that beautiful garden, with one dog crap in the middle of it, what you see is what you focus on. You can see the beauty, or you can focus on the shit. It's up to you to tidy that shit up. You hold the power to focus on the beauty. You have the power to clean up the mess. You have the power to create a life that you don't need distracting from.

Just as you have to accept that you are imperfect and that your physical Body is imperfect, you have to accept that life isn't perfect either.

Life is imperfect.
It ebbs and flows.

Every day you get to make the choice whether you sink, float or swim.

In the days that followed my brother's death I coined this term "Pockets of Joy" because while all the unbelievable amount of shit was raining down on us as a family, we still had moments of laughter. We still had moments of fun. We still had moments of joy, whether that was through someone saying "*Newborn like a baby*" or us taking Sam's boys to the beach and painting stones. Sometimes we would sit and tell stories about Sam and just fill our hearts with his memory. These little pockets kept us going. We knew even in our depths of darkness there were sparks of light. This has been true of all the shitty situations I've been in. Every time it felt like my world was crumbling, these little pockets of joy would pop up and give me relief.

It's easy to focus on this when life is plodding along nicely though. When the shit hits the fan and everything you try seems to be failing and life feels relentless- that's when it's extra hard to remember.

Trust...
Trust...
Surrender.

This is when you need to remember all that we've spoken about. Getting yourself in that place of gratitude. That you may not be getting what you want, but trusting that you are getting what you need.

Perfect Timings.

I don't believe in fate, but I do believe in perfect timings.

We are co-creating our future with the collective consciousness of the Universe. I believe the Universe wants us to succeed. She wants us to grow, expand, learn and love. She wants us to share our knowledge, support each other and grow together.

She gives us opportunities to grow with her every day. Sometimes in little ways, sometimes in gigantic ways. The Universe is constantly expanding and when one person's energy expands, the whole vibration of the universe rises. You are in control, but she is there to guide you.

In hindsight, everything happens for a reason and that reason is very nearly always a blessing. Hindsight is fucking amazing at giving you the proof of this, but when you are in the thick of it, it's hard. It's really fucking hard. It can be stressful especially if you feel things aren't happening quick enough or that life isn't being fair to you.

This is where trust plays an important role.

Let go of expectations and any timeline you have in your head. Always keep trusting that things will work out, that it will be at the perfect time, exactly when you need it. Sometimes it feels like the Universe is checking to see if the thing we are hoping for or trying to achieve is actually really what we want. Obstacles will come up or things will go wrong. It isn't a test, unless you believe it is. It's like she's simply asking: "*Are you sure?*"

It's really super helpful (note the sarcasm) because this will also happen when things aren't aligned, or it just isn't the right time for something to happen. This is when your trust and gut come into play again. Listen to your gut on the matter. Ask yourself if you have really tried everything or if your Body is protecting you in some way, trying to keep you small.

Reflect on what it is that you really want. What's stressing you out about it and why do you want it?

Is it to do with your ego or your Higher Self?
Are you aligned?
Are you following your soul purpose?
Are you acting out of fear or love?

Trust in your answers. No one knows you better than you.

Sometimes, we are not allowing our days to be easy. It's like we're addicted to the struggle. As soon as you break free from any expectations, trust in perfect timings, drop the "shoulds" and allow life to be imperfect, life will feel easier and that's a beautiful feeling. That's the place where it feels like magic can happen. That's the place where every day magic *will* happen.

Once your eyes are open, it's just your choice to make. Every day, no matter how you feel, no matter how shitty or good, no matter how you look, no matter what your money situation is and no matter what your health...you choose that you are WORTHY of feeling enough and ACT on it.

Unconditional living.

It's your choice what to focus on.
It's your choice what to have gratitude for.
It's your choice whether to have a kind voice.
It's your choice whether to choose Love.
Every. Single. Day.

Chapter Sixteen - Choosing Self-Love Every Day

Self-love is a feeling – a strong feeling, emotion, belief and knowing, which influences how we view and treat ourselves.

But it starts with a decision. It starts with a choice.

In order to have self-love, you need to first be able to see and decide that the way you've been taught to view yourself might just actually be wrong. The general view surrounding self-love is that people who have it are selfish, vain or up their own arses. We've been spoon-fed this belief for as long as we can remember. Choose to see the truth.

Self-love is not self-obsession or vanity. Self-love is merely having love, empathy and compassion for yourself (as well as others). It's feeling moved to care deeply about yourself, to care how you feel, to allow yourself to be imperfect while seeing the perfection in all that you say, think and do. It's to see yourself as worthy, to be able to be confident in your beliefs, goals, abilities and dreams.

It's the inspiration to be who you are and fulfil your dreams, without using a belittling or bitchy voice to get you there, it's appreciating your Body for more than just how she looks. It's all of these things wrapped up in just one feeling – love. Knowing that you are worthy, loved, supported and understood – right now, today - without having to change a thing.

For a lot of us, even the thought of that can be scary because we've never felt that type of love before. Maybe even your parents expected too much of you or were cold unless you followed their plan for your life 100%. Maybe you're in a marriage where your partner expects you to look or act a certain way. Maybe your friends are only your friends when they need something. Maybe you feel like you belong to a community or a religion, but you're only accepted if you behave like everyone else.

So many expectations and conditions surround us.

What would it look like to be loved without having to strive to be better, look better or have more? Who would you be? Who may you lose because of this? What would you decide to let go of? How would your world change?

This uncomfortable feeling is your Body once again protecting you from the unknown. Remember, she would rather be hated by you than take the chance of you being hurt by somebody else. But you can get through these uncomfortable thoughts by reminding your Body that no matter what happens, you will be safe. You will be OK.

Trust is a two-way street. At first your Body will need to learn to trust you as much as you will be learning to trust her! Tell her she is safe. Tell her you are doing this for her. Do this and prove to yourself and then you'll not just believe that you are enough, you will feel it. To trust you, your Body needs to see actions not just words.

So, just like all great starts, self-love begins with a tiny decision. To change the way you see the world, the way you see yourself and to allow the trust and emotion to grow. Just like falling in love, it's the decisions you make every day that add up over time to a feeling and deep belief. It's all the little actions that show love that accumulates into the deep love that grows deeper than you ever thought possible.

Self-acceptance is an important step, but just like everything, it's a million tiny decisions that add up to the final accomplishment. Except it's never final. It's a decision to make every day.

Why Imperfection is Beautiful

So, if self-acceptance is the first step, it means you will need to first step into imperfection and start to believe that it's actually OK to be imperfect. In fact, it's *more* than OK – it's human, it's life, it's beautiful, it's messy, it's perfect.

Imperfection is something we've been taught that humans "are" and that we need to expect it from everybody else. Yet when it comes to ourselves we can't help but feel slightly (or massively) disappointed, even for the most human mistakes or actions. It's like most of us have the belief that we can make exceptions for everyone else (sometimes massive ones), but it would be slipping up or weak to do so for ourselves. Being less than perfect is something we feel we should hide away or be ashamed of.

You are perfectly imperfect.

It's your imperfections that make you *more* loveable.
If we can have the belief for other people, can we for ourselves too?

ADMIT
ACCEPT
EMPATHISE
BE VULNERABLE
EMBRACE

If you can admit that, as a human being, you're not going to be able to attain perfection *in any area of your life*, no matter how hard you try, how hard you are on yourself, no matter how much money you throw at it, you cannot ever be perfect – then can you create the belief that it is acceptable that you are imperfect? Wouldn't that take a massive weight off your shoulders? Do you think your world would fall apart if you accepted that?

I admit I cannot be perfect.
    I accept my imperfections.
        I understand why I'm not perfect.

I believe in the perfection of my imperfections.
My imperfections make me so much more loveable.

Some people find that a world where the pressure is off is very scary. They think that without that pressure they'll end up "giving up", becoming a slob or amount to nothing. This couldn't be further from the truth!

We are much more motivated from our inner source than an external one. It can be good to have some pressure, but it needs to be *doable* or it's unhealthy.

So, if you're at the point of accepting your imperfections you now need to empathise with it – understand and feel compassion for yourself as to why you are imperfect in this area and give yourself grace. Realise that where you are right now is not where the story ends but also that where you are right now is still OK. You don't need to wait to improve yourself before you love yourself.

Next you have to get vulnerable with it. For many people, the pressure to be perfect allows them to not finish anything because the fear of others seeing them as imperfect is terrifying.

Allow yourself to get your imperfections out in front of people – not just online. Allow people to see the real you. Your strengths, your weaknesses, your emotions, your imperfections, the things that make you crazy about yourself – all of you.

If you ever believed being vulnerable was a weakness you will see you were damn wrong. Being vulnerable takes the most strength that anyone can have. Opening your beautiful, messy soul in front of people you love takes serious guts. You will be afraid – people *will* (not might) see you differently. You'll feel scared, open, liberated...*everything all at once.*

So, why do it?

Watch the people who truly love you, love you harder.
Watch people who hardly know you get inspired to love themselves.

Feel a true acceptance of yourself.
Feel the peace which comes from aligning the outside with the inside.
Feel the openness of speaking your truth.

Find a real "village".
Connect with people in an effortless, authentic way.

See other people opening up and feeling freer to speak their truth.

Feel completely free and strong enough to be, do and have whatever the fuck you truly want.
Know the beauty of unconditional living.

See the beauty of imperfection.
Be the beauty of unconditional love.

Feel the beauty of your unconditional enoughness in this very moment.

Imagine if everyone in the world had a white house. The walls were white, the furniture was white, and everyone wore white clothes and shoes. But you had a dog. A dog who loved rolling around in muddy puddles. Plus, toddlers. Kids who loved holding melting chocolate bars and eating Spaghetti Bolognese.

Because everyone else's homes and clothes are effortlessly spotless you felt like yours should be too. Trying to keep up with others meant it felt like all you did every day was contain, clean up or hide messes. You constantly run around after the dog, cleaning his paws, wiping down where he'd been, smudging muddy spots with wet fingers. You eagle-eyed the kids with wet wipes in hands, never being able to enjoy just playing with them.

Everyone is so spotless you must keep up.

You change your clothes so there would be no mess to be seen if people came round.

Cleaning would become your focus. White paint to cover over any marks/stains, getting stressed, shouty and obsessive, because if you let your guard down for just one minute people would realise you weren't really like them.

Then one day you go round your friend's and her toddler throws a chocolate bar, which hits her straight in the belly. Shock, horror! A brown stain in a completely white, sterile situation. You almost can't breathe and turn so you can't see her chocolatey stain. However, instead of freaking out, she laughs. Shocked, you turn and look at her and remember when your toddler did the same thing. The shame you felt, the embarrassment – you wanted the ground to swallow you up until you could clean yourself up and pretend to the world it never happened.

But not your friend. She's laughing. Then, she pulls out a big pot of paint and colours a beautiful splash on the stain – no cleaning up, no hiding. The stain now looks almost beautiful. She rubs her kid's head and chuckles as she says to them:

"Don't worry lovely, it happens to all of us."

You're taken aback. At first, you feel almost angry – how can she get away with this? Why isn't she upset? Then you notice little splashes of colour all over her house. Yellow over a muddy paw print, a rainbow messily painted on a clean white wall.

"This happened to me before," you tell your friend, *"but I was so ashamed."*

Your friend sits you down and looks you in the eyes. All of a sudden you can see a spectrum of colours covering her face, eyes, hair and clothes. She looks like a work of art. She looks messy, she looks wild, she looks free.

"These things happen to everyone", she says. *"It's not your fault. Now you know, it's your choice how to react to it. You can smile and turn the mess into something beautiful or hide it away and turn your mess into your biggest shame."*

You feel so relieved – you're not the only person feeling this messy.

You and your friend sit and laugh together about stories of your muddy dogs and crazy toddlers.

You feel more connected to your friend.
You feel the same as her.
You feel more connected to the world.

You feel lighter.
You feel not so alone.
You feel less stressed.

When a different friend comes to yours and your toddler throws spaghetti at your top, how do you react? After cleaning yourself up you notice a huge ugly tomato stain and you feel the pricks of shame at the back of your throat. But then you remember what your friend had said. It's your choice... Do you hide the imperfection away or reach for the coloured paint and enjoy making it beautiful?

It takes a leap of faith because you don't know how the other person will react, but if you're brave and grab the purple paint, what happens next?

As you walk down the street you notice other people who are living more colourfully – unashamed, open about their imperfections. You feel more drawn to them because you know they are like you. The more colours you see, the more beautiful and connected you see them as.

The *imperfection* is what connects us as human beings. The imperfections make our lives more colourful and make us more beautiful.

Imperfections tell a story: *"This happened to me and I'm OK"*. It gives us hope: *"I'm like this but can still find joy"*.

Allows us to connect: *"It's OK, I feel this way too"*

What about seemingly perfect people on social media? They may have huge followings but it's not about connection. People follow, then feel bad about themselves. It doesn't inspire – it creates false hope. You know deep down they're unauthentic, but you don't care because you want what they have. So, you compare and beat yourself up instead of seeing it for what it is: a show.

Turn it off. Find real people who inspire you, who you can truly *connect* with, not compete against. Once you realise just how beautiful imperfection is and how you can drop the belief that you are flawed for being imperfect, you'll live a much more colourful life and love yourself easier.

Can you fill your life with colour? Stand out different from the crowd? Can you see yourself through those kind eyes so you can see the beauty in yourself the way you see it in others?

It takes bravery, but with each splash of paint and each time you choose to accept yourself the way you are, not only are you allowing the light to fill you up, but you are making the world a more beautiful place to live in.

Your Brain Believes What You Want It To...

OK, this sounds too simplistic, but it's actually the truth.
If you say you want to believe you are amazing and you look in the mirror and tell yourself you're amazing, it's unlikely that you'll develop that belief. It's all too on-the-surface.

Like money affirmations, saying "*I am rich, I am successful*", if you look around and you're poor AF you're going to think "Well nothing has changed."

That's because deep down you don't actually want to believe you are rich because being poor is too real for you.

Ahhh shiiit...

I'm saying the desire to *believe* in a belief goes much deeper than a thought.

What you feel is stronger than the words you say.

Whenever I talk about self-love to friends, they say, "*I'd love to believe that about myself but...*".

So, in true DJ LANCE ROCK STYLE – let's break it down....

You saying that you'd love to believe in something is a thought that's just passing through your consciousness. It sounds lovely, it sounds idealistic – it sounds very different to the beliefs you hold about yourself right now.

Saying *"I'd love to believe that"* is actually saying *"it's impossible for me to believe that"*.

It's dismissive straight away. It's scratching the surface of your true beliefs and because you've dismissed the new belief before you've even thought it through, it means you don't even need to question your current beliefs which keeps you...yep, you've guessed it – *safe*.

New beliefs (even beneficial ones) are unsafe to your Body, so she wants you to dismiss them as quickly as possible. If you scratched a little deeper under the surface of your current beliefs, you would find a reason why you believe them.

"The brain believes what you want it to believe" doesn't mean that your conscious mind can make airy-fairy decisions to believe anything and everything or that the brain will fall in line and believe.

Oh fuck no.
Or does it?

Your brain is powerful enough to believe whatever you decide but most beliefs go deeper than that. You formed beliefs at a young age on a subconscious level to keep you safe, fed and loved. So, the desire to believe something new not only has to be strong, but you also need to be probing into your current belief and be honest about how it's serving you.

Going back to the money belief, if you've always believed you don't deserve to make a lot of money or that money is the root of all evil, but you really want to heal that belief so you can charge what you are worth or you just want to make tons of money to have a shit load of fun, just saying to yourself "I am rich" or "money is my friend" will not create any change in your beliefs.

This is because you're not probing into the *"why"* you want to believe it's evil or *why you believe that you're unworthy of it.*

If your desire isn't strong enough to enable you to be willing to get uncomfortable and look into how your current belief is serving you, it will be too easy for your Body to dismiss the new belief and protect you from change.

So, if you decide the new belief is worth the uncomfortable work, it goes like this...

Thought of new belief:
Dismiss or reflect

Thought of current belief
Dismiss or reflect

Compare current and new belief
Subconsciously weigh pros and cons
Consciously decide which belief serves you better

Feel fear and discomfort
Dismiss new belief or probe current one further

Go deeper into why your current belief has been serving you
What does it fulfil?
How does it keep you safe?
Why do you believe it?

CONSCIOUSLY DESIRE NEW BELIEF
Brain accepts that's what you want to believe and looks for proof of it.

If you decide daily to accept the new belief, the brain will feel your desire and look for proof. But expect the brain to default to your old belief if you feel weak or tired. Over time the new belief becomes your default current belief because it's been proven to you time and time again. You'll have no need to fall back on your old belief if the new one is serving you.

Now your brain believes what you want it to believe!

Your brain is hardwired to please you, but it puts your safety first. To get a thought (desire for new belief) to become a feeling (deep beliefs are felt) takes time. You will need to trust in yourself and your ability to handle whatever memories and feelings come up.

Once your Body believes you're safe enough, the brain will actively look for proof so your new belief can serve you better than your old one. But you may find it stirs up lots of shit so it's something which needs to be reflected on whenever life shows you your true belief.

Remember what you feel is stronger than the words you say. It's what you are feeling that life will show you the proof of.

This is actually a blessing because life shows you how aligned you are to your Higher Self. Every single day you have the opportunity to be more aligned in your beliefs and self-love.

It's your decision to make every day.

Like a full circle, we return to what I was talking about in Chapter 1 all those years ago now. Self-love is a commitment to love yourself unconditionally every day.

Back when I started writing this book it was my miscarriage which led me to find a new belief. In that one moment, I saw my Body's lifelong struggle to endure my hatred for her and to keep me safe no matter what. I had never seen my Body or my brain as loving companions. They had always been what I needed to battle against to live and have fun *in spite of*. Apart from looking good and working in the way I wanted her to work (which she still couldn't do), I didn't care about my Body one bit. It felt egotistical to care about myself – totally selfish to even want to love myself.

I'm a mum – my entire focus needs to be on my kids – not my broken Body or annoying mind. *Ain't nobody got time for that.*

But then I saw something I couldn't ever unsee – my Body's unconditional love for me. Her willingness to protect me no matter what. How could I continue to abuse her after seeing that? That was the moment I decided I needed to actually care about my Body. I didn't know what that would look like or what that would mean for me, but I just knew that's what my Body deserved.

That decision wasn't made and stuck to until this day. I've had to make a conscious decision to love myself every single day.

Some days, I've not lived up to that decision and I've slipped on many occasions. Sometimes just by not treating myself kindly, other times I've lost that love altogether and started back at the beginning all over again. Some days I've tasted that self-hate or seen myself through judgemental eyes, but because I've tasted that sweet alignment with my Higher Self again and again, and can see myself through the eyes of source, that pure love energy, it becomes easier and easier to bring myself back, forgive myself, chase the fun and give myself grace.

Self-love becomes the norm and it's so delicious, so incredibly satisfying, that nothing else will do. This belief, this knowing that I am where I am and it's OK to feel however I feel, has changed my life and it doesn't just apply to me, it applies to you too. It's possible for you. You are allowed to choose this for yourself every single day.

You can instil the belief that you are worthy and deserving of self-love, but the actual act of it – the daily practice, putting yourself first, spending money on yourself, giving yourself grace, allowing yourself to be imperfect and make mistakes over and over again? That's a thousand tiny decisions that start with just one.

Yes, I'm Already Enough. My enough-ness is warranting love. I am worthy of love. I deserve a loving inner voice. I deserve to feel good. I deserve unconditional love. I am allowed to be unapologetically me. I will be seen, I will be heard, I will be me.

Today, right now, without changing a thing. This decision is to be made consciously from the moment you wake up until the time you fall asleep.

You will need to make tiny decisions that you may feel will stop the earth from turning, but you'll find out they won't affect anyone much at all...*apart from you.*

They will have a profound effect on you. Each time you make a decision to love yourself – even in the smallest way – it's feeding into your belief system, guiding you, building up your kind inner voice.

It's OK if you make the "wrong" decisions sometimes, because there *are* no wrong decisions. Each decision you make sets you up perfectly on your path and your Body will love you regardless. It's OK if you fall from grace – your Body will love you regardless. It's OK if you totally mess up and hate on your Body for months or even years – *your Body will love you, regardless.*

Whatever you feel you are fucking up is just a beautiful unfolding, you are doing SO well. You can't do this wrong.

Your Body's love for you is unconditional. All she asks for or hopes from you is a little love back. Every day, regardless of the decisions you've made in the past, every day you get the opportunity to show her your love, even in the smallest of ways. Every moment you get the chance to prove just how grateful you are and just how compassionate you can be towards yourself. But she doesn't need the proof, she'll love on you anyway and your Higher Self will guide you, support you and embrace you regardless. You are so loved, whether you show yourself love or not.

Every day you choose how you talk to your Body, how you connect, how you treat her, how you feel your feelings or how you disconnect and block her voice. Every day you choose to step into your power and take responsibility or to give your power (and burdens) to your Body to cope with alone. Whatever you choose, she'll still be there holding you, working for you, loving you.

Every day you get to choose love or hate, to feel enough or feel like shit, to feel deserving or feel useless. Every day you get to choose to see yourself with compassion and empathy or to be critical and cold. Whatever you choose she'll still be there holding you, supporting you, loving you.

Every day you get to choose, by your actions, to inspire your kids and show them how to love themselves. Your actions towards yourself will inspire people you know or those you don't. But even if you don't, even if you sit in your pants all day eating Wotsits, your Body will still be there looking at you with loving eyes, protecting you, loving you.

Every day we get to choose self-love. Millions of times per day we get to choose self-love. It just starts with one tiny decision, and you get to choose right now...

Are you Already Enough?
Will you love yourself messy?
Are you ready for this?

You are so worthy, so deserving, so beautiful and so enough just as you are right now. Nothing to change, nothing to fix, nothing to long for.

Naked, strong, powerful, wonderful you.
With all your flaws
With all your mess
With all your amazingness
It's time for you to make that choice.
Unconditional living
Unconditional loving
Be satisfied, grateful and have fucking fun
It's time for you to decide you are allowed to love ALL of you.
Today's the day you make your choice,
Tomorrow, you get to make it again.

Will You Choose Self-Love?

The Never-Ending Ending

I want to write "The End" but it isn't the end.

It is the never-ending unfolding of loving the essence of who you truly are.

How fucking beautiful is that my lovers?

Already Enough.
Never ending enoughness.
Everyday pure fucking magic.

Printed in Great Britain
by Amazon

10535231R00210